Praise for *Aware*

"IN *AWARE*, Les Csorba provides a master class on self-awareness and leadership—where confidence meets humility to build true authenticity."

—JAMIE DIMON, *chairman and CEO of JPMorgan Chase*

"THE TRUTH HURTS—especially about yourself. We are generally unaware of our blind spot. Or we see them through a self-serving lens. Les Csorba's peerless acumen will expand your understanding of leadership and, perhaps also, yourself."

—THE HONORABLE CHRIS WRIGHT

"SELF-AWARENESS IS a critical quality for leaders at all levels, but particularly for those at the very top, and Les Csorba's *AWARE: The Power of Seeing Yourself Clearly* makes that point very effectively and convincingly."

—GENERAL DAVID PETRAEUS *US Army (Ret.), former commander of US Central Command, and former director of the CIA*

"IN *AWARE*, Les pinpoints a vital cornerstone of great leadership—self-awareness. Drawing on his unique vantage point as a trusted executive recruiter, White House advisor, and confidant to top leaders, he offers a compelling and practical guide for anyone seeking to lead with clarity and purpose."

—TRAVIS STICE, *executive chairman of Diamondback Energy*

"LES CSORBA IS the master of recognizing potential and placing it where it can shape the future. In this book, he distills a lifetime of wisdom from the highest levels of leadership into something every decision-maker needs to read. No one understands talent—real, game-changing talent—like Les."

—HAROLD HAMM, *founder and chairman of Continental Resources*

"WHAT SEPARATES GOOD leaders from great ones? Self-awareness. In *AWARE*, Les Csorba makes the case with clarity, wit, and just the right amount of blunt truth. I've known Les since White House days, and for over thirty years he's been in the room with Fortune 500 CEOs and Boards—helping them confront what they don't see about themselves. This book is bold, practical, and unforgettable, and you will be reminded that being the smartest person in the room isn't the same as being the best leader in it."

—THE HONORABLE ELAINE CHAO
former US secretary of labor and transportation and former CEO of United Way of America

"THERE ARE MANY books that will teach you leadership skills, but without self-awareness you will destroy everything you built, erode trust, and find yourself hurting people. If every leader read this book, there would be less pain in the world."

—DON MILLER, New York Times *bestselling author and CEO of StoryBrand.AI*

"LES'S BOOK IS a valuable reminder about the importance of integrity in leadership. *AWARE* shows that true leadership is about much more than intelligence and talent. It's also about making informed decisions and having the courage to stand by them. This book is a solid anchor for anyone looking to lead by doing what's right, even when it's unpopular."

—DARREN WOODS
chairman and chief executive officer of ExxonMobil

"IN *AWARE*, leadership expert Les Csorba shows that the goal for a leader isn't to control others—it's to control oneself. This important book teaches us that real power begins with the courage to look within."

—ARTHUR C. BROOKS, *Harvard professor and #1* New York Times *bestselling author*

"OH, HOW I wish I could have read this book during the twenty-five years I was former president George H.W. Bush's chief of staff. I, of course, learned so much from him, but reading Les Csorba's insightful and inspirational *AWARE* is like taking a master class in leadership. It should be mandatory reading for every MBA program in the country."

—JEAN BECKER, New York Times *bestselling author of* The Man I Knew and author of Character Matters … and Other Life Lessons from George H.W. Bush

"I ALREADY KNEW Les was the real deal, as a leader, husband, father, grandfather, and man of faith; but after reading *AWARE*, I walked away with fresh, practical lessons on self-awareness that I can apply immediately in my life and leadership. This book is a rare gift. Les weaves together decades of real-world leadership insight with ageless biblical wisdom, helping every reader confront their blind spots and lead with greater clarity, humility, and purpose. Honestly, I'm shocked this book hadn't been written before—but grateful Les had the courage and calling to write it now. Leaders—and those they serve—will be better because of it."

—WEST BRAZELTON
senior pastor at Grace Bible Church in Houston

"ABOVE THE ORACLE at Delphi, the words 'Know Thyself' were engraved. In this essential book, Les Csorba shows leaders that it's just as true now as it was then—and shows today's leaders how to acquire the self-knowledge that will allow them to be the courageous and ethical leaders the world needs."

—GAUTAM MUKUNDA, *lecturer of management practice at the Yale School of Management and author of* **Indispensable: When Leaders Really Matter** *and* **Picking Presidents: How to Make the Most Consequential Decision in the World**

"MY COLLEAGUE and friend, Les Csorba, not only proves the value of awareness using both his rich experience and rich data on leader performance but also lays out ways that this attribute can be cultivated and leveraged. The result is a super valuable toolkit—and a deeply engaging read."

—TOM MONAHAN
CEO of Heidrick & Struggles

AWARE

Diary of a Corporate Headhunter

AWARE

The Power of
Seeing Yourself Clearly

LES T. CSORBA

A Partner of the World's Premier Executive Search Firm
and Former White House Senior Advisor

AWARE: The Power of Seeing Yourself Clearly,
Diary of a Corporate Headhunter

Copyright © 2025 by Les T. Csorba

All rights reserved. No part of this publication may be reproduced, stored in a retrieval system, or transmitted in any form by any means, electronic, mechanical, photocopy, recording, or otherwise, without the prior permission of the publisher, except as provided by USA copyright law.

No patent liability is assumed with respect to the use of the information contained herein. Although every precaution has been taken in the preparation of this book, the publisher and author assume no responsibility for errors or omissions. Neither is any liability assumed for damages resulting from the use of the information contained herein.

All Heidrick & Struggles research cited is used with permission.

Scripture quotations marked BSB are taken from the Berean Standard Bible. The Berean Bible and Majority Bible texts are officially placed into the public domain as of April 30, 2023.

Scripture quotations marked ESV are taken from the ESV® Bible (The Holy Bible, English Standard Version®). Copyright © 2001 by Crossway, a publishing ministry of Good News Publishers. Used by permission. All rights reserved.

Scripture quotations marked KJV are taken from the King James Version. Public domain.

Scripture quotations marked NIV are taken from the Holy Bible, New International Version®, NIV®. Copyright © 1973, 1978, 1984, 2011 by Biblica, Inc.® Used by permission of Zondervan. All rights reserved worldwide. www.zondervan.com. The "NIV" and "New International Version" are trademarks registered in the United States Patent and Trademark Office by Biblica, Inc.®

Scripture quotations marked THE VOICE are taken from The Voice™. Copyright © 2012 by Ecclesia Bible Society. Used by permission. All rights reserved.

Published by StoryBrand Books, an imprint of Forefront Books, Nashville, Tennessee. Distributed by Simon & Schuster.

Library of Congress Control Number: 2025910231

Print ISBN: 978-1-63763-458-5
E-book ISBN: 978-1-63763-459-2

Cover Design by Mary Susan Oleson, Blu Design Concepts
Interior Design by Mary Susan Oleson, Blu Design Concepts

Printed in the United States of America
25 26 27 28 29 30 (LAK) 10 9 8 7 6 5 4 3 2 1

*To Anne—the most self-aware person
I've ever known and who proves
that true wisdom walks
hand in hand with grace.*

*(. . . and to Liesl and Lucy,
my two ever-loyal dogs,
whose affection raises my own awareness
not to take their overly generous
admiration too seriously.)*

Contents

Preface... 15

ONE   Subprime Leadership.. 25
When Leaders Fail: 28

TWO   The Other Man in Me.. 37
Old Grief: 40   Blind Spots: 43   Clear is Kind: 47

THREE   The Other Leader in You 51
Alter Egos in Leadership: 52   Breaking Bad: 54
In the Beginning: 57   Keeping Silence: 59
The Leader's Path: 62

FOUR   To Find Your Blind Spot... 67
Avoiding the Ditch: 71
America's Reckless Billionaire: 75
The Ungoverned Leader: 78
Drivers and Derailers: The Data: 80
The Path of Self-Awareness: 82

FIVE   The Leader with Backbone...................................... 87
Facing Our Flaws: 89   Objectivity over Bias: 94
The Strength That Lasts: 99   Specks and Planks: 102
Strong Back, Soft Front: 105

SIX   Your Superpower 109
"The Artwork of Your Life": 110
Superpowers, Common and Uncommon: 113
Cultivating Strengths: 118   Avoiding Derailers: 126

SEVEN   Captain of Your Soul 129
The Meta-Skill of Agility: 130   Foresight: 134
Learning: 136   Adaptability: 137   Resilience: 139
Execution: 143   The Agilist and the Conformist: 146

EIGHT The Fellowship of a Team 149
Team Awareness: 150
Interdependency Versus Independence: 154
The Elite Performers: 158
The Collaboration Dividend: 163

NINE The Invisible Crown 167
The Narcissistic Trap: 168
The Freedom of Self-Forgetfulness: 171
The Advantages of Humility: 176   Bench the Ego: 179

TEN Return to the Soil 187
Character as a Life Mindset: 189
The Self-Giving Spirit: 195

ELEVEN Making Others Feel Seen 201
From Empathy to Compassion: 202
The Three Ls: 206   Cultivating Compassion: 209

TWELVE From "Great" to Good 215
Where Greatness Begins: 217
Choosing and Persevering: 221
The Shadow of the Leader: 224
Return on Character: 229

THIRTEEN Cracking the Interview Code 233
Face-to-Face: 235   The Five Ps: 237
Controlled Energy: 240
Reflectiveness, Resiliency, and Red Flags: 243
Last Impressions: 246

FOURTEEN The Power of Your Story 249
Knowing Your Story: 251   Telling Your Story: 255

Epilogue: Consider the Raven 259

Appendix A: The Raven Rules 269

Author's Note: A Last Word on Awareness................... 275

Acknowledgments 281

Interviews.. 283

Studies 287

About the Author.. 291

Notes 293

Index.. 309

What you are aware of you are in control of.
What you are not aware of is in control of you.

—A<small>NTHONY DE</small> M<small>ELLO</small>

Preface

One day about thirty years ago, at the outset of my career in executive recruiting, I arrived at the office to find a courier-delivered envelope on my desk awaiting attention. Inside was a résumé, and nothing else. No cover letter, no word of recommendation, not even a Post-it note asking me to do anything.

But my name on the envelope was written in a familiar hand, and the return address confirmed the sender: "Office of George Bush, Houston, Texas." I had worked for the forty-first president in the White House, vetting candidates for presidential appointment. Clearly he wanted to help this person and knew I would get the message without more being said.

The résumé detailed service at the Departments of State and Defense. Some reading between the lines told me that this wasn't the whole story. These roles, I concluded, had been cover for a man working as a CIA operative. President Bush, who in the 1970s had served as CIA director, was being characteristically discreet, and trusted that I would know what to do. I took this as a mark of his confidence in my judgment, and within an hour I was talking to the former operative about his future.

That was George H. W. Bush's style as a man and as a leader: understated, trusting, supportive, gracious, considerate, discreet, and exceedingly self-aware. In these and many other ways, he remains an ideal for the kind of leadership I most admire. For years, I kept that moment to myself until his death—a little reminder of the President's humility and grace.

His close friend James A. Baker III, the former secretary of treasury and state, described Bush to me as the most self-aware person he ever encountered,[1] and I know just what Baker meant. It's an impressive sight when a man who rises so high in the world remains modest, unpretentious, and authentic. From an early age, he always reminded himself, "Keep your ego in check, George, and stay humble." That deep personal modesty was part of his greatness.

Few understood the art of keeping things low-key better than George Bush, the former Director of Central Intelligence himself. In professions like national security—or executive search—trust and confidentiality are the bedrock. Operating in the shadows isn't just an expectation; it's an unspoken responsibility. Frankly, there's probably an unwritten rule somewhere that executive recruiters should avoid writing books like this altogether.

As it turned out, my work for him in the Office of Presidential Personnel was a prelude to decades of matching leaders to top jobs in the private sector. Headhunters, as we're colloquially known, are in the business of placing talent where it can do the most good. The stakes can be pretty high in getting the right fit, and we develop an eye for leadership styles and personality types.

One thing I noticed, no doubt influenced in part by my association with George Bush, is that the flashiest leaders are by no means always the best. You learn to look for a subtler mix of traits to fit the bill of solid, reliable leadership. You want the type of leader who doesn't regard him- or herself, as a complete, finished product. The most effective leaders have the self-awareness to keep striving and improving—they recognize their flaws and confront them, defer to those who complement their skills, and deploy their best to bring out the best in others.

But here's the catch: Every leader wants to be known, yet many are terrified of being truly *seen*. That's where the real work begins. You can control what you are aware of; what you are unaware of controls you.

The Japanese have a saying about the "three faces" we wear: The first is the one we show the world, the second is for our close friends and family, and the third—the truest version—is the one we keep hidden, even from ourselves. That third face? That's where the magic happens, where self-awareness and growth as a leader begin.

The finest leaders, as I have observed time and again in my career, are hardly free of flaws and blind spots. What sets them apart is the awareness and determination to show up as the best version of themselves, whether they run a small team, lead a major organization, or have just stepped into a long-sought dream job. Most anyone in charge of an enterprise can see the limitations and shortcomings of others; self-aware leadership sees one's own limitations and shortcomings—and gets serious about correcting them, never simply giving up.

In our professional lives, the main barriers to success aren't always external—often they are internal. It can be our own blind spots, insecurities, bad habits, and complacency that hold us back. Every leader is locked in a tug-of-war between outward achievements and inward growth. The best leaders don't ignore that inner struggle—they embrace it. They dig deep, confront their flaws, and do the hard work to improve. Why? Because self-awareness, paired with the courage to change, is what sets exceptional leaders apart.

This book, based on my dealings with thousands of leaders, is meant to help you in that effort.

It's useful to remember, as I hope to show with many examples, that great leadership is aspirational; it takes relentless effort, honest reflection, and the humility to fail yet keep trying. The most

Preface

impressive leaders I've studied weren't perfect, but they had at least two traits in common. They had unwavering self-belief without falling into self-absorption. And they were alert to personal weaknesses, confronting their faults directly. This combination of strengths opens the path for a leader's personal growth. In business, as in other callings, successful leadership is not a point of arrival but a journey where we make progress by refusing to quit and being at least a little better than we were yesterday. And the best leaders aim to become the kind of leader they'd want to follow—not just a carbon copy of past role models.

> *Self-awareness, paired with the courage to change, is what sets exceptional leaders apart.*

Darren Woods is a great example. When offered the CEO role at ExxonMobil in 2016, he hesitated, saying he didn't feel the *need* to be in charge. The board's response? "That's why we believe you're perfect for the role."

Leaders of this caliber aren't the sort who just check off tasks; they think not only about what they want to *do*, but also about who they want to *be*. Working with that attitude is actually ancient wisdom, as in the advice of the Stoic philosopher Epictetus: "First say to yourself what you would be; and then do what you have to do."[2] By *self-awareness*, as I use the term in this book, I mean this reflective, intentional state of mind that sees the kind of leader we can be and doesn't settle for less.

Every aspiring leader has blind spots—it's just the physics of leadership. I've certainly had to deal with my own, and there was no avoiding discussion of these in this book. The faults we all contend with can become derailers, in our careers and for the teams and whole companies we're supposed to serve. Instead of addressing them with humility and honesty, we sometimes try to rationalize or to place the blame with others. This lack of self-awareness only lets problems fester, leaving us stalled when we and our teams could be advancing. No executive ever starts the day thinking, *How can I derail my team today?* More often, they give no thought at all to how their conduct and attitude are affecting others.

You'll find some very familiar names in the chapters ahead, from our own and earlier eras, all in their different ways offering key lessons in how to cultivate strengths or work around limitations. These are leaders of abundant natural gifts who nonetheless saw weakness that had to be overcome if their talents were to be put to full use.

Take Elon Musk—often hailed as a modern-day da Vinci—who admits to an Achilles' heel: He's *a little too optimistic*. In a moment of self-reflection, he acknowledged, "I'm a little optimistic about timeframes."[3] Now, optimism is a fantastic quality for leaders, especially trailblazers working on game-changing ideas. But when dialed up too high, it's a "derailer." For someone like Musk, whose vision seems ripped straight from a sci-fi novel, that optimism (which he confessed is almost "pathological"), can lead to setting sky-high expectations that are nearly impossible to meet—and even risky.[4]

Still, credit where it's due: Musk knows this about himself and owns it. And honestly, who can blame him? Between building reusable rockets, rolling out autonomous cars, and tinkering with humanoid robots, implantable brain chips, and advanced AI—not to mention digging futuristic tunnels, championing free speech, and driving government efficiency—he's got *a lot* on his plate. Sure, his optimism might stretch timelines a bit thin, but isn't that part of what makes him, well, Elon Musk? After all, it's hard to shoot for the stars without a little extra hope in your corner.

Warren Buffett, the legendary "Oracle of Omaha," has openly confessed to one of his flaws: being a bit *too* agreeable—what some call "Nebraska nice." He's admitted that his loyalty sometimes makes him slow to part ways with underperforming managers.[5] While his hands-off, trust-filled style has been a cornerstone of his success, even Buffett knows that every strength has its flip side. His self-awareness and humility, though, are what truly set him apart as a business icon.

Then there was Steve Jobs, whose management style sparked endless debate. Love him or not, Jobs always knew one thing about himself: He wasn't cut out to work for anyone else. Long before Apple was born in his parents' garage, he embraced this truth. Over time—after plenty of trial and error—Jobs cracked the code for pairing his visionary leadership with the operational genius of Tim Cook. Together, they formed one of the most dynamic leadership duos in history, proving that even the most brilliant minds need balance.

Dwight Eisenhower, the five-star general turned US president, had a flaw that's almost too relatable: a fiery temper. But Ike didn't let it control him. Instead, he turned to a simple yet effective routine—he'd write down the name of the person he was furious with, then toss the note in the trash. Over time, this quirky ritual and a lot of self-discipline helped him master his emotions, turning a personal weakness into one of his greatest strengths.[6]

Teddy Roosevelt's recognition of his erratic behavior as a young assemblyman in New York highlighted his exceptional self-awareness and capacity for growth. Early in his political career, the fiery "Bull Moose" was notorious for his aggressive, combative approach, often bulldozing through debates and alienating colleagues with his confrontational tactics. However, Roosevelt's willingness to reflect on his actions and acknowledge the ineffectiveness of his bullying style marked a pivotal moment in his development as a leader, ultimately becoming a towering, Rushmorean figure in American history.

Leading and navigating uncertain times require a powerful mix of self-awareness, adaptability, and the courage to pivot when needed. I once worked with the CEO of a $10 billion energy company who, despite his accomplishments, struggled with shyness and introversion. His reserved nature unintentionally created distance from his team, leading to a dip in morale and productivity. Recognizing this blind spot, he took a creative approach: He removed the chairs from his office. This forced him to leave his comfort zone—literally—and engage more intentionally with his team. Over time, he became what my extra-extroverted wife wryly calls me: a "high-functioning introvert."

On the other hand, some leaders resist confronting their blind spots, often to their own detriment. Take the senior executive I was coaching at a gas pipeline company when he was in the running for CEO. When presented with 360-degree feedback revealing him as "controlling," he spent an entire hour disputing the data rather than reflecting on it—the "feedback would have been different by recutting the data with other raters." The unwillingness to face the truth cost him the top role, leaving him stuck in the shadows of his own potential.

I'll also introduce you to some other executives I've come to know personally, whose stories illustrate the themes of this book in action. Before they held positions of enormous professional responsibility, and in some cases before they became hugely successful and wealthy, many of these men and women had to persevere through tough personal challenges. All found ways to get around obstacles in the journey, or to grow past weaknesses that were holding them back. The secret to unlocking your full potential is owning your imperfections, learning from them, and taking bold steps to grow. Even a small dose of humility and self-reflection can be transformational.

This shift from what has been known as a kind of transactional leadership to something more meaningful—call it the *Ted Lasso* effect—is what truly sets great leaders apart. *Ted Lasso* is a heartwarming comedy about an optimistic American football coach who transforms a struggling English soccer team—and the people around him—through kindness, resilience, and unwavering belief. The show's runaway popularity says a lot about what people crave today: leaders who are kind, empathetic, and make their teams feel valued, but who also know how to be direct when feedback and correction is necessary. Think of it as leading like a great coach, focusing not just on wins but on the people behind them.

Along the way, the book touches on agility, backbone, empathy, vulnerability, self-forgetfulness, and other traits you'll find in self-aware leaders. And in an epilogue and appendix, I venture a summary of the book's message along with forty principles of action I call, for reasons I'll explain, the Raven Rules. My last word reflects Anthony de Mello's work on awareness, namely, that self-observation is not for the fainthearted or the closed-minded.

This book pulls together insights from decades of experience at Heidrick & Struggles, the worldwide executive recruiting and leadership consulting firm. I drew from over 75,000 interviews conducted using our META leadership framework (Mobilize, Execute, Transform with Agility); my own notes from hundreds of candidate interviews, informal conversations, or interviews with more than fifty leading CEOs; and reflections from my personal leadership diary. I hasten to add that while the ideas and argument of the book are a product of my experiences at Heidrick & Struggles, in the opinions offered here I speak only for myself.

In writing the book, I've also learned a great deal about leadership from Jamie Dimon, Darren Woods, Chris Wright, and other

Preface

CEOs who were kind enough to make time for me. Many of these leaders are from the energy industry, for the simple reason that my recruiting and coaching work at Heidrick & Struggles has centered on that demanding, highly volatile, and risk-heavy sector. Occasionally, the stories and profiles in the book are personal in nature, recalling loss and past grief, and these are shared with permission.

Writing about leadership, I should say upfront, is a bit like walking a tightrope—you have to be careful because even the best leaders, whether they're historical icons or people we admire personally, are bound to slip up. As the saying goes, history doesn't repeat itself, but human nature does. Even the most self-aware, well-intentioned leaders aren't immune to stumbling now and then. Warren Buffett, in his 2024 Annual Letter to Berkshire Shareholders, said something executive recruiters can easily relate to: "People are not that easy to read," and "sincerity and empathy can be easily faked."[7] It's a humbling reminder that no one—not even legendary leaders—have it all figured out.

In these pages, I'll share some of the highs and the lows in my own experience, moments when I felt I was thriving, times when I fell short, and lessons I'm still learning. Growing in self-awareness takes work, and if I'm certain of anything it is that the effort is worth it. Some of the ideas that follow have changed my career and life for the better, and I hope that you might benefit as well from the mix of reflections, stories, and practical advice that follows.

The book is meant not just for CEOs or boardroom executives. Whether you're climbing the ladder, striving for greater impact, hiring, developing talent, or just starting out and surveying your career prospects, this book is meant for you as well. In a way, it's my long letter to the next generation of leaders so they can understand the truth in Cicero's words, "Not for ourselves alone, are we born."[8]

I have been very lucky in my career to work with incredible leaders in government, business, and the nonprofit sector. I've seen

Preface

the qualities that make leaders stand out. I have also seen the opposite—toxic leaders who teach us what *not* to do. Poor leadership can end in derailment for a career or a company, but the consequences are sometimes much more far-reaching, doing grave harm to the economy and to the lives of millions.

Here and there in the book, we'll recall some infamous cases of the ruin that reckless business executives have left in their wake. As many Americans learned in the aftermath of the 2008 financial crisis, one man's blind spot is not necessarily just one man's problem. The uncorrected flaws of a few can become everyone's burden. For this reason, I've tried to make this more than just another self-help book for aspiring executives. As much as ever, the business world needs people of character and moral ambition in positions of responsibility. In a financial crisis whose consequences many people are still feeling today, just about everything that could go wrong did go wrong, and it all started with a failure of leadership.

ONE

Subprime Leadership

Corporate America might get a bailout, but no one was going to bail me out.

—Julia

September 15, 2008, will forever be remembered as a day of economic infamy. Lehman Brothers, a 158-year-old institution that had weathered the Civil War, two World Wars, and the Great Depression, declared bankruptcy. The ensuing Great Recession brought about the most abrupt destruction of wealth since 1929, wiping out $10 trillion in asset value.[1]

Home values collapsed, retirement savings vanished, and a lot of people learned the hard way that some so-called "safe investments" were nothing of the kind. Among the millions caught in the fallout was a woman named Julia, whose story, a decade on, was related in the *Financial Times*. Her crash course in How to Survive a Financial Apocalypse started with a simple home purchase, made just before the Lehman disaster. As a small business owner and a mother of two, Julia thought she'd played it safe when buying a house in Melbourne,

Florida. "I qualified for more," she told the *Times*, but she had opted for something modest.

At first, life was manageable. Her web-design business was picking up, and the mortgage seemed doable, especially with her husband's income in the mix. "We've got this," she told herself confidently. But that was before faraway events undermined her whole life plan. The economic calamity changed everything. Her business dried up, and her husband—a spouse apparently not built for tough times—ran off with their savings. Julia was left to deal with it all herself: a six-year-old child, a two-year-old child, house payments she couldn't make, and a business that was going nowhere.

With poor credit, a house worth half its previous value, and no good options, she declared bankruptcy. She moved back in with her parents, reenrolled in school, and worked three jobs, getting by on little sleep and barely enough time to breathe, let alone pray. Looking back on ten hard years, she told a *Times* reporter:

> I feel less safe now than I did before the crisis. We haven't kept up with inflation, education is much more expensive and it's a struggle to maintain a middle-class lifestyle. I learned from experience that the little guy is not the priority. Corporate America might get a bailout, but no one was going to bail me out.[2]

While the big banks were deemed "too big to fail," people like Julia were, in effect, dismissed as too small to matter.

Among the millions, like Julia, caught in the fallout was Yu Lia Chun, a sixty-six-year-old retiree in Hong Kong who discovered that her "rock-solid" savings had been tied to a now-defunct American firm she'd never even heard of. One day, she was planning for her golden years; the next, her $155,000 nest egg was gone, leaving her wondering if she'd ever trust a banker—or anyone else in a suit—again.[3] In China, unpaid workers took matters into their own hands, kidnapping Israeli managers from a hotel construction site when a promised Lehman loan vanished into thin air. A guilt-ridden private equity executive in London, distraught over leaving his firm's funds in a doomed Lehman account, tragically stepped in front of a commuter train. In Arizona, a bankrupt CEO chose to meet his end dressed to the nines in a tuxedo, proving that even in despair, he wouldn't let standards slip. A Connecticut stockbroker leapt from his office window.[4]

The crisis didn't just steal money—it took livelihoods, hopes, and lives, leaving behind tales even more grim than the recession's spreadsheets. "The world breaks everyone," Hemingway wrote. "But those that will not break, it kills. It kills the very good and the very gentle and the very brave impartially."[5]

The economic collapse of 2008, and all that followed, changed the political landscape in ways few could have imagined at the time. From the aftermath of the Great Recession in 2010 and onward, America entered a simmering populist era, a stage set for an age-old drama: the haves versus the have-nots, and the protected versus the unprotected. On one side stood the Julias of the world—everyday Americans weathering an unforgiving economy. On the other, Wall Street bankers, the credentialed elite, and the expert class, all vying to safeguard their share of what was left of the American dream.

Nothing prepared the way for the eventual election and reelection of President Donald Trump like the bitterness and disillusionment left by the financial crisis. Hardworking, responsible people understandably felt forgotten and taken for granted, as *Wall Street Journal* columnist Peggy Noonan observed,

> The protected make public policy and the unprotected live in it. And the unprotected are starting to push back powerfully. The protected are the accomplished, the secure, the successful, those who have power, or access to it. They are

protected from much of the roughness of the world. More to the point, they are protected from the world they have created. They live in nice neighborhoods—in safe ones [and] they are insulated from the many of the effects of their own decisions. . . . Social philosophers are always saying the underclass must re-moralize. Maybe it is the overclass that must re-moralize.[6]

At the time of the collapse, of course, banking executives were quick to place the blame elsewhere, seeking to spread it as widely as possible. Lehman's CEO, Richard S. Fuld Jr., confidently declared, "It's not just one single thing—it's all these things taken together . . . the perfect storm."[7] Translation: "Don't look at me; it's the universe's fault!" If there's one thing we've learned from history, it's that when the going gets tough, the so-called tough go soft and blame the weather. Why bother with self-reflection when you can craft a narrative that makes fate the real villain? Like Dostoevsky's Raskolnikov, the self-deceptive character in *Crime and Punishment*, these financial masterminds found it far more convenient to point fingers at an angry cosmos than to acknowledge their own hubris.

When Leaders Fail

Looking back, it's clear that many banking executives were too preoccupied with their bonuses to see the great unraveling they had set in motion. It was Bill George, the truth-telling former CEO of Medtronic, who put it best: The crisis wasn't so much about subprime mortgages as it was about subprime leadership.[8]

Lehman Brothers is an example for the ages of reckless, self-seeking, and unreflective people running the show. Under Fuld's fearless (and accountability-free) leadership, Lehman Brothers became a masterclass in hubris, with the board more like a cheer squad than a governing body. Nine members were retired, four were over seventy-five, and only two had actual financial services experience. The rest? A theater producer, a retired Navy admiral, and, best of all, an actor from the 1957 Katherine Hepburn flick *Desk Set*. Sure, they were accomplished—just not in, you know, finance.

When the stakes were sky-high, the folks tasked with steering the ship seemed better suited to staging a Broadway revival than navigating the murky waters of risky credit and complex financial instruments. Fuld's empire crumbled under the weight of poor oversight and misplaced confidence, proving once again that a fish rots from the head down—or in this case, from the headliner and the supporting cast.

The Lehman board's financial experience? Let's just say it came from a simpler time, when the most exciting "innovation" was maybe a new kind of savings bond. Modern financial wizardry—credit default swaps, CDOs, and derivatives—might as well have been written in ancient Greek.

But there's more. During the critical years of 2006 and 2007, as Lehman was busy turning its real estate portfolio into a ticking time bomb, the board's risk committee met . . . twice a year. Meanwhile, analysts everywhere were practically screaming about the potential for Lehman's collapse, especially after Bear Stearns imploded in March 2008. But instead of doing anything proactive, Fuld and the board collectively shrugged. Even when Treasury Secretary Hank Paulson (whose reputation for running toward problems surely prevented a global depression), waved his arms and suggested *actual solutions*—like selling the business or raising capital—they passed. Multiple suitors showed interest, but Fuld apparently felt the offers weren't flattering enough. A 25 percent stake to Korea Development Bank? Too low. Half the company to China's CITIC Securities? Still not good enough. Turns out, holding out for a better deal works great—right up until your entire company becomes worthless.[9]

To be fair, Lehman wasn't the only contestant in the "Who

Can Wreck the Economy?" Olympics. They had stiff competition from Bear Stearns, AIG, Merrill Lynch, and even government-backed giants Fannie Mae and Freddie Mac—all deemed "too big to fail" and handed lifelines in the form of bailouts or mergers.[1] Bank of America even got the memo, swapping out seven board members in 2009 for actual banking experts, proving that maybe—just maybe—having good governance is a good idea.

The Great Recession was a group effort, with a cast of characters straight out of a dark comedy: politicians and lobbyists pushing "affordable" homeownership via Fannie Mae and Freddie Mac, predatory lenders preying on naive homebuyers, corporate boards napping on the job, CEOs chasing bonuses instead of long-term stability, and credit rating agencies doing their best impression of watchdogs asleep at the gate. Turns out, when everyone's chasing short-term gains, the long-term fallout hits *everyone*. Jack Welch summed it up best with a nod to *Murder on the Orient Express*: There might have been only one victim (the economy), but there were plenty of suspects—that is, the ones who were in charge.

The seeds of this fiasco were planted back in the 1980s when corporate America had its "Aha!" moment and decided to tie executive pay to short-term shareholder returns. What could go wrong? Cue a cultural shift toward self-interest and instant gratification, leaving long-term value creation and proper risk management in the dust. Somewhere, Adam Smith and Milton Friedman were probably shaking their heads, wondering how their free-market dream—built on fair competition and no fraud—turned into a twisted game of "How Fast Can We Cash Out?" The result? A crash course in what happens when leaders trade long-term health for short-term gains.

---

[1] Secretary Paulsen was reluctant to approve a bank bailout, but he did so in 2008, known as the Troubled Asset Relief Program (TARP). The bailout was eventually repaid in full, with the government even making a profit on certain investments. While certain investments lost money, the overall TARP initiative resulted in a net positive return. "Final Report on the Troubled Asset Relief Program," Congressional Budget Office, April 2024, https://www.cbo.gov/publication/60220.

Subprime Leadership

The rise of the "Imperial CEO" wasn't just a coincidence—it was practically a corporate fashion statement of the era. Charisma? Check. Absolute power? Double check. Governance experts today practically shout from the rooftops about the dangers of combining Chair and CEO roles, precisely because it can lead to these unchecked ego-fests. But back then? It was all systems go, with boardrooms prioritizing quick wins over relationships, instant gratification over patience, and hubris over humility. CEOs weren't reflecting or leading—they were basking.

Michael Burry, the legendary investor who foresaw the 2008 housing market collapse (and was portrayed by Christian Bale in *The Big Short*), had no illusions about what had happened and who was at fault. Lenders had lowered standards just to churn out more loans, a strategy no responsible executive team would ever even think to pursue.

To this day, Fuld's undoing remains a cautionary tale in the executive recruiting field, recalling a time when sharp and flashy leaders were preferred over grounded and genuine ones. These days recruiters look for self-awareness, empathy, humility, and authenticity, because everyone remembers what can happen when such qualities are completely missing in a business leader. Leadership is about character, not just execution, and failing spectacularly on both fronts nearly sank the global economy. Being "the smartest person in the room" isn't the same as being the best leader in it. The two great lessons about CEOs during that era: too much hubris, too little self-awareness.

Yet even now, too many leaders in business seem to crave attention and applause instead of accepting the sacrifices that real leadership requires. We still see the same weakness for short-term wins that make the top guy look good, at the expense of harder, behind-the-scenes decision-making that truly serves the long-term interests of stakeholders. When a leader becomes his own biggest fan, everyone else ends up paying a price. As the saying goes, there's no smaller package than a leader wrapped up in themselves.

Ambition in a leader is natural and often admirable, provided, of course, that it is tempered and well directed. In business, growth and profitability are obviously essential, but how they are achieved is hardly an incidental consideration. The great economist Milton Friedman explained that the social responsibility of business is to increase profits, but, he stressed, only within the boundaries of ethical conduct and what moral common sense recognizes as the rules of the game.[10]

Remember Jeff Skilling, Enron's CEO, who clearly skipped the fine print? Fueled by a mix of pride and envy, his ambition wasn't just to grow Enron—it was to make it *the* biggest company in the world, no matter the cost. The cost was sky-high, involving deception, fraud, and a catastrophic collapse. Turned out, the real villain of the Enron saga wasn't just plain old greed, but the far deadlier sin of hubris. Charlie Munger wisely pointed out, it's envy—not greed—that drives much of the world's bad behavior.[11] And Skilling's downfall proved it: He didn't just want success; he wanted everyone else to eat his dust.

Fast forward to 2023, and Silicon Valley Bank (SVB) followed suit, proving that hubris and leadership blindness never really go out of style. The SVB collapse wasn't quite the financial earthquake of 2008, but it was powered by the same force lurking beneath the surface: unchecked hubris. Turns out, when leaders stop listening and start believing their own hype, the fallout tends to come with a hefty price tag—for everyone else, of course.

Testifying before Congress in 2023, SVB CEO Greg Becker had a surprising take on his role in the bank's collapse: He was just a humble "custodian," swept up by forces beyond his control. Those who knew Becker's bold leadership style were baffled by this rebranding. After all, "custodians" don't pull in eight-figure salaries or sit idly by while risks pile up like overdue paperwork. Michael Burry, ever the master of the mic drops, nailed it with a tweet:

2000, 2008, 2023. It's always the same—people full of hubris and greed take stupid risks and fail. Then money is printed because it works so well.[12]

Meanwhile, SVB's demise played out like a high-speed car chase. Within forty-eight hours of signaling a liquidity crisis, $42 billion vanished in a frenzied bank run led by nervous startups and tech investors, exposing just how fragile the tech sector really was. Even Mark Zuckerberg couldn't resist a jab, joking that the tech industry had "moved so fast, it broke its own bank."[13]

One of the best ways of keeping the boundaries ever in mind is to stay close to people who would never cross them. In the words of the proverb, "As iron sharpens iron, so one man sharpens another."[14] We all are shaped, for good or ill, by the company we keep. Every leader—especially CEOs and board members—needs a mentor, coach, or even a *consigliere* to give candid advice and keep him or her grounded in reality. One thing a self-aware leader knows for sure is that when your team agrees with you 100 percent of the time, when your every idea or even passing thought is received as bold and inspired, it's not the truth you're hearing.

One of Richard Fuld's former associates at Lehman said of him, "He was brilliant in many ways, but couldn't admit where he fell short." Another insider described him as being stuck in a "bubble" of power where inconvenient truths and warning signs received no attention. Margaret Heffernan, in her book *Willful Blindness*, called this the "manufactured cocoon of superiority,"[15] allowing leaders to tune out risks, delude themselves, avoid conflict, and cling to their status no matter what. It's straight out of Plato's *Allegory of the Cave*, but instead of chained prisoners misinterpreting shadows, you've got CEOs mistaking reckless decisions for genius.[16] How many leaders today have slipped into bubbles of their own, insulated from hard realities or signs of trouble?

A sharp contrast is Jamie Dimon, CEO of JPMorgan Chase, the rare banker whose reputation never took a hit during the financial crisis. Among much else, Dimon is known for a level head and for keeping his ego in check—notwithstanding his occasional righteous anger. "Self-awareness is essential in leadership," he told me in an interview. "It's not everything, but without it there is nothing."[17] Dimon takes it further with the "OODA Loop" framework—Observe, Orient, Decide, Act—borrowed from US Air Force Colonel John Boyd. For him, the "orient" phase is all about sharpening self-awareness to navigate tricky decisions. Knowing what you don't know might just be the ultimate leadership hack.

This helps explain his cautious approach to risk management and constant focus on maintaining balance-sheet flexibility, both of which were key to guiding his firm safely through the crisis. Jamie Dimon's genius lies in his relentless focus on execution. It is driven by rigorous business reviews and a healthy paranoia that sharpens both his self-awareness and his keen understanding of emerging risks. His personal leadership style—marked by accessibility, including his famous "Heartland" road trips and open-door policy—also steers him far clear of the isolated power structures that have doomed so many other executives.

Dimon told me about a small moment of revelation he still remembers. He was at home on a call with colleagues, losing patience with them, when his middle child began to cry and asked, "Dad, why are you so angry?" If his own child had this reaction, he wondered, how must his colleagues feel about being spoken to in such a way? It woke him up, as Dimon told me, and from then on he was determined to present himself with more calm, self-control, and sensitivity to others. He was on a "mission," he said, "to ensure the team felt trusted, respected, and valued."[18] Turns out, sometimes the best leadership lessons come not from management books but from a teary-eyed kid with a knack for cutting through the noise.

Self-awareness has been crowned the "meta-skill of the 21st century," and with good reason. According to Tasha Eurich in her book *Insight*, only 10–15 percent of leaders actually possess it.[19] That tracks with a study from Heidrick & Struggles, which pegged the real number at 13 percent.[20] In other words, most leaders are confidently winging it. Eurich pointed out the usual culprit: self-deception or mistaking your illusions for reality and thinking everyone's buying it.

Crises like the Great Recession weren't just failures of decision-making but failures of self-awareness, character, and courage. Leaders willing to develop these strengths don't just weather storms—they avoid disasters altogether. True awareness—the kind that demands stepping back, reflecting, addressing blind spots, and aligning actions with a sense of responsibility—can make leaders not just resilient, but too aware to fail.

> *True awareness—the kind that demands stepping back, reflecting, addressing blind spots, and aligning actions with a sense of responsibility—can make leaders not just resilient, but too aware to fail.*

But let's zoom out for a second: Leadership isn't just about those in power. It's about the countless people who rely on them—ordinary folks who rarely get the safety nets or second chances that leaders do. That's the heart of this book: a reminder that the real purpose of leadership is serving those who depend on it, not just securing a corner office.

Take Julia, for example. The Great Recession knocked her down hard—she lost everything. But instead of staying there, she dusted herself off, reenrolled in school, and earned her degree without adding a single dollar to her debt. Now, that's something the financial leaders of 2008 could've learned from. More cautious and self-aware, Julia developed a resilience and depth of character that far outshone those who let her down in the first place. She's living proof of the proverb, "He who conquers his own soul is greater than he who takes a city."[21]

That quality has never been more at a premium, and executives who combine awareness, agility, empathy, and good judgment will be the ones to thrive. A powerful business leader's influence can affect the lives of so many other people, from day-to-day colleagues to innocent bystanders in the economy, like Julia. All of them have a lot riding on a leader's success, and true leaders will be tenacious in the commitment to never let them down.

TWO

The Other Man in Me

Well, I've learned the lines of the great American songbook
And I wear my leather shoes every day
Better with time, getting better with time
Just like the other man in me . . .

—Thomas Csorba, "Another Man in Me," 2020

Although the best leaders are always praised for being forward-looking, it can be just as valuable to stay attuned to the past, looking back now and then to reflect on the distance traveled. The most capable men and women I've encountered as an executive-search professional are un-self-regarding as a rule, but they also tend to be self-aware, knowing their own strengths and weaknesses alike. We all have to live our lives forward, as the philosopher Kierkegaard observed, but really we can only understand our lives backward.

For me, the story starts with my parents, who landed in Canada as refugees from communist Hungary in the 1950s. Life in Hungary had been anything but rosy—more like gray, grim, and suspiciously quiet. Growing up in a Stalinist police state meant you didn't just mind your manners; you minded your words and your neighbors because you never knew who might turn out to be an informant. One innocent comment could lead to a very awkward family meeting—hosted by the secret police.

After World War II, Hungary's first dictator, Matyas Rakosi, was an ardent communist known as "Stalin's best disciple." True to Rakosi's teacher, his regime during my parents' childhood presided over the mass imprisonment of hundreds of thousands and the deaths of many more. Torture, spying, and terror spread throughout the villages and larger cities.

Mom was twelve and Dad fifteen when college students and other brave young Hungarians revolted in October of 1956. Almost miraculously, Rakosi's regime and his henchmen were forced out of power. Some were hanged for their crimes against humanity. For one glorious week, Hungary was free.

What happened next is one of the sorrowful stories of the Cold War. Hundreds of Soviet tanks appeared, and in the space of a day—Sunday, November 4, 1956—it was all over. Thousands of heroic men and women were massacred in what still stands as one of Soviet communism's most ruthless crimes.

My teenage father fled his hometown of Apostag ("village of the apostles") and, with two school friends, headed on foot to the Austrian border. Three days later, with holes in his shoes and in the dark of night, he crawled under a barbed wire fence while holding another refugee's infant in his arms.

My mother's father was an educated man—an engineer and English interpreter. He was able to arrange a safer pathway for the family from Budapest into Austria. Eventually, both Mom and Dad made their way to Canada, where, in a close-knit Hungarian community of refugees, they met and married.

For all the drama of their passage to North America, my parents were grateful for their blessings and made a happy life for their children. Hungarians are lively and demonstrative, as any visitor to our house could instantly see. My childhood recollections are a mix of laughter, music, family gossip, passionate arguments, and horsing around with my younger brother. All this plus a constant stream of visitors and dinner guests. Picture a scene out of the film *My Big Fat Greek Wedding*, substituting Hungarians for the Greeks, and you've got the idea.

Especially vivid memories center on the cooking—all the savory, peppery aromas of chicken or beef or pork smothered in roasted Hungarian paprika. The scent of goulash in our three-room apartment made the place indistinguishable from our favorite Hungarian restaurant a few blocks away.

The bright orange-and-red color of that finely grated spice, paprika, was omnipresent. It was painted on the plates, pictured on the linens, etched on Hungarian paintings. And it always seasoned our food—the *paprikás csirke* (chicken paprika), cucumber salads, eggs for breakfast, goulash for supper. Normal families have salt and pepper shakers on the table; we had salt and paprika, and my dad could discourse at length on its endless dietary benefits.

To Dad, I also owe my boundless pride in Hungarian culture. I grew up hearing him hold forth about all the great Hungarians who stood as giants of history, arts, sports, and science. The list included Szent-Gyorgyi, who discovered Vitamin C, after extracting it from—that's right—paprika! There were more—Joseph Pulitzer, Franz Liszt, Edward Teller, Leo Szilard, Erno Rubik, Harry Houdini, "Broadway Joe" Namath, even "Columbo" (Peter Falk) and Zsa Zsa Gabor. In my dad's telling, most every achievement of civilization had a Hungarian behind it.

My dad was a larger-than-life character—think again of *My Big Fat Greek Wedding* and the character Gus Portokalos, with his Windex cure-all philosophy. He was proud, opinionated, and, well, let's just say, not shy about being the center of attention. Mom, on the other hand, was the understated, sensible one who kept everything (and everyone) running smoothly. Dad enjoyed being pampered—okay, coddled—and Mom happily obliged.

She made it her mission to ensure family and friends were happy, entertained, and always well-fed. Even after I was tucked in for the night, I'd hear the clinking of dishes and the gentle hum of her cleaning up the kitchen, determined not to let a single pot or pan sit unwashed. Mom's version of "resting" was making sure everyone else was taken care of first.

Dad was the life of every party and family gathering, though given at times to excessive drinking and flashes of anger. Mom was big on responsibility, and very big on hugs—and always knew when we needed them. Dad brought my brother and me with him to shady bars; Mom took us to Catholic catechism and taught us bedtime prayers. Dad brought home the bacon and taught us in Hungarian: "*Aki nem dolgozik, ne is egyek!*" ("If you don't work, you don't eat."). Mom, who worked at a modeling agency and a photography studio, was the picture of grace and motherly devotion. Dad was my hero. Mom, my saint.

Old Grief

As a sixteen-year-old, I showed promise on the tennis court and had the opportunity to train in Southern California. I still have the many precious letters my mother wrote to me during that time. One of them brought the sad news that she and my father were divorcing.

No doubt it helped ease the pain to be far away at the time, spared from the scene of my parents' parting. I felt that I had been left on my own, hurled into a world that would never be the same, yet not imagining the far worse turn life was about to take.

One day when I was eighteen, a senior in high school, and still far away from home, I heard that an uncle was frantically trying to reach me. When he finally tracked me down, he told me that my mother had been taken by ambulance to Vancouver General Hospital after a seizure. Trying to keep me calm, he said, "It's just probably just a calcium deposit on her brain." But, he added, "You should come home."

Between my departure and arrival, the surgeons discovered much more than a calcium deposit. Like a thief in the night, stealing the one whom I had loved more than any other, a malignant tumor had spread throughout her brain. It had all happened very quickly, and she had little time left.

When I arrived at the hospital on that dreary, rainy afternoon, I was beaten down. In a harshly lighted ICU room, quiet except for the sounds of life-support equipment, my beautiful mother was nearing her death. As family and friends gathered in the room, I escaped to the hospital chapel to be alone. When I returned, a priest had arrived to administer last rites. Mom never regained consciousness; I had no chance to say goodbye. Worse, as the eldest son, it fell to me to sign the papers to release her from life support and let her go. She was thirty-nine.

Oddly, my grief was held at bay, as though my heart wasn't ready to fully acknowledge what had been lost. In the days after her passing, I didn't cry—there was only an aching emptiness, a void that swallowed everything. It wasn't until after the burial service, when I found myself alone in her bedroom, surrounded by the remnants of her life—her favorite perfume on the dresser, her well-worn sweater folded neatly on the chair—that the weight of her absence crashed over me.

That was the moment it truly hit me: She was never coming back. The dam broke, and grief surged forward, raw, and unrelenting. I wept as though trying to pour out the unbearable truth with every tear. My aunt must have heard my cries, for she rushed in and gathered me into her arms, holding me as tightly as if she were trying to piece me back together. Her voice, steady and full of love, whispered words that would stay with me forever: "Let it out, all of it. She loved you so much."

Of course, none of us get through life without experiencing our share of sorrows. And we learn that time can be our friend, slowly lifting the weight and letting us live on. Dostoevsky, whose own travails included the death of a two-year old son, offered this powerful thought in *The Brothers Karamazov*:

> It's the great mystery of human life that old grief passes gradually into quiet tender joy. I bless the rising sun each day, and, as before, my heart sings to meet it, but now I love even more its setting, its long slanting rays and the soft tender gentle memories that come with them, the dear images from the whole of my long happy life.[1]

Her memory has always been with me, and it touched me in a special way during a recent family trip to Israel. We were in the fishing village of Magdala, on the Sea of Galilee, where a church stands in honor of great women of the faith. This church was built next to the remnants of a first-century synagogue where we know Jesus would have taught his disciples. Our guide, the Reverend Eamon Kelly, asked us to close our eyes and recall the special women in our lives who shaped our faith. "Take a few minutes," he said, "and consider those women."

I thought of my wife and daughters, who were standing with me, and I was filled with gratitude for my beautiful mother. Old grief returned in that moment, but also the gentle recollections of all that she gave me and still means to me. After losing her at such a young age, I have wanted my life to matter. I started my career not sure what work I would do, but one aim has always been fixed in my heart: I wanted to excel in a way that would honor my mother and make her proud.

Blind Spots

In sharing all this, I encourage you to consider your own story and how it has shaped you. Adversity is our least welcome instructor, but often the wisest. We all need to look back sometimes, especially to our hardest moments. As the prophet Isaiah told us, "Look to the place from where you came, the rock out of which you were shaped and the quarry from where you were mined."[2]

Over the years, I've discovered a few things about myself that both helped and hindered my career. The strong combination of divorce and a parent's death can, I am told, leave a pattern of forever trying to "fit in." When a family is shattered, the remaining members feel isolated. It's not unusual to develop a longing for acceptance and attention, a constant drive to measure up and belong. In time I came to recognize that my tendency to overcompensate, my desire to please to the point of overdoing it, was a blind spot.

> *Adversity is our least welcome instructor, but often the wisest. We all need to look back sometimes, especially to our hardest moments.*

Had the divorce of my parents and the death of my mother left a void that I was constantly trying to fill by winning the approval of others? Was I trying to prove something to my highly demanding and opinionated father? Or trying to overachieve and honor the legacy of my loving mother? Whatever the case, it was a quality that called for reflection and self-improvement. More than just a minor flaw or quirk of personality, the trait was a problem.

Time passed, and frankly as a young man I didn't do much to correct what I knew was a weakness. Things moved fast in those years, and "getting in touch with my feelings" wasn't high on the agenda. The pace really picked up when I became a new husband and then a father of one, two, three, and then four, all in the same years when I had left a White House job to serve as a partner in a leading global executive search firm. So preoccupied was I in those days, with work, travel, and getting ahead that my wife and I used to joke about one of our most coveted possessions: a card that gave us elite Global Services status with United Airlines. With each annual renewal of this status, Anne would say with approval, "I guess I'll stay married to you for another year."

If you'd met me during that period, you would have noticed the constant approval-seeking impulses. But dealing with blind spots cannot be put off forever, even when life and career are going well. The hinge moment for me came one day at a meeting with one of the firm's senior partners. We were discussing leadership succession in the office. A top biller for our company, this senior partner was one of those people you hear described as a "force of nature," with a mix of impressive and occasionally off-putting qualities. In other words, a straight-talking, no-nonsense guy without much tact or anything in the way of a filter. Once he had even come to blows with a colleague. He was the kind of partner clients loved and colleagues preferred to avoid.

He was in usual form when I sat down with him that day to talk over future leadership at the firm, a matter that involved my own prospects down the line. The guy held nothing back and got right in my face, saying "You're a brownnoser!" I was a "nice guy," he continued, "but you'll never make it here." He explained that the office needed a managing partner who was "tough as nails," and I didn't fit that description. "People-pleasers never make for good leaders," he told me. What the office needed, in his view, was someone with a sharp eye for talent and the backbone to push back on "corporate."

The source of this criticism made it easy to write off as bluster. The fact that this guy was terminated before year's end spared me from confronting the truth of what he had said. He had been shown the door—what did he know about me or about leadership?

I filed all this away in my mind, never really thinking about it again until long afterward when the firm identified me as a "high potential" leader, a designation given to only twenty or so junior partners who were then screened through an assessment program. Two senior partners interviewed me for three hours; then came a 360-reference report and a battery of psychometrics. All this data was reported back to me, along with the unattributed comments of colleagues, which had a familiar theme: "High in conflict avoidance." "Frequently holds back from expressing opinions with key stakeholders." "Resistance to making tough people decisions." "Reluctance to deliver direct feedback or outline clear expectations of underperforming employees." And so on.

It did not make for happy reading. The people-pleaser was in full view. I might be "well-liked" at the firm, but in the assessment of the report that hardly made me leadership material. What makes a leader, among much else, are directness and clarity. Yes, colleagues want their leaders to be considerate and respectful, and I met those criteria. But when they fail to set clear expectations or enable poor performance in fear of upsetting things or giving offense, that does more harm than good in any professional setting. That's where people-pleasing had gotten me at the firm: Nice guy but no leader.

The report identified me as a well-understood personality type. In the plus column, people-pleasers are generous with their time, energy, and effort. They eagerly take on extra work, may be more self-giving than others, are often peacemakers in an organization, and work harder than most to find ways to get to "yes." Downside: They beat around the bush. They have trouble saying "no." They might want to do the right thing but sometimes lack the nerve to follow through. They are generally more agreeable than others but can also be duplicitous in little schemes to avert or smooth out conflict. And in the end, their agenda of pleasing everyone and protecting themselves can hold an organization back.

It's not often in life when a personal flaw is so thoroughly documented as it was for me in this assessment by the firm. I wasn't exactly the Eddie Haskell type, to recall the two-faced kiss-up from the early sitcom *Leave It to Beaver* (more recently, Dwight Schrute from *The Office*), but after an initial period of denial, I knew I had some thinking and changing to do.

I kept reading about the people-pleasing type. One story resonated with me. A former people-pleaser tells how she was bitten by a snake and ended up in a hospital for three days. She and her family were camping, and, barefoot, she accidentally stepped on a snake, which bit her. Her dad was nearby but was deep in conversation with some fellow campers, and she thought it would be rude to interrupt. Instead, the woman walked three hundred yards back to her campsite to inform her mom that she had been bitten. "If it wasn't too much trouble," could she be taken to a hospital?

At the extreme, people-pleasing is a habit of subordinating self even to such a ridiculous extent—going so far that you'd set yourself on fire if that would keep others warm. Many who struggle with this tendency have experienced neglect, a traumatic event, or even abuse as children. It leads them to believe that their needs and wants are not that important. Alternatively, a child may begin to learn how to people-please by first learning how to "parent-please." During their formative years, as one expert writes, people-pleasers "likely received validation and approval when they fulfilled their parents' needs creating a link between self-worth and meeting external expectations."[3]

For me, it was perhaps both a yearning to belong and an imitation of my mother's unconditional love. The way she put others first, giving all and expecting so little in return; the way she never complained or found fault with anyone else. As she used to say, "*Ha nincs valami szép, ne mondd*" ("If you don't have anything nice to say, don't say it."). These were beautiful qualities in her, but they had become something different in me and they were hardly serving me well.

Clear Is Kind

Of all the blind spots in leadership I have encountered in decades as a corporate headhunter, the people-pleasing tendency is probably the most common, no doubt because it is so subtle and low-key. You run into all kinds of other blindspots—obsession with control, perfectionism, the devaluing of others, unconscious bias, and so on. It's easy enough to spot micromanagers and know-it-alls, but the people-pleasing type can elude attention for years.

The trait has even been a subject of polling. In one survey of 1,000 Americans, half self-identified as people-pleasers. In today's hyper-connected world, there seems to be a deepening need to please and to be liked. Women (56 percent) are more likely than men (42 percent) to see themselves this way. And by far most Americans recognize some of this tendency in themselves.[4]

Our own research at Heidrick & Struggles also confirms a trend toward people-pleasing in leadership, likely reflecting a social media–dependent culture. Coveting "likes" as if they were dopamine hits and obsessively posting our "perfect lives" on Instagram might both carry a hint of narcissism, but they also reflect a craving for approval and acceptance. The culture in this way rewards the very qualities that an aspiring leader needs to avoid—because you can't lead if your top concern is being liked. Real leadership does not show itself until the day you are confronted and opposed, and the disapproval of others doesn't throw you off your game.

In the sitcom *Everybody Loves Raymond*, the main character, played by Ray Romano, is the ultimate panderer. One episode is called "Somebody Hates Raymond." Romano's character, a sports columnist, is astounded to learn of someone who can't stand him. His pal Andy works for a popular sports-radio host who so dislikes Raymond that he refuses to ever book him on the show. As the story plays out, we see how panicked a people-pleaser becomes upon realizing that someone's approval has been withheld. When he finally confronts the issue, in a painfully awkward conversation, it's a scene I can relate to.[5]

As I sought to get rid of my own pandering tendencies, I also came across the writings of Dr. Brené Brown. Her book *Dare to Lead* reads as if written expressly for people like me. A lot of other readers must feel the same—her books are blockbusters and her TED Talk on "The Power of Vulnerability" has had more than thirty-five million views. At Heidrick & Struggles, we've even adapted the "Dare to Lead" program internally.

"Dare to Lead" starts with the understanding that an organization needs leadership at every level. Daring leaders have empathy, but they also know how to have hard conversations and hold themselves and others accountable. They take smart risks that make innovation possible, reset quickly after setbacks, build trust, and always give and receive feedback, even when that involves difficult conversations.

One of Dr. Brown's mottos is "Clear is kind," meaning that when we obscure hard truths we are doing no one any favors. As she bluntly put it, "Feeding people half-truths or bullshit to make them feel better (which is almost always about making ourselves feel more comfortable) is unkind."[6] And putting on the "armor" of avoidance is the opposite of the daring leadership that so many organizations urgently need.

For most of my career, I thought that I was good at giving feedback to others, and that I was encouraging that practice throughout the firm. In reality, I had a lot to learn, and it was this idea that "clear is kind" that really hit home for me. The full impact comes when you begin to think about the flip side—that to be unclear in a work setting, to withhold the full truth from others, is not a helpful way to treat colleagues. Moreover, as Brown observed, "Choosing our own comfort over hard conversations is the epitome of privilege, and it corrodes trust and moves us away from meaningful and lasting change."[7]

While her insight may have seemed simple, it sparked an internal battle for me to overcome my compulsion to please others and adopt a more transparent and straightforward approach with colleagues. This struggle persisted for quite some time, with mentors like the straight-talking and legendary Heidrick & Struggles Vice Chairman, John T. Gardner, frequently challenging me on it. After all, recognizing a blind spot is only the first crucial step toward finally overcoming it.

Perhaps you have been blinded, as I was, by the pull of seeking the approval of others, no matter what pretenses or deceptions that might involve. Or it might be another kind of blind spot that diminishes you as a colleague or as a leader. There are so many different tendencies that can undermine us: The micromanager. The authoritarian, controlling type. The perfectionist. The overly emotional type who creates needless drama. The office cynic who deflates the ideas and efforts of others. The colleague with the short fuse whose careless words alienate others and spread tension. Or maybe you're the easily distracted type, losing focus when colleagues are talking.

Whatever your blind spot, the crucial thing is to see it, name it, and treat it with zero tolerance. There's another, better person within each of us who is waiting to be heard. Once we start listening, it can change a career and even a life.

THREE

The Other Leader in You

I learned to recognize the thorough and primitive duality of man; I saw that, of the two natures that contended in the field of my consciousness, even if I could rightly be said to be either, it was only because I was radically both. . . . Good and evil are so close as to be chained together in the soul.
—Robert Lewis Stevenson,
The Strange Case of Dr. Jekyll and Mr. Hyde

In his classic *The Strange Case of Dr. Jekyll and Mr. Hyde*, Robert Louis Stevenson gave us the alter egos that have become modern-day shorthand for two-sided personalities. These opposites also capture a recurring challenge for anyone aspiring to be a leader.

Dr. Henry Jekyll is an upright citizen wrestling with his inner self. He is frustrated that the bad in him threatens to overpower the good. This "incongruous compound" of good and bad is driving him mad.[1]

A chemist, Dr. Jekyll creates a drug that separates himself into two distinct personalities. The good side is Dr. Jekyll; to the bad side, he gives the name Edward Hyde. Dr. Jekyll goes forth during the day; Mr. Hyde owns the night.

Of course, the experiment goes awry, and the doctor quickly discovers that his evil side is more monstrous than he had imagined. Though at first Mr. Hyde can be kept in check, eventually he dominates. He finds that every thought is centered on himself. Spiteful, vengeful, narcissistic, malicious, he is a liar and a cheat, he manipulates and then murders. Dr. Jekyll is ruined. "I was tenfold more wicked than I ever thought," he realizes.

As Stevenson explained through Jekyll's character, "I discovered through this process that man is not truly one, but two. It wasn't that I was a hypocrite . . . both sides of me were completely sincere."[2]

Alter Egos in Leadership

There is something in the Jekyll and Hyde story that we in the executive search business can recognize. It's far from the ultimate struggle between good and evil, but you do often find tension in leaders, and in candidates for leadership, between self-regard and service. Leaders must deal with two equally sincere sides of themselves and must always put forward only the side that best serves the interest of the organization.

An executive I once coached faced the choice of whether to accept a major leadership role in his company and was hesitant. This position offered a promotion in title and a way to give back to the firm by turning around an underperforming business unit. On the other hand, he realized the move would take him out of his well-settled routine and could also cost him financially in the short term.

He said, "I just don't think I can do it."

"Tell me more," I replied.

"Others have stepped into the role, and they almost always fail. And then they are screwed."

Still curious, I said "How does that make you feel?"

He paused. "Fearful." I let that hang in the air until he added, "Okay, maybe a bit selfish."

Now that we had gotten that far, I asked him to place himself in the shoes of the people in the struggling business unit. "They probably need you more than you realize, right?"

He could see the point. "I guess I never thought of it that way." In the end, he accepted the promotion.

As it happened, not even a year later the company was acquired in a $7 billion transaction. And because he had taken the offer and added critical new experiences to his résumé, more corporate headhunters came his way, his LinkedIn connections multiplied, and before long he landed a senior role in another peer company. His whole career took off because he had listened to his better self, accepted a sacrifice, and took a risk.

Good judgment and unselfish instincts are the mark of a leader. Tension starts to spread in an organization when a leader takes on a Jekyll-Hyde reputation and subordinates are never sure which one is going to show up on any given day. When your team starts to see that you are two different people, pleasant and purposeful one day and moody or volatile the next, everybody's energies divert toward managing you instead of advancing the enterprise. Suddenly colleagues are searching for excuses to stay clear of the boss. People disengage and pull back, the team loses cohesion and effectiveness, things unravel, and the story typically ends with new leadership.

Of course, it's not uncommon to encounter a leader who handles some situations much better than other situations. And even very capable people can show a darker side in moments of stress, exhaustion, conflict, or dejection. Our research at Heidrick & Struggles offers many examples of successful leaders who damaged their reputation in this way. And the harm isn't always done in total losses of control or other operatic scenes around the office; sometimes it's just a personal slight, an overbearing manner, a dismissive comment, or some other momentary display of unappealing qualities.

I was in a meeting once in Houston where our team was sitting down with a newly appointed executive who'd come in from New York. At the outset I made the usual suggestion that we go around the table and introduce ourselves. In a peremptory tone, our visitor said, "I think I know most of you, so we're good," and then plowed ahead with what he wanted to say. I made no objection, unreformed people-pleaser that I was, but I could tell his manner had turned off the entire room. For all the attention we paid him he might as well have stayed in New York.

The "dark side" of personality in leadership has been closely examined by Drs. Robert and Joyce Hogan, who compiled a set of traits associated with ineffective executives and often with career derailment.[3] When leaders exhibit the bright-side traits, they are "self-monitoring, behaving themselves, and motivated to do well and meet social expectations."[4] These leaders score high on conscientiousness and emotional stability, and they are more socially skilled and unflappable. The ones who show up with the dark-side traits are "less careful in managing their behavior and the impression it creates," or else they "simply don't care about how they are being perceived."[5] In other words, as the Hogans explained, we can't always define the traits that make a leader, but we can readily see the traits that true leaders would never display.

Breaking Bad

Another study of leadership traits, conducted by researchers at Michigan State University, turned up a paradox.[6] In a survey, employees were asked to describe the day-to-day behavior of their bosses. The study revealed a pattern in which leaders with reputations for being conscientious could now and then appear to disregard their own standards. How could it be, the researchers wondered, that the same leader might shine one day and "break bad" the next? The study proposed two explanations.

One is "moral licensing," the tendency of people to consider themselves so highly ethical as to be entitled to occasional exceptions, as if a practice of doing the right thing could buy a right to sometimes do the opposite.

> *Good and bad behavior are separate accounts; what accumulates in one can't cover what is missing in the other.*

In business, I've seen how moral licensing works. A former colleague of mine was exemplary in serving clients, but much less so in leading his team. Someone who calls it like he sees it, he was brutally transparent about candidate references and their flaws. He always gave clients the benefit of the doubt on fees and invoicing, even forgoing earned revenue to keep clients happy. He also set the highest standards of quality and execution. His search / completion ratio was second to none. And yet this same colleague seemed to grant himself license to behave differently with his team. Not only was he overly demanding, rude, and at times verbally abusive; he frequently had subordinates scurrying over to his house to care for his pets, pick up his laundry, and run other personal errands.

Distasteful as moral licensing can be, I've seen the fault in myself too. I remember once when I felt I had been quite generous with my time and money helping a local Houston charity, but then felt slighted when other donors were recognized and I wasn't. If I was entitled to complain at all, the way to do it was in a frank, private conversation with the lady in charge of the charity. Instead, I sent her an archly worded email conveying my annoyance, and, as if that weren't bad enough, cc'd everyone else who came to mind. I guess I felt that, having amply contributed to a good cause, I had the moral credits to offset this outburst, but of course it doesn't work that way. Good and bad behavior are separate accounts; what accumulates in one can't cover what is missing in the other.

It is common sense, after all, that self-control is not a constant, not always maintained at the same level. We all know this from experience. We start the day energized and focused on doing our best. We may even pray for the wisdom and strength to do it. Our reservoir of energy and goodwill is filled to capacity. Then as the day wears on our momentum slows; irritations and distractions that would have rolled off our back in the morning now hit us differently, and by day's end we are no one's example of poise and goodwill. This is what the study calls ego depletion.

I once saw a young colleague put in a star performance at the office. Moving from task to task and from meeting to meeting, he impressed everyone with his focus and enthusiasm. It didn't last, however, and by day's end he could be heard snapping at colleagues and griping about how "under-resourced" he was. Clients were expecting too much, colleagues weren't pulling their weight, and on and on. He went from office exemplar to whiny victim in a single day.

Sure, we all run out of steam as the workday draws on, and we all learn to make allowances for that. If we want to rise in an organization and be seen as leadership material, however, there's a higher standard to meet.

In the Beginning

It stands to reason that insight into leadership will always involve trying to better understand human nature. On that score, many people in the business world have lately drawn from the wisdom of a famous 1965 essay called *The Lonely Man of Faith*, by Rabbi Joseph B. Soloveitchik.

Biblical scholars have long noted the two accounts of creation in chapters one and two of Genesis. In the first account, mankind was created in God's image and given dominion over the rest of creation. We were called "to fill the earth and subdue it" in terms that depict humanity as a primary force in nature as God's plan unfolds. Chapter two gives a different picture. There, our Creator formed humanity from the "dust of the ground and breathed into his nostrils the breath of life." Adam was placed into the garden, soon to be joined by his mate Eve in a peaceful setting yet undisturbed by sin.

Genesis one gives us man as an active, dynamic presence in the world. It highlights our outer strength and our drive to control and reshape our surroundings. Genesis two presents a humbler, more pacific and inward-looking creature. And generations of theologians and philosophers, seeing the dramatic contrast in these two portrayals, have reasonably wondered how human beings could be represented by both.

In *The Lonely Man of Faith*, Rabbi Soloveitchik reflected on this question and on its implications. Essentially, he concluded that it was no mystery at all. The answer, he wrote, "lies not in an alleged dual tradition, but in dual man; not in an imaginary contradiction between the two versions but in a real contradiction in the nature of man."[7] There is not just one Adam, but two; not just one tradition, but two different traditions that speak to the realities of human nature.

It was Rabbi Soloveitchik who introduced the terms "Adam I" and "Adam II" that we hear often nowadays in discussions of personal growth and professional fulfillment. A key insight was that although different, these human types are not in complete opposition to each another. This isn't good versus evil, like Henry Jekyll and his opposite. The two Adams reflect the duality of God's character within us, and both are good. Yet one of them—Adam II—stands for qualities that are in urgent demand among leaders today.

Rabbi Soloveitchik's sixty-year-old essay might have been long forgotten but for the author and columnist David Brooks, who put Adam I and Adam II into the contemporary lexicon with his book *The Road to Character*. That book was a kind of revelation for me, drawing a clear framework for distinguishing the two general types of leaders I had encountered in my decades of acquaintance with business executives. I've met these two Adams many times in recruiting interviews and coaching sessions. Here is my summary of the way Brooks characterized each:

ADAM I NATURE	ADAM II NATURE
The ambitious and external side of our nature—he wants to build and create and innovate	The humble side of our nature—he wants not only to be good but to do good
Savors accomplishments	Savors consistency and inner strength
Asks, "how does the cosmos work?"	Asks, "why are we here?"
Asks, "how do things work?"	Asks, "what is our purpose?"
Believes in an external logic—input leads to output	Believes in an inverse logic—you must give to receive; to fulfill yourself, you must forget yourself

Brooks reminded us that we live in a world that favors Adam I and often neglects Adam II. And that is surely true in America's corporate culture. Businesses largely value work that is individualistic, competitive, and pragmatic—prizing results above all.

Edgar Schein, in *Humble Inquiry*, pointed out that we in the business world "claim to value teamwork and talk about it all the time, but the artifacts—our promotional systems and rewards systems—are entirely individualistic."[8] In our "do and tell" cultures, Schein observed, we become "impatient"; and with the power of technology to increase productivity, "we are even more impatient."[9] The "do and tell" attitudes of Adam I pervade business today—transactions valued over relationships, telling over asking, hubris over humility—and it all comes at a cost as team members feel estranged from their organizations and leaders.

Companies that pour all their energies into greater efficiency and performance can quickly find themselves with low morale and little loyalty among employees. Leaders can't just crack the whip with the "how" of a company's work; they must reinforce the "why" with attention to unity and purpose. In the whole spirit of the enterprise, the forcefulness and ambition of Adam I has to be tempered by the reflectiveness and calm of Adam II.

Adam I, wrote Brooks, "is built by building on your strengths. Adam II is built by fighting your weaknesses."[10] And while many leaders I've encountered are the full embodiment of Adam I, the standouts always bring Adam II to mind as well. When a leader balances the formidable qualities of Adam I with the quieter, gentler virtues of Adam II, people notice. Hiring managers and boards of directors sit straighter in their chairs. Everyone listens because, frankly, it's a rare and quite impressive sight. And when that kind of leader aims higher, so does everybody else.

Keeping Silence

The question is whether such leaders are so rare as to represent a basically unattainable ideal. Even Rabbi Soloveitchik asked long ago whether it was even possible for the Adam II type to succeed in highly competitive environments tailored to the Adam I type—in a society so "enamored of quantitative method and bent on material triumphs."[11]

Adam I figures prominently in free-market capitalism. He's the founder of enterprises, the initiator, the problem solver, the disrupter, the change maker. I give ground to no one in my admiration for the strength and boldness that make for Adam I types. In his way, my father—with only an eighth-grade education—was such a man, his own life a story of risk-taking, hard work, and achievement. Yet as central as they are to human progress, Adam I qualities must never be given absolute rule. Surely the key is to recall that the two Adams are complementary facets of created man. They are meant to be kept in balance, and doing so in our working lives has always required intention and effort. The challenge can seem harder than ever in our technology-driven lives, with so many influences that are designed to keep us from reflecting. Adam I holds his usual dominant place in public attention, while the voice of Adam II is barely heard at all.

When I'm coaching executives, I often ask how much time they set aside for simply thinking—and whether that feels like enough. One can only be truly themselves and fully free when they are comfortable being alone. So many CEOs these days seem "switched on" at all hours, and some of them cultivate that very image. They seem to be everywhere, all at once, always in motion and ubiquitous. I prefer to point instead to the example of business leaders who consistently reserve time for reflection—Warren Buffett being a famous case in point. His colleague, the late Charlie Munger, explained once that Buffett often arranged his entire schedule around hours of quiet thought. When the head of Berkshire Hathaway's schedule said only "haircut," Munger knew that "haircut Tuesdays" was another day for nothing but thought.[12]

Buffett's bridge partner and friend, Bill Gates, is likewise well known for his yearly "Think Weeks," passed alone in a cabin reading books, a practice now widely emulated. John Donahoe, the former CEO of Nike, had his designated regular "thinking days," and Jeff Weiner of LinkedIn has two hours of "thinking time" every day. Of course, you don't need a secluded cabin or a week off to reap the benefits of intentional reflection. Whether it's an afternoon unplugged, a quiet walk, or even a morning journal session, carving out space to think can be a game changer for anyone, no matter the role or the resources we have. Regardless, asserting our Adam II selves against the pressures of an Adam I business environment is prudent and wise.

Many recent books have been written on this theme of getting away to reorient ourselves so that we are not merely slaves to the moment. It's the modern expression of ancient wisdom—going back to the reminder in Ecclesiastes that there is "a time to keep silence."[13] That time has inestimable value for any leader who feels stuck and in need of a reset, who is facing a major decision, whose business is in or nearing crisis, or who just needs to think about how he or she can do better overall. As Ryan Holiday wrote in his 2023 *Stillness Is the Key*:

> You have to disconnect in order to better connect with yourself and with the people you serve and love. People don't have enough silence in their lives because they don't have enough solitude. And they don't get enough solitude because they don't seek out or cultivate silence. It's a vicious cycle that prevents stillness and reflection, and then stymies good ideas, which are almost always hatched in solitude.[14]

Anthony de Mello, the Jesuit priest, and author of *Awareness*, called the practice of solitude or reflection a time of "waking up." To illustrate, de Mello shared the story of a father who knocks on his son's door:

> "Jaime," he says, "wake up!"
> Jaime answers, "I don't want to get up, Papa."
> The father shouts, "Get up, you have to go to school."
> Jaime says, "I don't want to go to school."
> "Why not?" asks the father.
> "Three reasons," says Jaime. "First, because it's so dull; second, the kids tease me; and third, I hate school."
> And the father says, "Well, I am going to give you three reasons why you must go to school. First, because it is your duty; second, because you are forty-five years old, and third, because you are the headmaster."
>
> Some of us grow up, and yet, we have been asleep the whole time. Wake up! We need to wake up![15]

No one I've ever talked to on this subject has ever told me that taking time for serious thinking and awakening is an overrated idea. Everyone who makes this a discipline is rewarded for the effort. "The quieter you become, the more you are able to hear," in the saying of one poet. Another effect is to turn our "To-Do List" into a "To-Be List," as we clear away the distractions and false priorities that a workday can throw at us to focus instead on the real demands of leadership. Reflection can be a way of regaining something that can so easily slip away in business: control.

The Leader's Path

Some leaders carry themselves with a kind of self-control that instantly catches the attention of a headhunter. There's a consistency and inner strength about them that stands out in any crowd. You get the sense you're dealing with someone with solid values who behaves the way he or she believes, and is always the same responsible, reliable person in any circumstance. At some point, they decided what kind of professional they wanted to be and stayed with it.

Ultimately, when we stop sleepwalking and become more self-aware, to build our strengths and overcome our blind spots, what we are really aiming for is integrity. In engineering, they define integrity as uncompromising adherence to a standard, and the same applies to that quality in business leadership. It's unmistakable, and there's a reason why it is always named as a prized value in surveys of Fortune 500 companies.[16]

Of course, integrity is less a single quality than it is a reflection of many other virtues. In one common definition, it means doing the right thing even when no one is watching. This is how it was taught to William, my four-year-old grandson, although instead of saying "when no one is watching" he mixed it up and said "watch out where you are going"—and I guess that's good counsel too. To be a leader of integrity, you've got to keep an eye out for things in your path that can easily trip you up.

Such leaders are generally more levelheaded and poised even when faced with setbacks, failure, or bad news. While not without flaws, their integrity allows them to manage both chaos and the mundane in the same way—with grace and steadiness. Consistency of character always allows them to show up as impartial and fair, especially at the CEO level. It's in their nature as well to speak truth when it is uncomfortable or goes against self interest.

I recall an uncomfortable situation I once found myself in while leading the search for a chief technology officer of a well-known company. The finalist, a former top official at a presidential cabinet agency, had come to Houston for her final interview. When I called the candidate at her hotel to be sure she was all set for the interview, something seemed off. She was testy and her speech was slurred. I began wondering if we should just cancel the interview.

I told myself she was probably just weary from a long trip, but clearly more was going on here and the explanation was sure to be found in her bar tab. Should I let it pass or was this something my colleagues should know about? I didn't want to ruin her chances, but I also didn't want to neglect a concern that maybe our client company should know about.

As it turned out, I did raise the issue, but not emphatically, and this woman got the job. She lasted about six months before being undone by her alcoholism. It was not one of my better calls, especially because I went against my instincts.

On another occasion, things got awkward when I received something I wasn't supposed to see. A new client had recently terminated one of our major competitors—and then, inadvertently, sent my team a batch of files containing confidential information about our competitor. I was concerned about this potential disclosure of trade secrets, even though some counseled me that the information had been seen before and was "essentially immaterial." Still, this time I went with my instincts and immediately returned the files to their sender. Keeping them just didn't feel right.

The finest leaders I have seen in action don't hesitate once they are sure of the right thing to do. They stay firmly anchored to their values and understand their capabilities and blind spots alike. They know themselves, and different types must contend with different weaknesses. People-pleasers must get past the compulsion to always be liked and make it their rule to be direct. Micromanagers must learn to let go and to entrust authority to others. The more emotional types must learn resiliency and self-control. Those with an omniscience complex (a.k.a. know-it-alls) have to realize how this attitude can stifle discussion and dissent, instead allowing others on the team to think and contribute for themselves.

The "To-Be List" goes on. The easily triggered must learn how to manage frustration, disappointment, a bruised ego, or defeat. Some leaders find it hard to provide structure, and they must be intentional about creating boundaries and organizational systems. Still others prefer to go it alone; they must overcome their reluctance to ever ask for help. Those given to ascribing blame, habitually playing the victim, and pointing to the failures of others, obviously need to lose that habit and take responsibility. And finally, if we're the easily distracted type, diverted by the slightest stray thought or faintest alert notification, we need to think straight and start giving others the same respectful attention we expect of them.

We all have blind spots and dealing with those will always be enough to keep us busy, leaving little time for expounding on the shortcomings of others. Lest we doubt that, the chart below offers a reminder of common flaws in leadership, along with the opportunities for growth that might be right in front of us.

ENLIGHTENED LEADERS	**LEADERS STILL in the DARK**
Super aware	Oblivious to blind spots
Reflective	Impulsive
Ownership mindset	Deflects blame
Solicits feedback	Enables sycophants
Shows vulnerability	Pretends invincibility (avoids emotional exposure)
Wages war against flaws	Maintains a policy of neutrality
Faces fears directly	Stays anxious
Remains grateful	Complains regularly
Experiments with new solutions	Makes excuses
Seeks objectivity	Stays dogmatic
Impartial	Plays favorites
Keeps things real	Lies to themselves
Seeks to show up differently	Expects others to show up differently

From the C-Suite to frontline managers, no one willingly follows a Jekyll-and-Hyde leader who fails to consistently embody integrity. Leadership awareness demands recognizing that every hour of the day presents choices—choices that define us as individuals and shape the entire organization, for better or worse. These choices, like those illustrated in the chart above, include embracing enlightenment or remaining in ignorance; taking ownership or shifting blame; seeking constructive feedback or enabling sycophants; and striving for objectivity rather than clinging to dogma.

Remember, too, how high the stakes can be. Integrity in business leaders is more than a matter of growth and development in one person. It reaches the whole length of that person's power and influence. And when integrity is missing, the consequences can spread well beyond that.

FOUR

To Find Your Blindspot

Let them alone; they are blind guides.
And if the blind lead the blind,
both will fall into a pit.

—Matthew 15:14 ESV

The son of a prominent New York family, Richard Severan Fuld ascended to the heights of his profession: chairman and CEO of Lehman Brothers, the storied Wall Street investment firm and major player in global finance. And in all the annals of private enterprise, rarely has one man's blind spot resulted in more harm.

For context, Dick Fuld rose through the ranks at Lehman Brothers during an era defined by hubris, unchecked ambition, and moral vacuity—an age of relentless, even cutthroat, competition that extended to rivalries within their own firms. The ethos of Wall Street's aggressive banking culture in the 1980s and 90s was perhaps best encapsulated by the infamous saying from the Salomon Brothers days: "No one stabs you in the back around here; they come right through the front door and stab you in the chest."

This era was captured with razor-sharp precision by Tom Wolfe in *The Bonfire of the Vanities*. Through his satirical lens, Wolfe painted a vivid portrait of the "masters of the universe"—the swaggering, larger-than-life investment bankers and traders who wielded immense influence and reveled in their wealth and power. The novel delves into a culture consumed by greed and the pursuit of status, exposing the moral compromises and personal costs that often accompanied such relentless ambition. Sherman McCoy, the protagonist and a bond trader, stands as a fictional counterpart to figures like Fuld—a man enveloped in privilege and self-importance, whose carefully constructed world collapses with a single, catastrophic mistake.

Like other investment bank bosses leading up to the financial crisis, Dick Fuld single-mindedly pursued the enormous fees and profits to be made by repackaging America's mortgages into securities. Ignoring warnings that the nation's housing market was on the verge of collapse and that mortgage bankers were issuing loans to consumers who could never repay them, Fuld remained all-in. To get ahead of competition from other banks, he led Lehman into riskier and riskier debt, until the bank held less than a dollar in reserves for every thirty dollars in liabilities.

Even while all this was going on, there was still a way out. It required simply listening to those who were pointing to dangers ahead. Larry McDonald, a former vice president with the firm, told us that Fuld was warned three different times, but still could not be made to see a coming catastrophe of his own making. Both Fuld and Lehman president Joe Gregory were counseled by the "cleverest financial brains on Wall Street" to change course immediately. These advisors plainly saw the risks that Fuld and his team were blind to:

> Each laid it out, from way back in 2005, that the real estate market was living on borrowed time and that Lehman Brothers was headed directly for the biggest subprime iceberg ever seen, and with the wrong men on the bridge.

To Find Your Blindspot

Dick and Joe turned their backs all three times. It was probably the worst triple since St. Peter denied Christ.[1]

Chairman Fuld was sure he knew what he was doing. After all, even with all the subprime debt, the overall business was sound and profitable. As one of those unheeded advisors explained, the failure of Lehman Brothers, with 25,000 employees, came down to one sentence: "There were 24,992 people making money, and eight guys losing it—and unfortunately, most of those eight guys were very close to Richard S. Fuld."[2]

That the Lehman bankruptcy led to one of the most destructive global financial collapses ever may be old news, but its consequences linger. Millions continue to suffer the long-term effects of the Great Recession, and the lesson of over-levereaged balance sheets has not been fully learned. In the years after the crisis, Federal Reserve chairman Ben Bernanke employed quantitative easing (QE); his successor, Jerome Powell, continued QE during the Covid pandemic, arguing this was needed to make the nation's banking system safer.[3] Yet some analysts argue that Fed policy has made the banking system less safe, by holding interest rates artificially low for nearly fifteen years before inflation pressures forced them up again. These analysts fear that the accumulating losses on mortgages and bonds from the artificially low-interest rate environment could ultimately create the next crisis.

For many, it is still perplexing that many of the banking executives never faced prosecution. The court examiner in the Lehman bankruptcy case concluded that the firm had "manipulated" the balance sheet with an "accounting gimmick," namely the "Repo 105" accounting method that concealed $50 billion in liabilities. This made Lehman Brothers "effectively blind to its own danger."[4]

Some twenty years earlier, I sat in a stuffy Houston courtroom with my then fifteen-year-old son, observing the trial of Enron executives Jeffrey Skilling and Ken Lay. The courthouse was just two blocks from my office, and this was a chance to show my son just how wrong things can go when business ethics are cast aside.

This famous case of the era turned on the legal principle of "willful blindness." Lawyers for Skilling and Lay argued that the defendants did not know about the fraud and therefore could not have been held responsible. Judge Simeon Lake, a familiar face to many of us in Houston, gave instructions to the jury: "You may find that a defendant had knowledge of a fact if you find that the defendant closed his eyes to what would otherwise have been obvious to him." The judge added, "Knowledge can be inferred if the defendant deliberately blinded himself to the existence of a fact."[5] The jury returned verdicts of guilty.

The Enron case vindicated a long-established rule of law that probably would have applied had Dick Fuld and his top lieutenants ever been brought to trial. Fuld would later say he took "full responsibility," but also that he would not have done anything differently. He railed against "rumors, speculation, misunderstandings, and factual errors," and attributed Lehman's collapse to a "perfect storm" beyond anyone's control. It was the familiar spirit of blame-shifting, in that era when reckless institutions were "too big to fail"[6] and millions of responsible people with no role in the ruin bore the full weight of it.

Sorting out the epic scandals of that period is not my purpose here. What matters most is understanding what this and other disasters in business can teach us about overcoming blind spots and leading well. Leaders who cannot find the strength to do this are bound to repeat the errors of the past or else stumble into new ones. Leaders who identify and confront their blind spots will not only avoid that kind of grief; they will detect trouble far enough in advance to stay clear of it. Mindful of their strengths and weaknesses, far-sighted and well-grounded, alert to challenges that have undone others, they become almost too aware to fail.

Avoiding the Ditch

In Pieter Bruegel's well-known sixteenth-century painting *The Parable of the Blind*, we see a man unsure of himself leading several others who are equally unsure of themselves. It was the painter's visualization of the timeless parable in which Jesus asked: "Can the blind lead the blind? Shall they not both fall into the ditch?"[7]

As described by the novelist Gert Hoffman in his novel, also named *The Parable of the Blind*, the six men in the painting are "self-absorbed, withdrawn, bitter, and distrustful."[8] They cannot see that they are blundering, weak, and hopeless. They stumble around, bumping into one another. As the leader collapses, the man closest to him braces himself for a fall. The next two men are headed for the same fate and can already sense that something terrible is happening. The remaining two are relaxed and clueless, not yet aware of what lies just ahead.

The Parable of the Blind, Pieter Bruegel, 1568, Museo di Capodimonte, Naples, Italy

Worth noting as well is the church in the distance. The men are going away from it. And the farther they stray from the steeple, the closer they come to the ditch. To the Baroque mind, the imagery is unmistakable: The men have ventured dangerously far from their spiritual and moral home.

Of course, the painting and the original parable are no commentary on real, physical blindness. Indeed, I have known sightless people who have their own lessons to teach about clarity of perception. I think of a good family friend named Mary Farish Johnston, who has been blind most of her life. Mary has what neuroscientists call "enhanced auditory ability," among other heightened faculties that make her the most alert person in any setting. Once, in a crowded, noisy room, she easily made her way to my wife by following the sound of Anne's voice, and though I hadn't made a sound Mary turned to me and said, "Hi, Les." It's quite an experience, being seen by someone who cannot see. And that depth of awareness is just one attribute that any leader could stand to learn from my wonderful, kind friend Mary.

Bruegel's painting and its scriptural inspiration are both, in part, commentaries on human arrogance and foolishness. Metaphorically, blindness was attributed to the Pharisees, who were certain of their superior knowledge and piety and commanded others to follow. Pride and sanctimony were their blind spots. Lacking the humility to question themselves, to consider their own flaws, or to seek wisdom beyond their own fixed precepts, they fell into error and led others down the same troubled path.

Though more than five centuries old, this classic painting offers an image for our time. If the person in front cannot see the path ahead, or is heedless of his own limitation, then the whole group will come to grief. It's an allegory for the ages, and it keeps playing out in modern institutions. Invariably, the leader is the one who falls first and hardest. If you're taking cues from a leader with little or no self-awareness, who is so certain of himself that he is immune to growth and good counsel, you're probably headed for a ditch.

Searching ancient literature for an opposite image, we might recall Cassandra of Greek mythology—the royal who could see what others could not, though her warnings and prophesies went unheeded.

To Find Your Blindspot

Margaret Heffernan, in her book *Willful Blindness*, described certain types of people as "Cassandras," and explained what it is that can mark them as leaders. The Cassandras among us can see better, Heffernan wrote, because they "listen carefully to silence but don't succumb to it." These men and women, she observed, show that "while willful blindness may be part of the human condition, it need not define who we are."[9]

My friend, Mary, is herself a Cassandra, who can see what others cannot. A devoted wife, mother, and grandmother, she is a person after God's own heart—full of grace and truth. Blended into Bruegel's vivid tale, she would be the seventh figure in the painting pleading with the men to turn back toward the steeple.

Medically, a blind spot, or scotoma, is what obscures our vision. There is a spot in our retina where the optic nerve connects, and there are no light-sensitive cells. The absence of cells to detect light creates a corresponding field of vision that is invisible—our blind spot. When driving, it is that dangerous small zone of blindness that creates collisions when changing lanes or T-bones when your view of the traffic crossflow is partially obstructed.

When my youngest daughter, Molly, was doing drivers' ed as a fifteen-year-old, she got sick of me reminding her, "don't forget your blind spot." The middle child, she was never shy about expressing herself. "Dad, why do they make cars with blinds spots? It's stupid!" She has a point and was ahead of her time as newer vehicles built in the last decade have blind spot warning systems.

Innovative technologies in our smart vehicles have mitigated blinds spots, especially when leveraging and adjusting our mirrors. Drivers can adjust their rearview mirror to give a more direct view behind them. Such adjustments shrink the blind spot to such a small degree that it is no longer a debilitating factor in driving safely. The Blindspot Information System in my hybrid smart truck can enhance the safety of family members who trust me to avoid the modern ditch. Likewise, in leadership or human relationships, we can adjust our awareness to see the safer path.

To take a real-world example of a purposeful, self-aware business leader who confronted and overcame a serious blind spot, consider a case I have often cited when coaching leaders. Ken Olsen was among the pivotal figures who shaped the computer industry in its earliest days. The company he founded in 1957, Digital Equipment Corporation, or DEC, was at one point the world's second largest computer company. Bill Gates, among many others, expressed great admiration for Olsen and called him a "major influence" in his life.

For some years, however, there was another side to Olsen's reputation. You might have admired him from afar, but you didn't want to work for him. He was an autocratic CEO with a tyrannical streak that alienated his team. Yet over time, with coaching and getting outside his bubble, Olsen came to understand that this was a problem, and he addressed his blind spot in a serious way. He resolved to become a different kind of leader and restructured his entire company to reflect this radical change in style.

He created a nonhierarchal organization that back then, in the 1970s and 80s, was unique in corporate America. The formerly cold and impersonal CEO now brought a whole different attitude to the office. The sight of the boss approaching no longer put anyone on edge. Now, when Olsen stopped by an engineer's desk, he would ask in an offhanded way, "What are you working on?"[10] He was genuinely interested, and conversations with the boss were now productive and collegial.

The writer Edgar Schein, who worked closely with Olsen, remembered that "even when the company had over 100,000 people worldwide, Ken was well known and loved because so many people had experienced him as a humble inquirer."[11] Olsen himself has given the moral of the story in an interview toward the end of his career. "If you're blind to your weaknesses you get in trouble," he said. "You only learn if you're conscious of the need to learn."[12] In other words, no matter what it is, you can beat your blind spot.

"America's Reckless Billionaire"

After thirty-plus years of searching for executive talent, I could offer a good many case studies that turned out as well as Ken Olsen's. Yet there are a few sad cases as well, of headstrong, overconfident leaders whose flaws seemed clear to everyone but themselves. One example still hurts when I think about it.

Aubrey McClendon, one of the pioneers of the shale gas revolution, was an American CEO whose blind spot cost him his job, his fortune, and almost surely his life. Aubrey was a client of mine and I also considered him a friend. Known for his suave manner, sunny outlook, personal generosity, and silver hair, Aubrey was among the first to see the transformative possibilities of horizontal drilling and hydraulic fracking—the technologies that have made the United States by far the world's largest producer of natural gas. The company he founded in 1989, Chesapeake Energy, was second only to ExxonMobil in natural gas production by 2012.

Aubrey's warm and winsome style drew you in. And those who knew him recall, among other strengths, his peerless salesmanship. The Adam I drive and confidence glowed in him; his knack for making the sale or closing the deal was something to behold. Usually, it's the engineers and geologists who rise to top positions in the energy industry. Aubrey had been a history major in college, then became an accountant and an oil-and-gas landman—persuading property owners to lease their land for production. This landman-turned-CEO, Aubrey brought his own combination of gifts to the industry, plus zeal that never seemed to fade, and he stood out. In 2005, *Forbes* named Aubrey one of the top performing executives in the country. When his career took a different turn, the same magazine put him on the cover, with the heading "America's Reckless Billionaire."

It was true that he had a way of charging forward, often with more enthusiasm than deliberation, and that was one cause of his troubles. Another was a tendency to treat corporate assets as available for his own use. In a clear case of moral licensing, he took to using Chesapeake resources for his art collection and other personal indulgences. He was living large, even as problems came into view. Aubrey McClendon's philanthropic investments, I should add, helped transform Oklahoma City into a vibrant urban hub, revitalizing its downtown and propelling its emergence as a center for commerce, arts, and sports.

The man could also be a handful. His tedious management of every detail put his team to the test. And his friends and colleagues were treated as if on call 24/7. When I answered calls from Aubrey on Sunday mornings or late at night, my wife Anne told me I was just "enabling" him.

For years, Aubrey's business strategy consisted of acquiring more and more cheap leases, and drilling more and more wells. At about $8 million per well, this required a constant flow of capital, which in Aubrey's case meant a constant accumulation of debt. He just kept pushing it, one new project after another. An investor once asked him on a conference call, "When is enough?" Aubrey told him, "I can't get enough."[13]

The usual formula in business is to prepare for the worst and hope for the best. Aubrey McClendon always prepared for the best without imagining the worst. This was the blind spot that brought him to grief.

In the short version, greater supplies of natural gas on the market and the global crisis of 2008–2009 both put downward pressure on prices. By 2012 they were down 60 percent from their peak. As the economy started to recover after the Great Recession, demand for wells drove up the cost of leasing. Chesapeake was paying more for land even as it was taking in less cash for its production. The company's share price began to tumble. Carl Icahn, the investor known as "the most feared man on Wall Street," quickly acquired a large equity position in the company. Around the same time, Chesapeake found itself dealing with an SEC investigation and seventeen shareholder lawsuits.

To Find Your Blindspot

All this became a direct concern of mine after Chesapeake's board demoted Aubrey to CEO, replacing him as chairman with Archie Dunham, a man I knew well. Archie, who had once led ConocoPhillips, was trying to turn things around at Chesapeake when I was invited to meet him for breakfast in Houston in early 2013. Aubrey was about to be dismissed, he told me; could I quietly begin an executive search right away?

The story went on from there—Aubrey left the company and then promptly started another, American Energy Partners. He even leased office space in a tall building near the Chesapeake offices—so that, as his friends observed, he could look down on the company that he had founded. But the same blind spot yielded the same pattern: rapid growth, dangerous debt, and a second undoing with the inevitable next collapse in gas prices.

Worse, this time federal prosecutors were investigating Aubrey for allegedly rigging bids for drilling rights in violation of antitrust laws. A grand jury in Oklahoma City indicted him on charges that he had "orchestrated a conspiracy between two large oil and gas companies" between 2007 and 2012.[14] Prosecutors alleged that Aubrey and his coconspirators would "decide ahead of time who would win the leases," and that the winning bidder would still provide a cut of the leases to the losing bidder. Aubrey pledged to aggressively fight the allegations and clear his name.

The day after the indictment, Aubrey was due to turn himself in for arraignment at the federal courthouse at 11:00 a.m. Early that morning, he went to the office, "sent a few emails, then ditched his security detail and climbed into his 2013 Chevy Tahoe." Just after 9:00 a.m., traveling at high speed and not wearing a seat belt, he swerved off the road and crashed into an embankment. As one policeman described the scene, "flames engulfed McClendon's vehicle immediately." Aubrey, said the officer, "pretty much drove straight into the wall."[15]

I was in Heidrick & Struggles' New York office when I heard

77

what had happened. For all of Aubrey's friends, it's an awful memory. Over the years, I have been asked whether I thought it was suicide. I really don't know. He said he was determined to beat the charges against him, and that I can believe. He was also a man of faith, with a good family that he loved; suicide is hard to square with that side of Aubrey. In any case, Oklahoma authorities ruled the crash an accident and found no note or other evidence of suicidal intent. People much closer to the McClendons than I was could never believe he would take his own life. Aubrey was on another comeback—and if anyone could pull it off again, he was the guy.

He was just fifty-six years old, with so much talent, amazing energy, and plenty of runway for more achievement and growth. He wasn't given the time to fully correct course and match his many strengths to his full potential. Had life given Aubrey that chance, however, I would not have bet against him.

The Ungoverned Leader

One question a reasonable person would have asked, back when things at Chesapeake Energy started taking a bad turn, concerns the company's board of directors. Where were they in all this? Yes, they brought in Archie Dunham, the adult in the room, but not before the company had been badly damaged. Entire boards can develop blind spots of their own, leaving a leader's recklessness unchecked.

It can invite problems when CEOs also hold the title of chairman of the board, as Aubrey did. What can be lost is the healthy relationship between officers and directors. In such cases the CEO fails to properly leverage board members as real partners and risk experts whose independent views should carry weight. Instead of packing a board with loyalists and friends or viewing the boards as a hindrance to their own designs, the most successful CEOs I've known regard their boards as working partners and allies in governance.

To Find Your Blindspot

Recall the case of Dick Fuld and the board at Lehman Brothers. While the chairman and CEO plunged his firm into the turbulent waters of risky credit, unsustainable debt, and untested financial products such as mortgage-backed securities, a disengaged board was acting essentially as his personal fan club. Most members of the board had little or no experience in financial services. As Larry McDonald remarked, "It's pretty clear that the board was out of touch with 21st century financial products. These were people from another era, and they were sitting on top of $700 billion of 21st century risk. So, the question was 'why was that board selected by Richard Fuld and why didn't he pick a better board to sit over all of this risk that affected us all?'"[16]

While Lehman's board was flying blind, many outside analysts were saying as far back as March of 2008, when Bear Stearns failed, that Lehman was also in trouble. Fuld and his board had to understand the systemic risk and yet did nothing about it. Treasury Secretary Hank Paulson had strongly encouraged Lehman to immediately address the risk, perhaps by considering a sale or raising new capital. The board took a pass.

Stronger governance would likewise have made all the difference in averting the 2023 turmoil at Silicon Valley Bank. Just for starters, it wasn't a good sign that its CEO, Greg Becker, was a venture capitalist rather than a banker. That might help explain why SVB did not have a rigorous risk-management program. Many observers also highlighted Becker's decision to buy "risk-free" government bonds without actually analyzing the risks or holding a high percentage of accounts above the insured limit of $250,000 or cashing out millions of dollars in stock options weeks before the bank failure.[17] Thousands of employees, shareholders, and depositors paid heavily for the conduct of an overconfident CEO and a passive, compliant board.

New York Times reporter Maureen Farrell noted that just a week before the bank's collapse, Becker excitedly told investors and tech executives that the "the future of the tech industry was sparkling—and so was Silicon Valley Bank's place within it."[18] One day after that assurance, SVB booked a $1.8 billion loss. And two days later, the bank was ruined.

Becker later appeared before a congressional committee. What had SVB's CEO missed? Any regrets, any blind spots he wished he had addressed? Like Dick Fuld, however, he couldn't come up with any good answers—not one specific mistake made or lesson learned. What had become so obvious to others still didn't register with the guy who had been in charge. This was the man the bank's board had selected to be a leader.

Drivers and Derailers: The Data

Whether it's recklessness, an authoritarian streak, bravado, or a tough style that isolates an executive from his team, the blind spots in leadership are many. In fact, they are so common in the business world that their effects on corporate performance can be identified with some precision. That has been a focus of Heidrick & Struggles's research on the top performing companies in the *Financial Times* Global 500. In one study, our team assessed performance over three- and seven-year periods and zeroed in on twenty-three companies identified as "super accelerators" that consistently outperformed their peers. On close examination, we found the same accelerators of success: their ability to mobilize, execute, and transform with agility. We gave these factors the acronym META to serve as a framework for assessing organizations, teams, and their leaders.

Taking META a few steps further, these 360-degree analyses can now pinpoint what we call the "drag" and "drive" factors that can derail or advance an enterprise. Over time, we've surveyed thousands of executives and teams using our Leadership Acceleration Questionnaire (LAQ 360), and the result is a clear picture of forty-four major blind spots—and of the competencies needed to overcome them (pictured in the word cloud of common organizational blind spots.)

Coming across as distant; holding back from connecting with others

Holding back from expressing their opinion in public forums, with senior stakeholders, or when feeling they lack expertise

Making it difficult for others to provide feedback   Shying away from conflict and difficult conversations

Looking at symptoms instead of underlying root causes

Setting too many strategic priorities that overwhelm and confuse

Being too much of a perfectionist   Being too internally focused, neglecting the customer

Finding it difficult to adapt their approach across different interpersonal situations

Creating relationships that are only task and transaction focused

Missing key opportunities and threats facing the business

Taking on too much and overcommitting

Being overly cautious and risk averse   Not actively contributing to the development of others

Being focused primarily upon success within their own function or business unit

Having difficulty flexing between detail and the big picture   Making things complex

Micromanaging and doing work that can and should be done by others   Focusing on the short term at the expense of the long term

Not encouraging risk taking and having a low tolerance for mistakes

Falling back on established ways of working rather than embracing change

Undertaking too many innovation initiatives at one time

Failing to build the systems and processes to scale ideas quickly   Dictating change to others rather than involving them in the process

Avoiding the tough conversations with underperforming individuals

The Path of Self-Awareness

If blind spots and their correctives can be so thoroughly categorized, why are they so common, so persistent? The research suggests a fairly plain answer. Dr. Tasha Eurich, an organizational psychologist found that 95 percent of people think they are self-aware, but when objective criteria are applied only 15 percent actually meet that description.[19] And this finding squares with studies we've done at Heidrick & Struggles. To overcome blind spots, we must know ourselves. The reality is that many people in leadership are simply lacking in the wisdom and capacity to grow that come only from self-awareness.

Searching for explanations, Dr. Eurich wondered about the influence of a "me-centered" culture that tends more toward self-absorption than toward self-examination. "Recent generations," she observed, "have grown up in a world obsessed with self-esteem, constantly being reminded of their special qualities. And it is fiendishly difficult to examine objectively who we are and how we're seen."[20]

Matters are made worse, wrote Dr. Jonathan Haidt, author of *Anxious Generation*, by the new ways of the "phone-based generation." In this virtual, social media–obsessed world, he pointed out, "real relationships are neglected, self-esteem is magnified, and the sensitivities of the average person more easily triggered."[21] Constantly being reminded of our own special qualities and soothed by the dopamine high from social media "likes," can have the effect of making us too self-satisfied to even consider our flaws and blind spots. All this artificial stimulation has a way of crowding out real life and real human relationships. We don't know others as we should; *we know ourselves even less.*

Since the 1980s, moreover, all kinds of research have tracked another unpleasant societal development: a greater prevalence of narcissistic traits. Writer Zoe Williams, for the *Guardian*, gave us a depressing image for the behavior—depressing only because it has the ring of truth. The sure sign of narcissism, as she put it, is to view other people as if they were "items in a vending machine, using them to service their own needs, never being able to acknowledge that others might have needs of their own, still less guess what they might be."[22]

How do these trends play out in corporate America? One glaring issue we at Heidrick & Struggles see all the time is an avoidance of direct conversations and feedback within teams. This is often meant to "keep the peace," but in today's environment the effect can be just the opposite. Combine this with a culture-wide weakness for self-adulation and you end up with a burden that too many companies have carried, often to disastrous outcomes: leaders with an obviously false sense of superiority and an exaggerated opinion of their own abilities. They might be isolated, clueless, arrogant, and indifferent to risk, and yet they are surely among the 95 percent of people who confidently report in surveys that they are self-aware.

The untold wreckage of the Great Recession had many causes. And even though the aftermath was system-wide calamity, a primary factor traces directly back to the qualities of individual corporate leaders—leaders utterly unaware of their own destructive flaws. Happily, not every high executive with a blind spot can cause widespread economic harm. Yet every one of them does bear responsibility for their enterprise and for all the people who depend on it. Poor leadership always inflicts a cost in weakened performance, frayed relationships, pointless conflicts, and lost opportunities. For every team with a poor leader, there is always a ditch ahead.

It takes a self-aware leader to avoid such troubles. And obviously, becoming that kind of leader takes work. As with breaking any bad habit, reform starts with acknowledging our blind spot and deciding that it must be conquered. Better still, we can think in terms of adopting a new habit to counteract and replace an old and unwanted pattern. We achieve the needed level of awareness both externally and internally. The external tools include requests for regular feedback, or perhaps working with an executive coach who can keep us on our path, or casual inquiries to colleagues for candid opinions of how we're doing. The main internal tool is humble, honest reflection—not falling into what Dr. Eurich called the endless "self-analysis trap," when we overanalyze, ruminate, and become stuck in a loop of self-doubt rather than expecting more of ourselves in a healthy, forward-looking spirit.[23]

> *Reform starts with acknowledging our blind spot and deciding that it must be conquered.*

"Self-awareness is an essential quality for leaders at all levels, but especially for those at the very top," General David Petraeus told me. Widely recognized as the world's foremost authority on counter-insurgency warfare, Petraeus—who served as Director of Central Intelligence and commanded the successful Surge operation in Iraq—underscored the critical role of self-awareness in enhancing leadership effectiveness. He explained, "Self-awareness is vital to the performance of each task of a strategic leader: getting the big ideas right, communicating them effectively, overseeing their implementation, and determining how they need to be refined to perform them . . . again, and again, and again!"[24]

To Find Your Blindspot

All this can be pretty demanding, a daily discipline we won't always enjoy, with a "To-Be List" we won't always measure up to. But having finally thrown off my people-pleasing excesses, I recommend it to everyone striving to show their best selves at work. We never fully realize how much harm our blind spots are doing until we deal with them in earnest. I can testify that it will always repay the effort.

FIVE

The Leader with Backbone

Much of a man's character will be found betokened in his backbone. I would rather feel your spine than your skull, whoever you are. A thin joist of a spine never yet upheld a full and noble soul.

—HERMAN MELVILLE, *Moby Dick*

If you ask well-informed observers of American business to name a modern example of courageous decision-making, many would cite Steve Jobs's return to Apple when the company seemed just days from bankruptcy. Others might point to Elon Musk's audacious vow to make regular commercial space travel a reality, or to acquire Twitter and make it true to the platform's original free-speech principles. Still others, at least in my home state of Texas, would recall the steady determination of ExxonMobil's Darren Woods, who courageously was doubling down on oil-and-gas exploration despite intense pressure from climate and shareholder activists who were agitating to shut it all down.

But on the subject of courageous CEOs, the name you will almost always hear is James Burke, the CEO of Johnson & Johnson in the crisis year of 1982. It was Burke who decided to remove Tylenol from store shelves after it was discovered that some capsules had been tainted with cyanide, killing at least seven people. The tainted product caused a national scare and threatened to ruin a long-established brand in a matter of weeks. That one decision to recall every bottle of Tylenol cost the company $200 million in lost earnings. And yet it is still regarded as one of the great moments in corporate leadership.

Jim Collins, author of *Good to Great*, rates James Burke among "the ten greatest CEOs of all time" and helped us to understand Burke as a decision-maker.[1] Long before that gutsy public moment in 1982, the CEO had done some serious thinking about the company's mission and responsibilities. It was also a case of a leader catching his blind spot early: He excelled in marketing, having little insight into medicine or pharmacology, and so would have to resist the marketer's tendency to put product movement above all else. After he was hired by J&J in 1976, Burke made it clear to colleagues that he considered the company's original statement of purpose—written decades earlier by founder R. W. Johnson Jr. and displayed on office walls—to be definitive. That statement declared that the company's values included a higher duty to the "mothers and all others who use our products," and Burke intended to honor it. As he later recalled, "I said, 'Here's the credo. If we're not going to live by it, let's tear it off the wall. We either ought to commit to it or get rid of it.'"[2]

It might seem easy enough for a CEO to extol a company's high-minded credo in good times for the business. What sets this example apart is that J&J's CEO held to it when things got really rough. When the cyanide crisis came, the company didn't need to deliberate over whether to eliminate a small risk to customers at a very high cost to the company. That issue had been settled years earlier when Burke reaffirmed the uncompromising values his company stood for. He had put J&J on the right track before there was trouble, which is what saved it when trouble arrived.

After another cyanide death was reported, Burke accelerated efforts to develop the tamper-proof seal that would revive consumer confidence, restore Tylenol's market share, and establish a product-safety standard that is today's norm. To see Johnson & Johnson ranked by *Barron's* decades later as number five among the "World's Most Respected Companies,"[1] you would never know it had once come so close to completely unraveling.

When a company survives something like that, the lesson takes hold. Burke's successors at J&J have remembered; the company's core principles are still front and center in the workings of the business. The Tylenol crisis response remains the gold standard for handling public-relations disasters—not just for executing a crisis plan effectively, but for prioritizing integrity and doing what is right.

When dogs and cats were dying after consuming contaminated ingredients in pet food, the company, Menu Foods, recalled more than two hundred products. When tainted spinach sickened consumers, the packager Natural Selection Foods (sold under the Dole brand) also issued an immediate recall. When JetBlue passengers were stranded after a storm, in a highly publicized ordeal, the CEO announced that from then on the company would operate according to an explicit customer bill of rights. In healthy, well-led companies, it is second nature for CEOs to acknowledge an error and quickly move to make things right with their customers and the public.

Facing Our Flaws

To state the obvious, in moments of crisis a leader has to be alert and resolute. And facing a crisis is always easier for a leader who has already faced his or her own flaws.

---

1 "The World's Most Respected Companies," Barron's, June 22, 2013.

All our lives, we're each engaged in the project of building our character. It might be new construction for some, a renovation for others, but either way our basic tools are self-awareness and courage. That first tool represents the effort to know ourselves as we are. The second stands for the actions we must take to become our best selves. The tools work in combination; neither will get you far without the other.

Really it comes down to two simple tests that Heidrick & Struggles CEO Tom Monahan helped me consider that we can apply to ourselves:

TEST 1 for a leader is "Can you name your blind spots?"

TEST 2 for a leader is "Do you have the backbone to engage your flaws?"

As challenging as Test 1 can be, naturally, Test 2 is where the real work begins and where the rewards to businesses are greatest. I've observed this for myself in the executive recruiting field. It also requires the courage, as Tom argued, to surround yourself with people who complement your gaps and shore up your strengths. Many studies also attest to the essential difference that courage can make in a workplace. The Edelman Trust Barometer, to cite just one example, found that in high-trust companies—those with a culture of ethical and courageous conduct—employees are vastly more engaged and committed than people working in low-trust organizations.[3]

Our in-depth research at Heidrick & Struggles likewise shows that leaders who score highly in self-awareness, and in their success combatting flaws, find themselves and their companies accelerating much faster than peers. As for how flaws are overcome, our research identifies a process with three basic elements: *courageous action*, an *ownership mindset*, and *an aptitude for solving complex problems*.

Courageous action within a company, which we found is the most important of the three elements, means pretty much what you would assume: willingly stepping out of our comfort zones, seeking out new experiences and responsibilities, trying out new approaches, and so on. I've seen all kinds of examples of how this can work in ways dramatic and less so, and one story comes straight to mind.

The story involved a client who was very smart, at times even brilliant. The problem was, he would be the first to describe himself in such terms. Like the "smartest guys in the room" at Enron, this fellow was well aware of his sharp mind, with the difference that he was also coachable because he genuinely cared about how he came across to his team. He didn't want to be the know-it-all in every setting. Eventually he came to realize that others on the team had smart and useful things to say, if only he would learn to listen.

Working with this executive, we came up with an approach that required consistent effort and backbone to change a regular habit. At the next team meeting, he would do two things—or rather, *not* do two things. He would not sit at the head of the table. And he would be silent as much as possible.

As you might expect, as issues came up in the meeting, everyone automatically looked at him for the answer. But he said nothing. It was awkward at first, but after a while the others adjusted and started weighing in with their thoughts. Even his more reticent colleagues began to speak up and contribute. It turned out that a more balanced discussion around the table led to more good ideas.

What did this executive learn? That leading does not mean dominating. Before facing his flaw, he had been so overbearing that everyone expected his answers to be the final answers. He came to realize that his attitude and manner had been smothering the creativity of the team. When he made the effort to be more self-controlled, his colleagues made the effort to be more collaborative. This example shows all the harm that a single blind spot—an omniscience complex—can do, and all the good that follows when the blind spot is confronted.

The second element in the process of overcoming flaws, what we call an *ownership mindset*, also can require considerable effort. A key here is understanding how much the person in charge shapes the working environment of everyone else. The best leaders are the first to take responsibility for setbacks, the first to share credit for successes, and the first to uphold the standards of collegiality and respect that make teamwork possible.

I think of a CEO I coached. He had taken command of a huge energy company and had performed quite well at it, but he had never really taken ownership of all his responsibilities. After his 360-reference check, we briefed him on what impressions he had left on people who worked with him. The report gave a picture of a somewhat aloof and indifferent executive, which he conceded had a ring of truth.

This kind of detachment from subordinates is not uncommon among CEOs. They might view themselves as caring bosses, but sometimes the self-image doesn't square with day-to-day reality. An engineer by training, with an impersonal style and analytical cast of mind, this CEO told us that he wasn't one for "kumbaya" moments with his team, and that frankly he didn't think much about them beyond their function in the company. He didn't need us to tell him that this lack of interest and empathy was, as he himself put it, "a blind spot my whole career."

Having got that far, he still needed a little prodding to see how such a flaw might be holding him back as a leader. So, in our coaching, we followed the "practice makes permanent" principle to replace his indifference with a habit of showing concern. "You want me to fake empathy?" he asked. In a way, the answer was yes: if we pretend long enough to have a good quality, after a while the quality sinks in, becoming part of who we are. He agreed to give it a try.

For months thereafter, he made it his business to become better acquainted with the people who worked for his company. He told us it felt unnatural at first, taking time to chat and ask colleagues about their lives and families. But what he called "forced empathy" turned after a while into actual curiosity, and little by little he became a much more engaged and friendly presence in the office, with all the benefits to the organization that come with that. By the time he was finished methodically overcoming his blind spot, it would have seemed *unnatural* to go about his workdays without ever pausing to show interest in the people around him.

Overcoming flaws depends as well on the third element we have observed at Heidrick & Struggles: an *aptitude for solving complex problems*. And this can include problems that are psychological, such as the emotional barriers to our character growth as leaders.

A clear instance of this was my client mentioned earlier who, as the CEO of a large energy company, was so shy he could hardly interact with his team. This man could see how his personality was undermining morale and made the effort to change. To force himself to move around more and get to know colleagues, he actually took all the chairs out of his office. Since no one could come to sit with him, he had to venture out and became known as a "walk-around" leader; by sheer willpower, the isolated introvert became a high-functioning introvert.

We all have reluctance to deal with our own flaws. It can take real humility, effort, and sometimes even courage to close the gap between what we are and what we are capable of being. This is a theme in the research of Dr. Stephanie O. Lopez, who stressed vulnerability and a willingness to "descend" as qualities of leadership. Choosing vulnerability, Dr. Lopez explained, involves "demonstrating transparency" and an "openness to emotional exposure in relationship with others." Descent, in this sense, is necessary before the leader can ascend. Vulnerability, she wrote, is a human ideal that we must approach with thoughtfulness and care as we seek to become authentically connected to one another. These findings give us initial tools for building a generation of leaders that have the courage to descend into vulnerability when it might be unpopular to do so, but for the sake of becoming better versions of ourselves. By building up leaders with this quality, we have the opportunity to change the landscape of business and create organizations that are built on human connection and authenticity, instead of self-serving greed and achievement for the sake of nothing.[4]

Objectivity over Bias

Much as personal change takes clear thinking, clear thinking requires objectivity. At Heidrick & Struggles, our research on leadership consistently finds the same strengths among highly aware executives: They are reflective, open, inquisitive, and objective. When we separate them out, however, objectivity is the rarest of the four. Just 40 percent of leaders demonstrate this strength.

If they lack an ability to view facts without bias, recognize personal preconceptions, and remain uninfluenced by personal feelings or opinions, leaders cannot be counted on to make wise decisions. Even less, of course, can they reliably face their own flaws or see past honest disagreements to work effectively with others. You have to wonder why so many top-line executives have trouble with objectivity. Shouldn't they, of all people in an organization, be most attuned to reality and most equipped to distinguish fact from opinion? Of course they should. Yet how easy it is to become so settled and comfortable in our views that, at a certain point, we're not taking in new information any longer and we cease to be objective—even though we might tell ourselves that we are.

In my work over the years, I rarely doubted my own objectivity. In fact, I probably considered myself more objective and fair-minded than the average person. It was only when I zeroed in on this quality and what it means that I realized how many unconscious biases were affecting my judgment, sometimes to the detriment of colleagues. I had favorites in the office, which was fine except that I wasn't really getting to know everybody as a leader in the office should. So, I set out to spend time with the people beyond my circle, and for that matter outside predictable cultural groupings. Before long I was well-acquainted with the observant Muslim down the hall, the ethical vegetarian who brought her lunch to work, and others who had been off my beaten trail at headquarters.

You can work at a place for years and never get to know some people unless you try. And you won't try unless you're objective enough to shake off social biases.

It's the same with political differences, which can be important but don't have to spell the end of friendships and associations—or prevent them from ever forming. One thing I've always tried to do is keep a balanced diet of news and commentary, so as to understand what others are thinking even when I don't agree. My family's history with communist Hungary left me with a lifelong distrust of collectivism and wariness toward far-left ideas in general. Even so, I make the effort to hear the other side, and had always considered myself reasonable and fair-minded in engaging with colleagues who saw things differently.

In fact, I gave myself too much credit, as I finally began to realize. And again, the prime suspect was the people-pleaser in me, who was finding excuses to avoid those having other political views. To steer clear of conflict, I tried to stay away from anyone who might present a challenge to my thinking. It took a good friend and colleague at Heidrick & Struggles to help me see all of this more clearly.

One of my partners at the firm, Jeremy Hanson, stepped up to lead our Global Sustainability practice. That field, of course, is primarily concerned about the impact of industry as a factor in global warming. Jeremy, an avid outdoorsman and conservationist, was perfect for his position, although not in ways that always aligned us politically. Given that many of Heidrick & Struggles's high-volume client relationships have been large producers of oil and gas, and that leaders in those companies are my friends, Jeremy and I were not exactly fated to get along well. Yet we do. What the current political etiquette would rule out as a mismatch—two people with supposedly irreconcilable agendas—has turned out to be a great learning experience for both of us.

Jeremy and I have made a deliberate commitment to approach each other's perspectives with genuine open-mindedness, striving to examine areas of disagreement with objectivity. We've also agreed to hold each other accountable whenever one of us resorts to prepackaged phrases or political jargon that replaces thoughtful discussion. While I was never a climate "denier," my stance was more agnostic—I saw the issue as likely more nuanced. I believed that while human activity contributes to warming, it's not the sole cause, and I considered other crises—such as energy poverty and the tragic reality of a child under five dying every two minutes due to a lack of clean water and reliable energy—to be more urgent.

This is true, but I had more to learn, and working with Jeremy in our Sustainability practice made me appreciate how much the energy industry could be doing to significantly reduce greenhouse gas emissions. Jeremy, for his part, spent three days with me in Houston visiting CEOs of the largest energy companies, an experience that better acquainted him with the good this industry does and with the caliber of the people who run it. For much of humanity, the availability of affordable fossil-fuel energy makes the difference between poverty and opportunity. That's a case that critics of the industry never hear when they're just talking to one another.[2]

It's a lot harder to believe caricatures of people once you meet and get to know them. The energy leaders Jeremy met were clearly serious and smart people, committed to meeting a vital need of society, while also investing enormous sums to reduce emissions and develop cleaner energy sources. Likewise, thanks to Jeremy's influence, you will never hear me speak dismissively of climate change or the hazards of environmental neglect. Not surprisingly, this one sincere connection between Jeremy and me led to more, including the happy coincidence of becoming grandfathers at the same time. Though I doubt we will ever count each other political allies, I know I'm better off to have him as a colleague and friend.

The silver lining in these polarized times is the emergence of bridge-building initiatives like Mark Halperin's acclaimed video podcast, *Two-Way*. Offering a welcome break from the soundbite-driven chaos of cable news, *Two-Way* creates a space for meaningful conversations guided by the principles of "peace, love, and understanding." Rather than relying on the usual cadre of paid pundits, the podcast invites everyday citizens to share their perspectives on the pressing issues of our time—proving that genuine dialogue is still possible, even in a divided world. Corporate America and other institutions could take a page from this playbook, embracing "two-way" dialogues to encourage greater objectivity, connection, and understanding—or what we at Heidrick & Struggles call "bridging the boundaries that divide us."

When coaching executives who lack objectivity or carry unconscious bias, I point to the even more vivid example of Cornel West and Robert George. The first is an outspoken progressive

---

[2] One of the most rewarding executive search assignments of my career was *pro bono* work in 2024 to build the board of the Bettering Human Lives Foundation, which addresses global energy poverty. Over 3 million people die annually from indoor pollution caused by cooking with wood, manure, or agricultural waste (Source: WHO: The World Health Organization). The foundation provides low-interest loans to entrepreneurs in Ghana and Kenya to distribute clean-cooking stoves (propane/LPG) to some of the 2 billion people still relying on these traditional fuels.

thinker, the second a noted conservative legal scholar. When they first met, Professor West, now at the Harvard Divinity School, and Professor George of Princeton found themselves talking for hours—to the point, as West recalled, that it continued on into the parking lot, where George "held [his] hand on the car latch for another 30 minutes while we kept going at it."[5] Referring to each other as "Brother George" and "Brother West," they have since become close friends, and even teach a class together on the great books.[6]

When we defy conventional expectations in this way and meet others across typical dividing lines, it doesn't feel like we're doing anything especially courageous. Yet in a sense we are because these days there is so much pressure to follow fixed patterns and biases. Objectivity is part of the discipline of leadership; it takes real work. In like manner, self-awareness comes through effort and reflection. The simple chart below shows how, as these strengths are developed, a leader can rise among peers toward true self-mastery.

SELF—AWARENESS + COURAGE = SELF—MASTERY

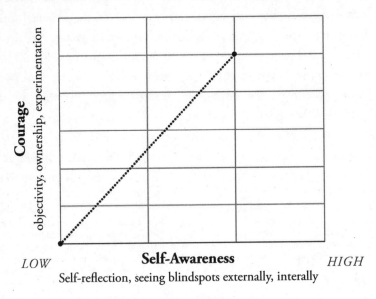

The Strength That Lasts

Deriding one of his fellow politicians, Theodore Roosevelt described the man as having "no more backbone than a chocolate éclair."[7] His meaning wasn't lost on anyone, because the idea of a soft backbone instantly evokes weakness, malleability, indecision, and ineffectiveness.

Conversely, few tributes speak better of a leader than when it is said that he or she has backbone. To know a man's character, Herman Melville wrote, "I would rather feel your spine than your skull; a thin joist of a spine never yet upheld a full and noble soul."[8] As an image in the study of leadership, "backbone" goes a long way, conveying sturdiness, balance, resilience, fortitude, and overall health. And those qualities, like the muscles of the spinal column itself, can be built up and reinforced over time.

This applies as well to the struggle involved in overcoming the blind spots that can hold us back. A leader needs backbone—courage—to overcome obstacles, learn from failures, adapt to changing circumstances, and persevere when it is easier to give up. In coaching, I sometimes liken the effort to long-distance running. I've done quite a bit of that, and the crucial point in training is to push beyond your comfort zone into what runners call the "threshold" zones. That's where you really start to feel the pain. Then you drop back to a more comfortable pace before pushing harder again and repeating the pattern over and over. It's the only way to build up your capacity and endurance, just as in the consistent effort it takes to develop strength as a leader. There's no reaching your best without pushing through the discomfort of the threshold zones.

In professional situations, there are always difficulties we'd rather avoid. It could be a tough conversation with a colleague, or raising important questions that others don't want to hear, or otherwise letting our own timidity or insecurity interfere with the standard of excellence we want to reach. We've got to keep "feeling the burn," as athletes say, until things that used to cause strain and dread gradually become second nature. To stay with the workout imagery, when we don't apply ourselves to dealing with our flaws, when we are not exercising intention and will, the muscles atrophy, and growing in leadership seems only harder and more hopeless.

One leader who trains himself this way is Alex Jackson, a partner with Quantum Capital Group, an energy private equity firm with $25 billion in assets under management. I've worked with Alex over the years, and I especially admire his relentless, purposeful self-improvement. We're often reminded these days to be fully "present" at every moment, and Alex is that kind of leader across the board. Whether he's bringing out the best in colleagues, creating value for limited partners, or just being a standout husband and father of three, Alex goes all the way.

Still, he understands how even such a stellar quality can become a derailer. Alex found himself stretched thinner and thinner, only in this case he was the first to see what problems this could cause. And in dealing with his blind spot, he was lucky to have the support of his firm.

Alex, who built a backbone, didn't want to let matters get out of hand, so we talked it over. In our coaching, we defined some clearer boundaries on his commitments, which in the extremely intense world of private equity can be very tough to do. To his credit, Alex's boss, Quantum's CEO, and founder Wil VanLoh, also intervened in the interest of both his colleague and his company. Wil is known in the industry for creating billions in value for his limited partners by investing in unconventional shale energy resources. His investment savvy earned him high praise from Tony Robbins in his book *The Holy Grail of Investing*. What showed Wil's true leadership, however, was the way he invested in the well-being of one of his company's rising stars by making sure Alex was energized for the long run. Even as the firm was at peak performance, Wil insisted that one of his protégés step away from the job for a while—a short-term sabbatical, before the demands of work became destructive to the rest of Alex's life.[9]

Ann Fox, CEO of Nine Energy Services and a former Marine, is another leader with backbone who knows the value of voicing hard truths. While embedded in Iraq, training Iraqi Security Forces in US counterinsurgency tactics, she observed low morale and troubling signs—soldiers were splintering, and some even abandoned weapons to insurgents. Summoned by General David Petraeus to debrief in the sweltering summer Iraqi heat, Ann's superior urged her to "sanitize" or downplay the challenges. But as a Marine captain who was aware of her limited career prospects in the military as a woman, she asked herself, "What do I have to lose?" Ann laid out the unfiltered reality. Petraeus, impressed, responded, "That's the kind of truth I need to hear." He later brought her into a special unit that would play a pivotal role in the major "Surge" operation that ultimately defeated the insurgency.[10]

General Petraeus shared with me, "Ann stood out from the day I met her. She never pulled punches with her assessments and didn't shy away from speaking truth to power, even when it wasn't what those above her wanted to hear." Her courage and candor made a lasting impression on General Petraeus—a leader renowned for identifying exceptional talent. So much so, that when he was appointed to command the Surge in Iraq, he personally recruited Ann and her team to return to active duty. "Ann seemed as though she was sent from central casting to take on the roles assigned to Team Phoenix," General Petraeus noted, adding, "she and her comrades achieved strategic effects that extended far beyond the tactical or operational levels."[11]

This story of fortitude highlights a lesson in leadership and self-awareness: Verbalizing an intention or facing a fear out loud can turn a thought into courage and action. Psychologists call this "metacognition"—thinking about our thinking—and it's a powerful tool for keeping ourselves grounded and focused. Just as Ann told herself to do the right thing, we, too, can use our own voice as a call to action, breaking habits of ease for the courage of doing what's right. Each time we summon self-control or backbone, we're building the lasting strength to overcome our blind spots. Sometimes the most commanding voice we need to hear is our own.

> *Each time we summon self-control or backbone, we're building the lasting strength to overcome our blind spots. Sometimes the most commanding voice we need to hear is our own.*

Specks and Planks

When I first began to think carefully about blind spots as a factor in executive recruiting and coaching, I was self-aware enough to anticipate an obvious hazard. Other people's flaws are always easier to identify than our own, and the last thing I wanted was a reputation as a full-time fault-finder oblivious to his own.

A recent example comes straight to mind, much as I'd like to forget it. A colleague came down hard on me in an email that he cc'd all around the firm. He saw fit to chastise me for some alleged misstep, informing one and all instead of raising the matter directly in person or with a call. He was known for this kind of thing—it was a clear blind spot we'd observed before—and this time it really got to me. I was livid.

As I resolved to confront him, however, I suddenly remembered something. Had I not done almost exactly the same thing myself not long before? Appalled at the thought, I started going through my sent messages and it all came back: Not only had I sent an intemperate email at another colleague's expense, I had cc'd others, including the same guy with which I was now so upset. He had been careless and inconsiderate, but who was I to point that out?

I guess one memory leads to another, and I think now of how I used to badger a college roommate for his habit of oversleeping and his rather casual attitude toward keeping commitments. Poor Peter had to put up with my mini sermons on the themes of sloth, responsibility, and the like, until one day he tired of the routine and made an apt reply to my hectoring. When I was giving him grief for not joining me in a college fellowship meeting, he said, "Judge, and you will be judged!" On another occasion, Peter hit me with the ultimate wisdom about confronting blind spots: "Why do you see the speck that is in your brother's eye, but do not notice the plank that is in your own eye?"[12]

Half a lifetime later, sitting in an office and simmering over a colleague's censorious email, that old truth came to mind again and helped me to get hold of myself. I knew he and I had to clear the air, but it took me a while to work up the nerve to do it properly—meaning with the humility of someone who was no better than he was, but who genuinely hoped we could both improve and up our games. Finally, one day we talked it over. Just having the conversation was enough to push me into my "threshold" zone. But we parted with a real understanding between us and mutual relief at putting our hostility in the past.

In the case of another partner at the firm, I could always sense his air of disapproval regarding my use of plastics. Every time he saw me walk off with a bottle of water from the office kitchen instead of using some ecologically enlightened alternative, he managed to convey his opinion with a look or a comment. It got to be pretty irritating, especially because he was hardly any exemplar himself: I'd seen the guy driving one of the highest-emitting SUVs on the market. That was the speck in his eye, but since I had enough planks of my own, I let the point go. When he and I finally got to talking about all this one day, it was a good-natured exchange and we both admitted that as "speck-spotters" we could each do better.

Among recent stories that show how utterly obtuse business leaders can be in this respect, and how damaging such conduct can be, consider one well publicized case. In 2023, the CEO of upscale furniture maker MillerKnoll taped a video message to be shared with all employees. She had heard complaints that employees would not be receiving bonuses that year, and she'd had enough of this—never mind that everyone knew this woman would be getting a bonus of more than a million dollars. "I'm going to address this head on," she began. With Covid, supply-chain delays, and bank failures, these were tough times and we "can control only what we can control." They could control "excellent customer service," "treating each other well," and "focusing on the future," which she assured them was very bright.[13]

As to bonuses, however, sales had not been sufficient to justify such an extravagance: "Don't ask me about 'What are we going to do if we don't get a bonus?' Get the damn $26 million dollars [in sales]." Her parting advice to employees? "So, people, leave Pity City. Let's get it done. Thank you. Have a great day."

Cancelling bonuses for everyone but yourself is never going to play out well. And this CEO certainly came to regret her behavior and choice of words. After the video got out, she apologized, in carefully couched terms, about having merely "seemed" insensitive, and even then not addressing the obvious unfairness of taking a bonus while everyone else got nothing. What did real leadership call for?

Forfeiting the bonus.

We can look at PR fiascos like the one at MillerKnoll and feel superior as we join in the disapproving commentary. But surely it's better to concentrate on the real lesson that we all have our share of mistakes and flaws to account for and correct, even if our bad moments don't wind up as viral videos. We all have blind spots, and dealing with those will always be enough to keep us busy, leaving little time for expounding on the shortcomings of others.

Strong Back, Soft Front

The popular maxim "strong back, soft front" in leadership resonates with me. As an executive recruiter, I have seen it in action. It's an alternative to the traditional approach of leading out front with forceful self-confidence. Instead, the emphasis is on empathy, compassion, and at times even the vulnerability to concede that as leaders we have plenty of room for improvement.

Good to Great author Jim Collins touched on this idea in his description of "Level 5" leaders—the ones who manage to temper an iron will with personal humility. Dr. Joan Halifax, an anthropologist and Buddhist teacher, has also advocated the idea to her large readership, reminding us that "all too often our so-called strength comes from fear, not love." She wrote, "Instead of having a strong back, many of us have a defended front, shielding a weak spine."[14]

A third piece of the picture comes from Dr. Brené Brown, who drew a contrast between "armored" leadership, which tends to be insular and self-protective, and "daring" leadership, which is bolder and more self-giving. She suggested the maxim be expanded to "Strong Back, Soft Front, *Wild Heart*." Leadership, as she put it, "is not about titles or the corner office. It's about the willingness to step up, put yourself out there, and lean into courage. The world is desperate for braver leaders."[15]

If such advice to be "daring" can sound vague at times, we should recall how it can play out in practice. Think again of James Burke, an executive who certainly must have been tempted to hide behind armor during a crisis as tough as any, but instead faced adversity with such an impressive mix of humility and courage. I think as well of Dr. Michael Burry, the physician-turned-investor who was a voice in the wilderness before the financial crisis of 2008. In an era of yes-men and banks "too big to fail," here was a true Cassandra, displaying the kind of courage and untamed spirit that Brené Brown was talking about.

Somehow, practically no one else on Wall Street could see what Burry knew was coming. As early as 2005, he was cautioning about the hazards of declining lending standards and a housing bubble. The man's warnings were ignored, dismissed, and scorned, in those years when others were imagining the riches to be gained as the house of cards grew taller. Burry withstood it all. And you must wonder: Insight like that is rare enough, but where does a man get that kind of backbone?

His story supports the idea that sometimes the strongest people have experienced personal pain. As a child, Burry was diagnosed with a rare form of cancer. Surgery saved his life but cost him his left eye. Such a background makes it all the more impressive that he grew up to become a physician before eventually leaving medicine to become a securities trader.

Author Michael Lewis, who spent time with Burry while doing legwork for *The Big Short*, saw a connection between Burry's reliance on a single eye and his ability as a financial observer to notice what others did not. The limitations on his vision had the effect of setting him apart in a more solitary life detached from crowds and free of groupthink. He became a bit of a loner, learning from his own reading and analysis, the type who prefers to figure things out on his own. Wall Street in 2008 could have used a lot of people like him, but it turned out he was more or less alone in discerning where things were heading. His deep reading and intuition gave him the feeling that a massive real-estate downturn was on the way. There being no tool to bet against subprime-mortgage lending, Burry set out to devise one:

> In the beginning, credit-default swaps had been a tool for hedging: some banks had loaned more than they wanted to General Electric because G.E. had asked for it, and they feared alienating a long-standing client; another bank changed its mind about the wisdom of lending to G.E. at all. Very quickly, however, the new derivatives became tools for speculation: a lot of people wanted to make bets on the likelihood of G.E.'s defaulting. It struck Burry: Wall Street is bound to do the same thing with subprime-mortgage bonds too. Given what was happening in the real-estate market—and given what subprime-mortgage lenders were doing—a lot of smart people eventually were going to want to make side bets on subprime-mortgage bonds. And the only way to do it would be to buy a credit-default swap.[16]

Burry stuck to his investment thesis and created enormous value for investors who stuck with him. By June 30, 2008, any investor who was long with Burry's firm, Scion Capital, from its beginning in 2000 had a gain, after fees and expenses, of 489.34 percent. Over the same period, the S&P 500 returned just slightly more than 2 percent.[17] While the Wall Street herd confidently thundered on toward the cliff, the smart money went the other way, on advice from a man too aware to fail.

SIX

Your Superpower

*Open your eyes . . . and see what
you can with them before they close forever.*
—Anthony Doerr, *All the Light We Cannot See*

I suppose all of us have had moments when we feel that we have just seen the best in the human spirit. Maybe a devoted friend fixed to your side when nothing was going right. Or it might have been some incredible act of compassion or generosity by someone who wanted nothing in return. Or—in a story many of us appreciate only in retrospect—the toil and self-giving of a parent. That's certainly where I start when I reflect on the best in humanity, with the loving mother I lost at eighteen.

Along these lines, I was quite taken recently by the Netflix series based on Anthony Doerr's novel *All the Light We Cannot See*, a story in which a blind teenager named Marie endures withering adversity in wartime France, while her beautiful spirit shines through it all. As the drama unfolds, this girl who cannot see is a light to others in the darkness of Nazi occupation. A fearful uncle and a conflicted soldier both draw strength from her resiliency, which passes every test amid the death and destruction in their midst. There is a goodness in Marie, something revealing humanity at its best, that cannot be overcome or taken away.

The effect of such stories is to remind us that we all have particular gifts we are meant to use, though in most cases we never have to bear up through the extreme circumstances of physical disability or war. When you stop to think about it, isn't much of life about trying to find that gift and to show all that it can do?

"The Artwork of Your Life"

This simple wisdom applies as well to anyone striving to grow as a leader. As much as self-awareness can reveal the blind spots that limit us, it can shine a light on our special gifts as well. Engaging your self-examining Adam II nature is not merely an exercise to reflect on what holds you back. Ultimately, the point is to discern and draw upon the combination of strengths that define you at your best.

To use a term that has caught on lately, we each need to know our "superpower" and make the most of it. The idea, with its exaggerated imagery, admittedly has a modern self-help ring to it. But to me it also conveys something real and deep about life: We are each here for a reason, with one chance to show our Creator's purposes in this world. In the work we do, there will always be others we look up to and know we cannot equal in ability. Yet our gifts, whatever they might be, are ours alone to use, signifying the path that is meant for us—an idea beautifully expressed in the Old Testament, where the Lord speaks to Jeremiah: "For I know the plans I have for you . . . plans to prosper you and not to harm you, plans to give you a future and a hope."[1]

What a waste it can be not to find our special strengths, leaving our superpower unrealized. Yet so much in modern life seems designed to do just that, by so often distracting us and discouraging self-awareness. Leader after leader will attest to this problem in our cultural environment. "Distraction," as the writer Arthur Brooks put it to me, is a "plague of our time." Brooks, the coauthor with Oprah Winfrey of *Build the Life You Want*, noted that "We are constantly distracted by stupid things . . . the things that just suck up our dopamine by distracting you away from the business of you." A cheerful advocate for a better way, Brooks saw that we have been "systematically disempowered by distraction," and offered this blunt advice:

> Do not waste another minute on the artwork of your life. No more scrolling. No more binging on some stupid television show you don't like, because all you are doing is creating another empty canvas you are never going to get to. Each one of us must see our life as the ultimate work of art. You are the start-up . . . you are the founder.[2]

None of us want to look back on our work in life and see mostly a series of blank or unfinished canvases. How sad and unfulfilling a fate to finally appreciate, only when it's too late, all the people who needed our care, all the causes that needed our service, all the great things we might have accomplished had we only been paying closer attention. Charles Dickens captured this awareness of squandered opportunity in his story for the ages, *A Christmas Carol*, at the moment when the ghost of Jacob Marley asks why, during his life, "did I walk through crowds of fellow-beings with my eyes turned down, and never raise them to that blessed Star which led the Wise Men to a poor abode! Were there no poor homes to which its light would have conducted me!" All that he desired now was to serve the good of others, and his misery was in knowing that he "had lost the power forever."[3]

Thinking of admirable people I've been lucky to know, altruism and selflessness stand out as the distinctive gifts of some. Others seem to have a depth of empathy that can be rare, specially attuned to need and suffering, and incapable of turning away. In still others, I wouldn't hesitate to call their ability to remain calm, steady, and decisive in difficult moments a kind of superpower. And then there's the amazing capacity of some people for intense, sustained concentration, a trait that places some business leaders in a realm of their own. Take any one of these gifts, and there's no telling how far-reaching its impact can be when fully applied.

Consider the impact today of Elon Musk, noted for superpowers that include uncommonly fast learning. How else could a man run three large and complex global businesses, yet still seem to be giving each his undivided attention? As profiles describe Musk, the man is a learning machine, constantly soaking up knowledge in many fields. You don't master the technology of reusable commercial rockets, automotive manufacturing processes, artificial intelligence, and neurological research, or drive government efficiency, without a prodigious mind and a lot of reading. Whatever else might be said of him, this is a man clearly deploying his powers to the utmost.

It's been noted that Musk can not only absorb information rapidly but is also proficient at a specific skill known as "learning transfer." That is, what he grasps in one context he can readily apply to another. By his own account, Musk always reads and learns with a tangible objective in mind. He even insists that "most people" could equal such feats of learning, but instead "self-limit" or else simply lack the confidence to try. Most of us are more capable than we imagine, he says. If you just "simply read a lot of books and talk to a lot of people, you can learn almost anything."[4]

Technology and the AI revolution is now giving individual powers that only big companies used to have. Peter Thiel, one of Musk's "tech bros," has implied that one person with the right tools can now do the work of an entire organization. He might be stretching the point, but it's certainly true that many of us self-limit before we have ever really discovered what we're capable of. In executive recruiting and coaching, I've seen how even very confident men and women can fail to realize what further strengths they could be developing. They can't always see it in the present, but down the road they might find themselves lacking that extra edge they could have sharpened.

Nearly two decades ago, my colleague Bonnie Gwin stepped from being a recruiter into a senior executive role within the firm—a tenure that proved shorter than we had all envisioned. Yet, where others might have seen a limitation, Bonnie saw an opportunity to reimagine her path and unlock a remarkable new path—and superpower. She conceptualized and built what has become the industry's most successful global board of directors search practice.

A towering figure in both industry and the community—having served as chair of the Make-A-Wish Foundation and on the board of the Cleveland Clinic, among other roles—Bonnie transformed her expertise and focus, emerging as one of the world's preeminent board recruiters. Her unmatched insights and influence have reshaped the field, making her indispensable to Fortune 100 companies around the globe, each vying for her strategic counsel and time. Bonnie's journey is a testament to the power of reinvention and the enduring impact of vision paired with mastery.

Aspiring leaders cannot be reminded too often that their superpower is there in reserve, waiting to be shaped and used. And the limit we all should be worrying about is not one that we impose on ourselves; it is the limit that every one of us encounters and answers to in the end: the finite amount of time we are given.

Superpowers, Common and Uncommon

A "superpower" is just a normal human quality or talent that is developed and deployed to the full. We all have them, and such powers at their peak can take leaders and teams to new levels of performance.

Consider the quality of resiliency, for example. This is a virtue we discover when we're tested most. Many a CEO discovered it in the last fifteen or so years, a time that brought both a global financial crisis and a global pandemic. And what about the millions of small-business owners who somehow managed to hold on, despite the disappearance of customers and financial pressures that wouldn't let up? They certainly showed deep reserves of toughness and perseverance.

> *And the limit we all should be worrying about is not one that we impose on ourselves; it is the limit that every one of us encounters and answers to in the end: the finite amount of time we are given.*

And though we don't typically think of vulnerability as an asset, much less a superpower, that changes when we understand its connection to authenticity and humility. In this sense vulnerability is the quality I've found most lacking in business leaders. And it's a refreshing sight when I do find it.

I think of Chris Wright, the dynamic founder and CEO of Liberty Energy, a $4 billion company, who became the United States Secretary of Energy under President Trump. Chris, an MIT graduate and self-described "energy nerd," is the first to admit he can be a little quirky. But for such a bright guy who might otherwise create distance from others, his disarming manner, and wonderful way of bonding with his employees is itself a unique power. In towns like Williston, North Dakota, and Midland, Texas, Chris will shut down company operations for a whole day just for big get-togethers for his workers and their families. As he put it to me, these are the "real people who make our economy work, the ones who keep the energy flowing so we can enjoy our air conditioning, lights, and electronic devices."

For Chris, staying connected with them is the "secret" of his leadership. "The tearful hugs I get from those folks in the field, and the employees who say, 'I have never been treated this way in my life,' just blows you away."[5]

They are not used to someone like this CEO, who knows that being the boss doesn't set you above anyone, who meets every member of his team as an equal, and who, as I've seen in many settings, is friendly and respectful to everyone he meets regardless of whether they can do anything for him. "The essence of being human," Chris told me, "is the magic that connects us with each other." Top executives don't usually sound like this, so sensitive and vulnerable, and for an executive recruiter such qualities are something to behold.

Over the years I've become attuned to instances of high-profile leaders showing flashes of self-awareness and vulnerability. Indeed, I keep my own list of examples. A notable one is Howard Schultz, the man who gave us Starbucks. During the worst of the Great Recession, Schultz, as CEO, was compelled to lay off some twelve thousand employees, a decision that brought him literally to tears. Later, as a guest on Oprah, he was asked about this moment of vulnerability and showed no embarrassment at all. "I think the currency of leadership is transparency," Schultz said. "You've got to be truthful . . . and there are moments where you've got to share your soul . . . and show them who you are, and not be afraid of it."[6] That kind of vulnerability does not convey weakness. It reveals genuine concern and empathy for others, which is always a strength.

Another word that's taken on some currency in business is "manifesting," which refers to the special kind of leadership that can truly turn ideas into reality. Certain names are practically synonymous with this superpower—Musk, Jobs, Bezos, Zuckerberg, Huang, and the like. For every great innovator whose name we know, there are no doubt thousands who had similar visions that just never materialized. Something set these few apart from the others and made them the ones who actually saw it through. Manifesting captures the boldness, intense focus, and determination that can make for that rare superpower.

And in tough circumstances, is there any superpower we admire more than simple calmness? In every kind of circumstance, for that matter, we've all seen some people who cannot be shaken or rattled. Their self-command and unflappability inspire confidence in the teams they lead, sustaining both morale and performance. Among executives I know, Darren Woods comes again to mind. As ExxonMobil shareholders and employees will attest, their CEO has never been unnerved by the perpetual barrage of criticism and pressure from foes of fossil fuel energy. Whatever the day brings, Darren can be found quietly leading an industrial powerhouse that consistently outperforms peers and delivers shareholder value quarter after quarter. Almost as impressive, he is understated in manner, not given to talking about himself, and reacted with typical modesty when I told him once that his steadiness under pressure was so exemplary as to be a kind of superpower.

Still another attribute that can become a standout strength in leadership is discernment—or, in day-to-day business, the ability to separate truth from the falsehoods, illusions, and sheer BS that can cloud the picture in executive decision-making. Indeed, the leaders we associate with this superpower tend to be super-successful, in the category of Warren Buffett and Charlie Munger, with their uncanny knack for knowing the difference between "cash cows" and "cash hogs" in prospective investments. Or John Krenicki, a Jack Welch protégé at GE now in private equity with Clayton, Dubilier & Rice. John's well-known talent for spotting BS probably owes, he told me, to a blue-collar background and the work ethic he learned from his parents. "It all comes out in the wash, Johnny," his mother once told him as a child.[7] The Krenickis lived in the real world, knew that nothing good came easy, and valued effort and honesty. All this left John with a good ear for the half-baked, oversold ideas that might take less discerning leaders down the wrong road.

Watch John Krenicki in action and you might notice another superpower: the ability to help others find and develop superpowers of their own. John seems to have picked up from Jack Welch an incredible knack for finding and mentoring top-flight executive talent.[1] It's a great gift in so many ways. For one thing, CEOs who develop the talent of their people consistently outperform their peers. And for another, the ability to identify potential in colleagues, and to clear the path for their growth and advancement, is the sign of a leader who has the confidence to look beyond himself.

Even a sense of humor has superpower possibilities, especially when we direct it at ourselves. Berkshire Hathaway investors still talk about the firm's 2023 annual meeting, which kicked off with a hilarious video showing Buffett arriving to work one morning but being refused entry by a security guard, played by Bill Murray, demanding Buffet's credentials. At the same meeting, the ninety-eight-year-old Munger was asked what question about the future held the greatest interest, and he replied, "All I want to know is where I'm going to die, so I'll never go there." My favorite recent example of humor in leaders came when Jared Polis, the governor of Colorado, was asked

---

[1] Jack Welch privately confided to close friends, including our former Heidrick Chairman Gerry Roche, that while the timing was never ideal, he had wished John Krenicki had succeeded him as GE's CEO. Krenicki's appointment as a director of Devon Energy remains one of our proudest placements, as he was highly sought after by nearly every major independent oil and gas producer at the time.

on CNN whether he would consider joining the 2024 Democratic ticket. He told the reporter, "If they do the polling and it turns out they need a forty-nine-year-old balding gay Jew from Boulder, Colorado, they've got my number."[8] Like the best kind of self-deprecation, the quip showed not just self-awareness but also a great way of winning people over.

Cultivating Strengths

Self-awareness goes a long way in leadership. And yet with a mere 13 percent of people qualifying as actually being self-aware when tested objectively, we're left with quite a gap between self-image and reality. The only upside is that such data can make us at least aware of our lack of self-awareness, which is a start.

Not to get too caught up in a wheels-within-wheels construct, but once we recognize our blind spots, we can also see ways to use the strengths they have concealed. That awareness becomes our chance to turn these hidden strengths into visible and active assets that might each develop into a superpower.

As you might imagine, our Heidrick & Struggles researchers have made close study of this. To complement the thorough listing of derailers, or blind spots, in chapter three, our research team has also identified at least one hundred strengths, or "capability spikes," which at their peak qualify as superpowers. Drawing on data from thousands of executive assessments at Heidrick & Struggles, this research also suggests some basic steps that turn capabilities and strengths into something even greater, accelerating performance all around.

Here we're talking about things needed to create the right conditions, often very practical things such as: delegating and prioritizing, to keep focus and enhance productivity; mentoring and coaching, to steer clear of micromanagement by developing talent and independence across the team; networking and engaging stakeholders,

Transparently shares their
personal values and purpose

Adapts their interpersonal approach to respond
to the demands of different situations

Takes personal responsibility
for setbacks and failures

Recovers from
setbacks quickly

Shows unrelenting determination to succeed

Makes others feel comfortable
to authentically be themselves

Delivers real value and impact for the customers

Acts as a role model for ethical standards

Maintains consistently high levels
of energy and optimism

Contributes beyond their area of direct authority

Willingly stands up for their own beliefs and
values, even with senior stakeholders

Proactively shapes customer thinking and needs

Builds close, long-term
relationships with customers

Adapts and transform their approach to leadership

Stays ahead of the competition to
deliver great solutions to customers

Creates compelling value propositions for the customer

Builds influence within the industry to shape
customer thinking about future possibilities

Makes strong personal connections
with a diverse range of individuals

Seeks out customer
ideas and feedback

Actively listens to others to find out
what they are thinking and feeling

Shows sensitivity and regard for others' feelings

Actively shapes their surrounding environment

Manages their own emotions to
avoid passing stress onto others

to broaden a leader's impact beyond just one sphere; adopting a "work-in-progress" mindset to keep developing new skills; holding to a clear vision that gives direction and motivation; building strong, trusting professional relationships; and at every turn maintaining the strategic focus that tries to see beyond the horizon instead of just operating in the present.

Do all this, said Dr. Kate Malter McLean, director of psychology at Heidrick & Struggles Digital Labs, and a lot of good things will follow for any organization. In this way, she told us, "Leaders can then transform their strengths into true superpowers that drive both personal and organizational success."[9]

The research squares with my own observations over many years in executive recruiting. If a leader really wants to bring forth a superpower, he or she will stay mindful of the following four intentions, which are hardly original by themselves, but in combination can keep any executive on an upward path:

1. *Know your strengths and put them to use.* "Hide not your talents, they for use were made," Benjamin Franklin wrote—adding, "What's a sundial in the shade?"[10] An image he might employ in our day would be solar panels: What good are they if they're always in the shade? This wise advice takes on urgency when we are still trying to figure out what our true strengths really are.

    How exactly can we do this in a rigorous, objective way? Well, there's a lot to be gained from a thorough 360-feedback report, or else from going directly to colleagues for their frank opinions and feedback. There's also the fairly new field of psychometrics, which offers tools such as the Clifton Strength Online Talent Assessment, devised by the Gallup organization and used by millions. The VIA Institute on Character has a similar survey to help users hone in on their most promising attributes and virtues. And then there's the Hogan Personality Inventory, a regular feature in Heidrick & Struggles's assessments of personal qualities and executive potential.

A reasonable question in any self-improvement journey is whether to focus on extending strengths or eliminating weaknesses. Expert opinion varies. Some lay greater stress on developing strengths; others argue that weaknesses need the most attention. And obviously, as a matter of common sense, there's a lot of overlap, since building and refining strengths and battling against those flaws that limit us often come to the same thing. For my part, I'm a little wary of a purely strength-based approach that goes too heavy on personal affirmation, energizing us with talk of our stellar qualities while neglecting the self-awareness and humility it takes to face and erase a flaw.

2. *Find what you love to do and do it.* As Steve Jobs famously told Stanford's graduating class in 2005, Don't settle. . . .

> Remembering that you are going to die is the best way I know to avoid the trap of thinking you have something to lose. . . . Your time is limited, so don't waste it living someone else's life. Don't be trapped by dogma—which is living with the results of other people's thinking. Don't let the noise of others' opinions drown out your own inner voice. And most important, have the courage to follow your heart and intuition. They somehow already know what you truly want to become. Everything else is secondary. . . . You have got to find what you love.[11]

As a practical matter, the careers we follow usually involve a lot of chance, and the positions we hold can seem less than ideal at times. But the goal to keep in mind is to find work that is fulfilling and worthy of our efforts. That's been my experience, anyway, and I am lucky to have ended up in a calling that helps others find their calling. When I read about "kingmakers" in history who were content to guide others into positions where they could shine, I know the feeling.

Chase Untermeyer, my White House mentor in the Office of Presidential Personnel—where applicants for thousands of presidential appointments are vetted—used to joke that "every appointment earns me nine enemies and one ingrate."[12] And it's true that when you have to make choices and recommendations for coveted jobs, there are a lot of sensitivities to be aware of. The upside of recruiting, though, is the regular satisfaction of pairing executive responsibility and power with ability and character. I've seen case after case of people doing work they love, and when that happens everything else tends to fall into place. Charlie Munger was again on to something when he remarked, "In my whole life I've never been good at something I wasn't very interested in. It just doesn't work. There's no substitute for strong interest."[13]

I spent time recently with Jamie Dimon, who as chairman and CEO of JPMorgan Chase is no doubt the world's best-known banker. You'd have to search far and wide for anyone in so powerful a position so perfectly matched to work he loves. A 360-report on Jamie, as if one were needed, would highlight the singular focus, personal drive, tenacity, and approachability for which he is already widely admired, both within the bank and well beyond. What struck me wasn't just his intellect or influence. It was his unmistakable presence. Jamie carries himself with a focused energy and enthusiasm that's hard to miss and even harder to forget. A cancer and heart surgery survivor, you feel that. He knows time is precious and doesn't waste it. In a world where many top leaders drift into isolation, Jamie does the opposite. His open-door policy isn't a soundbite—it's how he leads. He stays close to the people who power the business, listens deeply, speaks directly, and leads with humility. He doesn't see leadership as being above others, but among them.

There may be no greater example in the history of business of someone truly loving what they do than the titan John D. Rockefeller. His legendary success as a "conqueror" in industry is well-documented, but what sets him apart from other "robber barons" of his time was the respect he showed for his team and employees—an approach that was far from common in that era.[14] Rockefeller once famously remarked, "Do not many of us who fail to achieve big things . . . fail because we lack concentration—the art of concentrating the mind on the thing to be done at the proper time and to the exclusion of everything else?"[15] He found his passion in his work, and his dedication was unparalleled. In fact, throughout his life, Rockefeller wrote thirty-eight personal letters to his son—never intended for publication—including one at age ninety-six where he spoke about the dignity of work and the importance of finding what you love to do.

3. *Reflect on life lessons.* This intention forced me, as I recounted earlier, to confront flaws and do battle with them, while also getting a better sense of my strengths and how to use them. People whose opinions I value have told me that I have a thirst for learning, a tenacious side, and the mindset of a striver even if I don't always hit the mark. Since my youth, I've felt a need to be a better version of myself, and at least I keep trying. Surely, too, it took some toughness—more than I knew I had—to move on after the loss of my mother in living a life that would have made her proud.

You might even say these traits set me in the direction of

my current firm. For some years, I worked at a smaller executive search firm where I was content. After the prospect of joining Heidrick & Struggles materialized, something in the pitch from the partner I spoke with, Linda Heagy, got me to wonder whether being content was enough. Known in our business for her charisma and direct manner, Linda asked, "Do you want play triple AAA ball or play in the Major Leagues?" As she laid it out to me, I had already worked at the White House and dealt with all kinds of high-level officials. So, at this point in my career, asked Linda, "Why settle? You can be whoever you want to be in this business." In effect, she was telling me that if I loved this work then I should stretch myself to do it with the best. She was right. I had been persistent and ambitious thus far in my career, and there was no good reason to let up now.

I've found self-reflectiveness to be a common theme in the leadership journeys of others. One of the standout executives I came across in handling presidential personnel is Elaine Chao, whom you might recall as a cabinet secretary under Presidents George W. Bush and Donald Trump. When I met her in 1991, she was under consideration to serve as Peace Corps director for President George H. W. Bush, and I was happy to make that recommendation. Here, after all, was a highly capable woman who had come to America thirty years earlier on a cargo ship from Taiwan, traveling with her young mother and three sisters and just a few belongings. Yet starting out with almost nothing, not even a knowledge of English, Elaine excelled as a student, earned a White House fellowship in the Reagan years, and by 1991 had clearly shown the ability and character needed for a presidential appointment to a Senate-confirmed position.

Even in her family's early years of struggle in a new country, Elaine told me, there was always an expectation of success. It was a given that with hard work and discipline, the Chao children would rise in the world. She recognizes now what a difference this work ethic has made in her life, allowing her to take on ever greater and more complex assignments. Indeed, she said, "almost every assignment I had was a stretch assignment," each job demanding more than the last. Her experiences, Elaine recalled, taught her "humility and empathy toward others," but also a "determination for excellence." As she explained an attitude that has guided her career, "Coming from a disadvantaged background, I just remembered that I had to learn to be observant and become my own teacher."

Even with the strengths that such a background can build, she has stayed alert to faults. "Self-awareness has always been an indispensable part of who I am as a person and a leader." Chinese culture, she noted, expects a leader to be "forceful" and to "know all the answers," which can make for a cold and overbearing management style. She regards "impatience" as a flaw to resist, and over the years kept in view the goal of being a "servant leader with high expectations"—an ideal that anyone who knows Elaine Chao would say she has lived up to.[16]

4. *"Use it or Lose it."* Though it might be a little trite, like most clichés the saying has truth to it. What we use develops; what we don't use fades away. So it is with self-awareness that we can shape a strength into a superpower.

Writing in *Psychology Today*, Susanna Wu-Pong Calvert of Virginia Commonwealth University said that a superpower is developed by "pursuing your deepest, most heartfelt purpose using your natural talents and abilities." Doing this takes "commitment, effort, experimentation, and growth." She advocated an approach she called "integrate and iterate," with an emphasis on repetition and consistency akin to athletic training.

"Sometimes you will 'fail,'" Dr. Calvert said, but failure itself has things to teach. "Superpowers don't emerge overnight, won't make you perfect, and don't allow you to substitute magic for hard work," she continued. "Rather, they create a greater sense of ease and fun as you learn, work hard, and continually push the margins of your comfort zone."[17]

Of course, this insight of modern psychology merely restates some ancient wisdom. Aristotle told us long ago that "we are what we repeatedly do." Excellence, the philosopher observed, "is not an act but a habit."[18]

Avoiding Derailers

Can even a superpower be stretched too far? Sure, it can. Overused, a strength that propels us can also derail us.

Take, for instance, a person with a great gift for empathy. He or she can listen beyond just hearing, instead conveying sincere concern and solidarity. That quality, wonderful as it is, can also lead one to indulge the faults of another and fail to treat that person as responsible and accountable—which isn't doing a colleague any favors. Such excessive empathy, warned Nietzsche, is a form of "pathological softness" that leads to siding with those who might harm society, including criminals.[19]

Similarly, those whose strength is a capacity for high performance at a rapid pace might be prone to assuming that everyone can meet such a standard. But people do their work in different ways, according to their own set of strengths, and the hard-charger who doesn't get that can do more harm than good to the enterprise—turning his own asset into a derailer.

It happens to the best of us. Recall that Warren Buffett is well-known for empowering his managers and trusting them to run their businesses without constant intervention from Omaha. That is one of his great strengths, yet Buffett himself has acknowledged that it may have caused him to move too slowly in addressing poor performance. Elon Musk, likewise, has said that his "pathological" optimism and way of manifesting has sometimes crossed the boundary into impossible timelines and unfounded expectations. And then there's Steve Jobs, who could be so difficult and demanding that, as he himself freely admitted, he could never work for anyone else. A man who knew himself, he also acknowledged that his confidence could easily veer into arrogance—a distasteful quality even at the heights of success.[20]

It's a little sobering to reflect that even our finest qualities can be subverted to bring out the worst version of ourselves in a professional environment. We might think we're impressing someone with our special strengths or talent, but the effect is exactly the opposite—they find us tiresome and predictable, seeing not an asset to the enterprise but a derailer.

The more we understand our own strengths, the more we will want to temper them and give them direction. In practice, we can do this in two ways. Externally, we should never shy away from candid feedback or the rigor of a formal 360. Internally, it's a matter of personal resolve and the self-checks that come with honest self-reflection. Nor should we hesitate to engage an advisor or coach who can help sharpen our objectivity and judgment. In all this, the basics of self-awareness in leadership should be kept in clear view, and a simple acronym might help:

- **A**lert to blind spots
- **W**ill to overcome flaws
- **A**ttentive to strengths
- **R**eflect on risks / derailers
- **E**xercise superpowers to make others shine

Making these steps your mission can be a tough journey, especially in a culture that sometimes encourages self-absorption and even narcissism—qualities a world away from mature, self-reflective servant leadership. But completing that journey will be rewarded many times over, for executive leader and team alike. To have seen so many men and women aim high, even when it seemed too hard or unrealistic, is one of the blessings of my profession—the experience never gets old. For the executive headhunter, there is nothing more fulfilling than the sight of a leader coming into his or her own, finding a superpower and showing all that it can do.

SEVEN

The Captain of Your Soul

It matters not how strait the gate,
How charged with punishments the scroll,
I am the master of my fate, I am the captain of my soul.
—William Ernest Henley *Invictus*

Among distinctions in the modern world, few are more widely admired than the Nobel Prize, awarded for achievement in science, literature, economics, medicine, and—most notably—the pursuit of peace. The title "Nobel Laureate" commands attention anywhere. Recipients of the peace prize include such names as Theodore Roosevelt, Albert Schweitzer, Martin Luther King Jr., Norman Borlaug, Mother Teresa, Nelson Mandela, and Jimmy Carter. That's the kind of company you're in when your name is attached to "Nobel."

In the well-known history of the peace prize, Alfred B. Nobel, the Swedish explosives manufacturer who invented dynamite, directed in his will that his fortune endows this annual recognition of high achievement "to those who, during the preceding year, shall have conferred the greatest benefit to humankind."[1] It's a remarkable story, and you're not the first to wonder how a guy who got rich making weapons of war made his name synonymous with the highest hopes of humanity.

You might say Alfred Nobel had an unusual form of luck. When his brother Ludvig, an oil industry pioneer known as the "Russian Rockefeller," died in 1888, newspapers mistakenly ran obituaries of Alfred. Reading of his own passing, and of his legacy as little more than a merchant of death, afforded him a clear view of the life he had led. He'd been given a gift, a chance to reimagine his own obituary and fill it out with service to high ideals. In that moment of clarity, he became the "master of his fate," and because of that his name is honored to this day.

Had Nobel ever come under review at Heidrick & Struggles, one trait we would have recognized right away is *agility*. What business leader has ever made a faster or more successful pivot? And talk about self-awareness. As a wake-up call to strive for our best selves, there's nothing to match the experience of reading one's own death notice.

In less dramatic ways, every leader will have opportunities to show agility, and it's a quality that can have a "multiplier effect" across an organization. Our research at Heidrick & Struggles has found that no other factor in leadership is more impactful than the ability to discern a wrong direction, master one's circumstances, and fundamentally change course. All the more in an ever-changing business landscape, agility can be an indispensable skill.

The Meta-Skill of Agility

"Change is the law of life," as John F. Kennedy said, and this certainly makes a good adage for today's business environment.[2] More than ordinary change, in fact, we're often presented today with extreme unpredictability.

The Captain of Your Soul

Nassim Nicholas Taleb was more prophetic than he realized in his 2007 bestseller *The Black Swan: The Impact of the Highly Improbable*. When the financial crisis hit the following year, suddenly everyone was talking about "black swan" events. The term refers to occurrences nobody imagined before they happened. Yet they also have a way of seeming inevitable in hindsight. We were blind to the housing bubble that Michael Burry foresaw until the full global calamity was upon us. As Taleb wrote, "a prophet is not someone with special visions, just someone blind to most of what others see."[3] Clarity like Burry's, in other words, comes from paying attention to what really matters, not the mass of hype and illusion that everyone else mistakes for reality.

Since the Great Recession, other unforeseen events might be viewed as "black swans" that seemed to come out of nowhere: the Brexit vote in 2016, the global pandemic of 2020, Russia's invasion of Ukraine in 2022, and the sudden invasion of Israel and massacre of its civilians on October 7, 2023.[1] It's reasonable to wonder why such events appear to characterize our era.

Today, the interconnectedness of global systems creates abundant ground for the influence of randomness experienced by many. Whatever the reason, what we know for sure is that such a time places a special premium on agility in leadership.

One unforeseen event in one country can drive events, or even upend lives, in so many other places. Consider how reliant our lives have become on networks—the internet, GPS, energy grids, data storage systems, and of course social media. A breakdown in one network can cause havoc in an instant, even for nonusers. When a

---

[1] The attacks by Hamas killed more than 1,300 Israelis and foreign nationals, including at least twenty-nine Americans, in a country whose population is less than ten million. In America, this would be equivalent to killing forty thousand—thirteen times more than the number of Al Qaeda victims on 9/11. In Israel, a country whose width is less than the daily commute of many Americans, not a single family was untouched by the attack, either directly, through a neighbor, friend, or classmate. Robert Satloff, "Why 10/7 Was Worse for Israel Than 9/11 Was for America," The Washington Institute, October 15, 2023.

widespread Microsoft outage occurred in the summer of 2024, the disruption impacted airlines, banks, and media outlets around the world. The cybersecurity firm CrowdStrike was accused by Delta Airlines of "negligence," as Delta was forced to cancel thousands of flights and lost almost $1 billion in revenue.[4]

The pace of change is also increasing. A prime example is the impact and ethical complexity of artificial intelligence, which Elon Musk has predicted will soon outperform human intelligence. Executives and many others will be left to make some quick pivots, even in the essential skills they look for in hiring. By one estimate, as many as 375 million people globally will need to change roles and update their skills because of AI and all the automation and innovation that comes with it—and that's just in the next five years.[5] One thing AI will not make obsolete is the heightened awareness that leaders will need. As black swans multiply, agility will become an asset only more prized.

> *One thing AI will not make obsolete is the heightened awareness that leaders will need.*

No less than 92 percent of business leaders, according to one study, said that organizational agility, an ability to respond rapidly to external factors, is critical to success.[6] When Federal Reserve chairman Jerome Powell was grappling with intense inflationary pressures in the fall of 2023, he described the board's task as "navigating by the stars under cloudy skies."[7] Some argue that his hesitation in tightening monetary policy added to the problem, but all agreed with Powell that the circumstances called for agility.

The contemporary way of explaining our complex world is the "VUCA" model, developed by Warren Bennis and Bert Nanus in their 1985 book, *Leaders: The Strategies for Taking Charge*. Popularized by the US Army War College in 1990, the VUCA model ("Volatility, Uncertainty, Complexity and Ambiguity") described our world after the Soviet Union collapsed, or what was prematurely labeled as the "end of history."[2] What may have been the end of the long and tense Cold War—something to celebrate—was also the beginning of other unforeseen and unintended geopolitical consequences—something to be wary of.

At Heidrick & Struggles, we view agility in leadership as a combination of foresight, learning, adaptability, and resilience. From my own experience, I would add a fifth element: execution. It's not enough to grasp the urgency of a pivot; the leader must act decisively and execute. Otherwise, it's like dashing for your car to make a last-minute journey but then idling for hours in the driveway.

A noted military strategist offered another useful way of thinking about agile leadership. Air Force Colonel John Boyd developed the "OODA Loop" of decision-making: "Observe, Orient, Decide, Act." With OODA, it's all there—self-awareness, agility, and execution—which is why Jamie Dimon and other executives have applied the framework with such great success. Dimon told me that while "self-awareness is fundamental in leadership," it can only take you so far. A leader must also "orient" as new information requires adaptation and change. At that point, said Dimon, decisiveness and execution are everything.

---

2 In Francis Fukuyama's 1992 book, *The End of History and the Last Man*, he argued that liberal democracy and the market economy had won the competition with its defeat of fascism and communism. The theory, popularized and much trumpeted at the time, has since been debunked with the rise of international terrorism, the proxy wars sponsored by the Mullahs in Iran and its nuclear weapon program, and rising autocracies and threats from Russia, China, and North Korea.

As with OODA, there's an acronym for the agility framework I've just described. FLARE, for me, conveys a sudden burst of energy and light that can help leaders find their way forward:

- *FORESIGHT*
- *LEARNING*
- *ADAPTABILITY*
- *RESILIENCE*
- *EXECUTION*

Foresight

In a 2021 study, my Heidrick & Struggles partners analyzed thousands of assessments and found that the largest gap in the agility framework is foresight. To measure agility potential,[8] they used a video- and game-based methodology that allows an assessment of behavior in real time.[9] This gaming study showed that fewer than half were strong in any of the four traits of agility (foresight, learning, adaptability, and resilience), but not even 15 percent of the executives Heidrick & Struggles assessed had the strong "developed creative solutions" that underlies foresight—or "thinking dexterity."[10] The upshot is that foresight turns out to be a pretty rare attribute.

When I think of the trait, Wil VanLoh comes to mind. At age twenty-eight, Wil founded Quantum Capital Group, and over the last twenty-five years has gained a place among the private-equity elite. Admired for building a culture of integrity and performance, Wil also has a keen eye for timely investments that have yielded billions of dollars in value for his limited partners (primarily pension funds for firefighters, teachers, and university endowments). With over $35 billion in enterprise value of their active funds, Quantum's combined production from their oil and gas portfolio companies, would collectively be among the largest private energy companies in the world, producing approximately 800,000 (BOE) barrels of oil and natural gas per day equivalent.

Wil rated as "highly accelerating" in the foresight category of our leadership assessment, with a personal 360-report showing a clear pattern of "thinking dexterity." Colleagues observed that "Wil has a gift for decoding signal from the noise," and that he "can quickly get to the root of any issue more than most."[11]

He was mentored by the legendary A. V. Jones, known as the "Warren Buffett of energy investing," and follows the Jones model of simplicity and humility in his approach to both investing and life generally. That model in action, combined with Wil's intense curiosity, have made for some impressive displays of agility.

Wil was among the first to see major investment potential in renewable energy. Without pivoting away from traditional oil and gas investments entirely, he started the firm's Quantum Innovation Fund to navigate the complex transition to a low-carbon future. Wil's strategic diversification of Quantum's energy portfolio to an "all of the above" approach to energy has set a standard that many investors have adopted as their own.

That kind of foresight is hard to teach. Somehow Wil acquired it growing up in Temple, Texas, where, as he put it, folks didn't have very much but "we didn't even know we didn't have very much." A model of the small-town work ethic, his father, Wil recalled, was a man who almost never bought himself anything. His mother was a little less careful with money, and at times this could lead to disagreements at home. It was not until he arrived at Texas Christian University that Wil realized how less well off his family was than others and resolved that money would never be a source of tension or discontent in his adult life or when he married. That desire supplied him with a healthy ambition for financial success.

At TCU, Wil started as a premed student, but even then displayed agility in switching to finance when he realized that his true talents were entrepreneurial. He paid his own tuition and expenses by starting several businesses and managed to graduate debt free. From there it was on to the hugely successful career in which we find him today.[12]

Foresight, like prudence, is a strength we usually acquire through experience. But it can also be consciously developed; we can train ourselves to think ahead and see around corners. The key, as in Wil's case, is to live and work with a learning mindset that sees openings when others don't.

Learning

With a learning mindset, we are aware of what we know and of what we don't know, which allows for quick adjustment and self-correction. Elon Musk, as agile as leaders come, warned that "some people don't like change, but you need to embrace change if the alternative is disaster."[13] Musk's own willingness to change hinges on a clear and constant sense of purpose. This is a man who never wakes up wondering how he can fill a day.

Sam Walton, the founder of Walmart, was also renowned for his quick learning and agility. Jim Collins recounted the story of a Brazilian businessman who wrote to the CEOs of ten US retailers in the 1980s requesting a visit to observe their operations. Everyone turned him down, except Sam Walton.

> When the Brazilian and his colleagues stepped off the plane in Bentonville, Ark., a white-haired man asked if he could help. "We're looking for Sam Walton," they said, to which the man replied, "That's me." Walton led them to his truck and introduced his dog, Roy. As they rumbled around in the front cab of Walton's pickup, the Brazilian billionaires were pummeled with

questions. Eventually it dawned on them: Walton had invited them to Bentonville so that he could learn about South America. Later Walton visited his friends in Sao Paulo. Late one afternoon there was a phone call from the police. Walton had been crawling around in stores on his hands and knees measuring aisle widths and had been arrested.[14]

Who else but Sam Walton would go to such lengths or be so eager to learn better business practices? This was a man who could have rested on laurels for the rest of his days. He'd achieved immense business success, received countless accolades, and had become a genuine celebrity beyond what most CEOs could ever imagine. Yet at heart he remained the small-town shop owner that he was in the beginning, always interested in what changes could be made to win a few more customers, meeting anyone who could teach him something, and bringing Roy along for the ride. Leaders are humble enough to understand that in any kind of business, there is always more to learn.

Adaptability

It is usually the habitual learners, of course, who are quickest to adapt. And the quality of adaptability, as we've found at Heidrick & Struggles, is closely related to what we call social agility, meaning a mix of attributes such as assertiveness and self-confidence balanced with empathy and personal warmth.

Adaptability, in building agility, also relies on keen self-awareness. To pivot quickly with precision, leaders need to heighten awareness of old mental models as well as biases that pervade their organization. So, when Albert Einstein said that the greatest "measure of intelligence is the ability to change," he was likely considering emotional intelligence (EQ) not just the cognitive kind.[15]

We've all encountered the kind of leaders who don't check the empathy box or score high on EQ, like the drill sergeant in an old story who is called in one day by a superior:

"Sarge, do you have a man in your unit named Dumbowski?"
"Yes, sir, I do."
"Well, we just received word that his mother has died. You're going to have to break the news to him. I know this isn't your style, but, Sarge, please do it as gently as you can."
"Yes, sir, I will."
So, the sergeant returns to the barracks and orders his recruits to line up.
"All right, listen up now: I want all of you whose mothers are still living to take one step forward—not so fast, Dumbowski!"

Empathy, as we've seen earlier, doesn't come naturally to some CEOs. Reaching the top job calls on the harder virtues, and more sensitive types often never get there. Yet among the best of our time you'll find a disposition to adapt and bring toughness and empathy into balance.

Jamie Dimon has patterned this style for almost twenty years as CEO of JPMorgan Chase. Reflective yet decisive. Principled yet adaptable. Tough but fair and empathetic. This latter trait, he told me, was instilled early on by the example of his parents, who, he remembers, treated everyone with courtesy and respect. Thinking more about the influences that shaped him, Dimon credited his direct, straight-talking manner to his Greek American mother, who, he said, had a way of teaching by asking questions—about basic assumptions and motivations. The Socratic method sharpened his intellect and made him more independent and objective in his approach to questions and problems of every kind. He has never been one to be drawn in by fuzzy thinking or corporate groupthink, which helps explain why people in the business world pay close attention when he speaks.

His annual shareholder letters are usually widely reported news. In 2024, Dimon's letter stressed "strategic thinking, leading with heart, and *adaptability*." The success of the bank during recent black swans, Dimon wrote, can be credited to resilience and adaptability, two keys of agile leadership.

The same letter urged leaders to disregard "sacred cows, seek out blind spots, and challenge the status quo." Often, he observed, people use their "brains to justify existing biases rather than finding the objectively correct answer;" we should instead engage with naysayers to "seek out where they may be partially right."[16] He considers curiosity to be a healthy "form of humility," requiring us to ask questions on the usually safe assumption that we don't have all the answers. In fact, every year, Dimon takes what the company calls his Heartland bus tour to visit with JPMorgan Chase employees, clients, and other stakeholders. This keeps him alert to what's in the air and helps him adapt to changes that other executives might not see coming until they're headlines in the *Wall Street Journal*.

Resilience

J. Paul Getty, the oil and gas pioneer who was once known as the world's richest man, offered this formula for success in the industry: "Rise early, work hard, and strike oil." Getty left behind this adage as well: "The meek shall inherit the earth, but not its mineral rights." Oil and gas exploration is still that kind of industry—it sifts out the faint of heart and usually reserves its biggest rewards for the most resilient.

Among leaders I've known in that industry, one of the more impressive is Doug Lawler. It was Doug whom we recruited to take over at Chesapeake Energy in June 2013 after Aubrey McClendon was removed as CEO. Arriving to that position, he faced what was by all accounts an extremely tough leadership challenge.

When Doug replaced Aubrey, the *Wall Street Journal* landed the scoop as their lead story for their Marketplace section. America's premier business journal knew what industry leaders understood: The Chesapeake job was the greatest leadership challenge in the oil and gas industry. Then the second largest natural gas producer in the country, the company was on the brink of bankruptcy with a mountain of debt, deteriorating morale, and Wall Street's disfavor. Chesapeake was the worst performing oil and gas company in the world by any measure—a bottom quartile performer.

Months earlier, McClendon was forced out from the mounting pressure of Carl Icahn, who announced to shareholders that "now more than ever the company needs the stewardship of a strong board—a board that can instill confidence in the shareholder base and restore accountability and credibility."[17] The company also got a new CEO in Doug Lawler, whom Icahn embraced and gave full backing to make the changes he needed to make.

"Despite all your best due diligence," Doug shared at a luncheon with industry leaders, "what I found when I got inside the company was much, much worse than I thought." Typically, a headhunter like me takes pride in knowing all the details of the company—the good, the bad, and the ugly. Certainly I was familiar with the good (the quality of the assets) and the bad (the debt that was drowning the company). I knew less about the ugly, namely, the entanglements of complex midstream agreements and commitments Aubrey had made that would take years to unwind combined with no financial, operational, or cultural discipline.

Despite the progress Doug made in the first year and an equity market increase of roughly 50 percent, the "crude collapse" which occurred in November 2014 when OPEC surprised the market by not opting to cut production, set in motion a commodity price environment for oil and gas that had long-term, punishing consequences to Chesapeake and the industry. The company was back on its heels. While Doug and his team kept fighting by reducing capital expenditures, improving capital efficiencies, and reducing operating costs, the mountain of legacy debt was a massive, lingering challenge. When asked by a reporter when he thought his honeymoon with Icahn would end, Doug responded, "it will end when I stop driving the greatest value for shareholders, and then I fully expect him to fire me when that happens."[18]

At the time, Doug likened his situation to that of Ernest Shackleton, the British explorer who led expeditions in Antarctica in the early 1900s. Shackleton is remembered for his bleak recruitment notice: "Men wanted for hazardous journey. Small wages. Bitter cold. Long months of complete darkness. Constant danger. Safe return doubtful. Honor and recognition in case of success." Why would Doug take the helm of a company when everything looked so grim? The short answer is that he is a man built for tough times.

The next several years was a tale of highs and lows, tough calls, even bankruptcy when Doug gritted his teeth once more. He encouraged employees, "by working together . . . we will not only survive this, but we will thrive." To Doug and his team's credit, the company successfully emerged from bankruptcy in early 2021 with the same discipline and strategic plan that had been in place for eight years. Commodity prices recovered and optimism abounded, yet instead of being celebrated for his perseverance and strategic agility, the new board decided that Doug's services were no longer needed.

What shocked the industry wasn't just the news itself, but the fact that bondholder-led boards often change leadership post-bankruptcy—despite the effusive praise Doug received from both the board and industry veterans for navigating the storm. While the sense of betrayal stung, Doug, known for both his steeliness and modesty, simply chalked it up to "the Lord's plan."[19]

That the board ended up tapping Doug's CFO, Nick Dell'Osso, as the CEO fully validated Doug's strategic turnaround plan.[3] Industry peers still stunned by the news were certain that one of the most highly sought-after CEOs in the industry would land on his feet. Sure enough, legendary oil man Harold Hamm, the seventy-nine-year-old founder and CEO of Continental Resources, persuaded Doug to join Continental as its president in 2022, becoming CEO less than a year later.

But even this turnaround doesn't tell the full story of why I so admire Doug Lawler. Back when he was starting out as a petroleum engineer, Doug's wife, Heidi, was diagnosed with brain cancer not long after giving birth to their daughter. After three years of surgeries, radiation, and chemotherapy, she died, leaving Doug to tell their little girl that "Mommy had gone to heaven." His determination to "make the most of every moment" with his daughter—which included bringing her flowers every week—became the defining commitment of his life. "My prayer," he said, "was that God would help me do the very best for her."[20]

When a man or woman has walked through a wall of fire like that, the pressures of professional life will never get the best of him or her. Doug's focus on the things that matter most kept him grounded and oriented, forging the resilient spirit that powered him through the upheavals of a troubled company and the wild swings of a highly cyclical industry. I'm happy to note that Doug married again, had triplet daughters and a son, and that his first daughter not long ago had a child of her own, a girl she named Heidi, after her mother.

---

3 When Chesapeake Energy's closed its acquisition of Southwestern Energy on October 1, 2024, it was renamed Expand Energy and continues to be led by its CEO, Nick Dell'Osso.

Execution

Being adaptable and resilient does not, of course, mean letting go of fixed principles or losing focus on the demands of day-to-day execution. On the contrary, for agile leaders like Jamie Dimon, core principles inform every major decision or move. Leaders who are quick on their feet, adaptable, and durable set themselves apart by an ability to execute on plans and deliver sustained performance.

By those measures, few CEOs have records to equal that of Darren Woods of ExxonMobil. Consider that in October 2020, the first year of the Covid pandemic, the total market value of ExxonMobil was actually less than that of Zoom Video Communications. Here was a universally known American energy producer, with a presence everywhere in a fundamental sector of the economy, and for a brief time it was worth less than a videoconferencing site that few people had even heard of a year earlier. Even industry veterans, accustomed to uncertainty, were a bit rattled by the extent of the volatility and hardship that oil and gas companies faced in that time.

Far from panicking, Darren pivoted and adopted a countercyclical investment strategy. He used the pandemic to trim $5 billion from annual operating costs and made targeted investments while energy prices were low. While this added to ExxonMobil's debt, the company was still able to raise its dividend payment for a thirty-ninth consecutive year.[21]

In the short of it, Darren kept his eye on the fundamentals. Zoom might have been trendy for investors, given its sudden usefulness in pandemic circumstances, but even that ubiquitous platform wouldn't last a day without the energy and materials produced by companies like ExxonMobil. Darren executed with confidence that the market would again reflect this reality. And, sure enough, by September of 2024 ExxonMobil was trading at around $550 billion market cap, compared to Zoom's, at $17 billion, or 0.03 percent of ExxonMobil's value. No one in the fall of 2020 would have predicted such a recovery for the company, and the scale of it owes to the vision and execution of the CEO.

Seeing Darren at the helm today, you'd never guess that he almost quit his first job at Exxon (as it was then known). He was an electrical engineering graduate of Texas A&M and earned his MBA from the Kellogg School at Northwestern University. After he joined the company as a planning analyst, his boss told him that the way to succeed at Exxon was to "keep your head down." Darren didn't like the sound of that advice—he wasn't the type to lie low and stay passive—and he remembers telling his wife Kathryn that he was starting to feel he might be working in the wrong place.

His father had worked with the military, with all the relocations that usually involves. Adjusting to one school after another wasn't easy; there was bullying, a feeling of always being the outsider, and constant attempts to fit in. Yet somehow, as Darren recalled, the sum effect was to give him a certain self-assurance that's clear to anyone who meets him. He treats people as he expects to be treated and refuses to simply conform to the thinking or the ways of others. As he put it, long ago Darren decided "I was going to be me and do what is right."[22]

Darren's mother, he recalled of his teenage years, "felt guilty for putting us kids through those challenges. She expressed regret." He told her that, looking back, those experiences were "for my own good," and "made me the person I am today." Mature—or I should say, aware—beyond his years, Darren rejected people-pleasing tendencies, a choice that would serve him well years later. The conflict of those early years would sow the seeds for the operating chops and resilience that resulted in him not only be named chairman and CEO of ExxonMobil in 2016 but also had a lot to do with him being named "one of the top CEOs" in America.[23]

It was the influence of his father, who taught Darren to never "be a quitter," that kept him from leaving that first Exxon job. He didn't keep his head down, but instead handled each assignment in his own way, pushing back when necessary and producing results that gained him both attention and regular promotions. When the day came in 2016 and he was offered the top job by outgoing CEO Rex Tillerson on behalf of the board, Darren insisted that he really didn't need or aspire to be the company's new leader. Tillerson replied, "That's why you are the perfect man for the job."

ExxonMobil is known for its operating discipline and accountability culture; Darren added his own trademark touches of greater transparency and consistency in execution. When commodity prices collapsed during the pandemic and shareholder activism threatened to upend the boardroom in 2021, Darren never let external pressures throw him off course. When a hedge fund landed three new directors on the ExxonMobil board, Darren addressed investor concerns diplomatically while standing his ground on the oil strategy, low carbon aims, and other purposes he has set for the company. By 2022, Exxon was handily beating its peers—Chevron, Shell, and BP—and remains far ahead of them to this day.

Since Darren Woods became CEO, ExxonMobil's total shareholder return has been more than 87 percent, or $150 billion return to shareholders in dividends and share buybacks. Here's how *Barron's* summarized his executive record: "By pursuing a countercyclical investment strategy in recent years—putting money to work during downturns and despite claims that fossil fuel is in decline—Woods has given Exxon a financial edge."[24] That's the performance of a company lucky to have a leader who understands that big goals and objectives are meaningless without steady and purposeful execution. "I am not sure I have ever seen a more effective CEO than Darren who operates with complete objectivity driven by facts and data," said Larry Kellner, a current director of ExxonMobil.[25]

The Agilist and the Conformist

The elements of FLARE—foresight, learning, adaptability, resilience, and execution—are one way of understanding agility in leadership. Another way of thinking about agility is to compare two basic types we find in most organizations—the *agilist* and the *conformist*.

The term *agilist*, a neologism originally referring to an engineer who develops agile software, is the type who embraces change and shows adaptability, and is thus able to move a business forward in the face of uncertainty. The agilists are always looking out on the horizon for what could go wrong, even during the best of times. They're the most likely to ask, "What's working and what's not?" Or "What can we be doing differently?" And even "Are there opportunities in crisis?" As with Warren Buffett's proven countercyclical investment strategy over the decades, or Darren Woods's reinvesting in oil exploration when prices were collapsing, the agilist mentality is forever questioning and planning for change.

The *conformists*, on the other hand, are comfortable with the status quo and seem more interested in keeping up with the herd, as when banks followed other banks headlong into subprime mortgages, or when energy companies invested in non-core businesses during the Enron era, putting their balance sheets in jeopardy. At their worst, the conformists are like lemmings, the small, furry-footed rodents known for recurrent mass migrations in the Norwegian sea, who in the lore of the species follow the ones ahead to their demise.

Applying these categories, we would surely have to term Dick Fuld a conformist in the context of the financial crisis for having doubled down on subprime mortgages, and Jamie Dimon an agilist for his hyperfocus on maintaining balance-sheet flexibility and buying other banks on the cheap. Agilists like Dimon are comfortable and secure in examining preconceived notions and keeping their doors open to hear contrarian views. Fuld preferred to keep being told what he wanted to hear.

Conformists invite trouble because they are so prone to groupthink, discounting and pushing away objective, independent judgment. Worse, the unwillingness of conformists to question authority can soon become a tolerance of unethical practices. Agilists, on the other hand, are more self-reflective, inclusive, innovative, creative, and productive. They question authority respectfully, are team players, and thus stand out in the way of Darren Woods and Jamie Dimon. They are more likely to adapt and pivot in changing business environments later in their careers. They tend to keep their egos in check and so are more inclined to collaboration.

Agilists, in my experience, have the advantage of heightened self-awareness—not only knowing their own blind spots and superpowers, but also being far better attuned than conformists to organizational vulnerabilities and emerging opportunities. Striving to increase awareness, they don't fall into the trap once described by Ann Landers as accepting "your dog's admiration as conclusive evidence that you are wonderful."

Although he established no prize for agilism, Alfred Nobel would have grasped its meaning at once—no doubt with some self-recognition. He had the unique experience of reading the verdict on his life before it was over, and surely his was one of the great pivots in history. What aspiring leaders don't stand to learn from that example in striving to use their time, talents, and opportunities to the full?

EIGHT

The Fellowship of a Team

The world is indeed full of peril, and in it there are many dark places; but still there is much that is fair, and though in all lands love is now mingled with grief, it grows perhaps the greater... The Company of the Ring shall be Nine; and the Nine Walkers shall be set against the Nine Riders that are evil.

—Haldir, an Elf of Lothlorien,
in *The Fellowship of the Ring*

Leaders trying to enhance their awareness and agility are working on strengths that come from within. There is one strength, however, that comes only from without: the power of teamwork.

On this theme, we get a vivid example from one of my favorite works, J. R. R. Tolkien's *The Lord of the Rings* trilogy. It's a saga with much to teach, and one of the essential messages has to do with a unity of purpose forged among vastly different groups. The story centers on "The Fellowship of the Ring," revealing how qualities of greatness are instilled in its members.

The nine unique characters in the Fellowship represent the Free Peoples of Middle-Earth. These characters set out to destroy the evil One Ring. This Fellowship includes an elf, a dwarf, men, and hobbits, all with different skills and superpowers. Some are empathetic guides, like Sam Gamgee, the gardener hobbit from the Shire. Others are fearless heroes like Frodo, the playful and upright hobbit and chosen bearer of the One Ring.

At the appointed hour, Frodo goes forth to complete the quest. The Fellowship, also called "The Company of the Ring," numbers nine in order to counterbalance the nine evil "Ringwraiths" they must contend with. The effect of this epic tale is to make readers see the beauty and goodness of the world as reflected in the unity and camaraderie of the nine companions. Their sense of fellowship, which grows stronger in the face of adversity and sorrow, presents the very ideal of what teamwork can mean and accomplish!

The capacity to work and excel in teams is more critical than ever in today's business environment. So, it's a little concerning that, among teams analyzed by Heidrick & Struggles, just 13 percent qualified as the strongest performers in our top category of "accelerating" teams. And fully one-third were "derailing" or "lagging" in teamwork.[1] Leaders in every kind of business organization should stay alert to this problem. We don't have Ringwraiths to fear, but there are plenty of disruptors, uncertainties, and potential black swans that can spell the undoing of an organization where teamwork is weak or missing altogether.

Team Awareness

Think of some of the most effective and admired teams in history. The very best all have one thing in common: They were acutely *aware* of their mission and the combination of skills that they brought to it.

The Fellowship of a Team

For many Americans, the first team that comes to mind are the scientists and engineers of the Manhattan Project, who, in secrecy and with the highest possible stakes, developed the weapon that brought an enemy to surrender and ended a war.

Others recall NASA's Mission Control Center during the Apollo 13 crisis in 1970. Led by flight director Gene Kranz, the mission-control team, through improvisation and sheer tenacity, worked almost as one mind to overcome the odds and bring the astronauts safely back to earth.

> *Think of some of the most effective and admired teams in history. The very best all have one thing in common: They were acutely aware of their mission and the combination of skills that they brought to it.*

Still others would cite the triumphant team at Ford Motor Company that designed a vehicle to challenge the Ferrari racecar dynasty. With intense collaborative energy, Ford's next-level experts stunned the Ferrari team in 1966 by placing first, second, and third at Le Mans.

And while sports fans might argue the point, perhaps the greatest of teams was the UCLA Bruins basketball dynasty under coach John Wooden, which won ten NCAA championships in twelve seasons. The team's key success factors were each man's selfless character, discipline, sense of personal responsibility, and awareness—qualities instilled by the wisdom of Coach Wooden. A team can go a long way when each member is constantly striving to bring his or her utmost to the enterprise. As Wooden used to say, "The best competition I have is against myself to become better."[2]

On the other hand, asked to name the worst kind of teamwork, we might think of Dunder-Mifflin, the paper company in *The Office* managed by the Steve Carell character Michael Scott. The least self-aware character imaginable, Michael asks in one episode, "Would I rather be feared or loved? Easy. Both. I want people to be afraid of how much they love me."[3]

Another episode finds Michael hiding behind his office door. As a colleague walks by, Michael says to the camera, "I don't understand how someone can have so little self-awareness."[4] Often hilarious in its self-mockery, *The Office*, many viewers commented, made you want to avoid ever conducting yourself in a way that reminded colleagues of any character on the show.

And if a lack of self-awareness can make for absurd extremes, it's the virtue of self-awareness that keeps things rational and well-directed. Our Heidrick & Struggles research shows that self-awareness not only accelerates a leader's performance but also helps teams decide, collaborate, and manage conflict more effectively. In fact, as an asset of leadership, this quality has been shown to matter more than an MBA.[5] Evaluating more than one thousand leaders in more than eight hundred global companies, another study showed that higher self-awareness correlates with greater authenticity and integrity. Highly aware teams outperformed low-awareness teams on the quality of their decisions (68 percent versus 32 percent), collaboration and coordination (73 percent versus 27 percent), and conflict management (65 percent versus 35 percent).[6]

The Fellowship of a Team

As an individual pursuit, effective leadership development depends on experience, feedback, and coaching. This kind of individual effort, for the good of the whole, is clearest in the setting of team sports, where one excelling player tends to up everyone else's game. Our research shows the same effect in business environments. Greater team performance comes about with a clear understanding of what each team member can do at his or her best.[7]

Phil Jackson, the Zen master basketball coach with eleven NBA championship rings, was famous for emphasizing self-awareness—developed, in his case, from a study of Christian mysticism, Zen meditation, and even some Native American rituals. "The more aware I became of what was going on inside me," he wrote, "the more connected I became to the world outside. I became more patient with others and calmer under pressure—qualities that helped me immensely when I became a coach."[8] His famous "triangle" offense was centered on mindful awareness and the selflessness of each player.

With the Chicago Bulls, Jackson was intentional in creating this ethic and culture, "bonding people together and awakening the spirit," as he put it. Coach Jackson needed a "sanctuary" where his team could escape outside distraction. As if all these concepts weren't enough, the coach also subscribed to Maslow's hierarchy of needs, with its idea that the highest human need is to achieve self-actualization, defined as "the full use and exploitation of one's talents, capacities, and potentialities."[9] This background helps explain the title Peter Richmond gave to his best-selling biography of the coaching genius, *Phil Jackson: Lord of the Rings*.

The success of the Zen master coach in leading the Chicago Bulls to six NBA championships surely has a lot to do with the "awareness and selflessness gospel" that he preached. He built a fellowship that was more than a team—and, of course, having Michael Jordan didn't hurt either.

Interdependency Versus Independence

In general, we don't think of corporate leadership in quite the same way we once did. It's no longer the image of one commanding figure, above and superior to underlings. This has given way to our era of networked leadership teams that shape the fortunes of organizations. MIT social psychologist Edgar Schein was an early advocate of today's model of "interdependency over independence," living long enough to see it take hold before his passing in 2023 at age ninety-four.

Most of us operate in organizational cultures and teams that have certain tacit assumptions. Over time, these are taken for granted and applied without need of explanation.[10] Although we often claim to value teamwork, Schein observed that our promotion and reward structures are fundamentally designed to recognize individual achievements rather than collective success. As he wrote,

> The U.S. culture is individualistic, competitive, optimistic, and pragmatic. We believe that the basic unit of society is the individual, whose rights have to be protected at all costs. We are entrepreneurial and admire individual accomplishment. We thrive on competition. Optimism and pragmatism show up in the way we are oriented toward the short term and in our dislike of long-range planning. . . . We are impatient and, with information technology's ability to do things faster, we are even more impatient. Most important of all, we value task accomplishment over relationship building and either are not aware of this cultural bias or worse, don't care and don't want to be bothered with it.[11]

To help us think clearly about all this, Schein offered his own construct: Leadership is relational at two levels. Level 1 relationships are "civil and transactional"; at Level 2 they are much more "whole person to whole person." Level 1 leaders are "reasonably open with each other while maintaining professional distance and trust that neither will harm the other as they transact business."[12] The hallmark of Level 2 leaders is a "deeper level of openness and trust."[13] Schein's son and collaborator, Peter, noted that America's post-war industrial success has been based on a "linear machine model" in which few relationships get past Level 1. But in our day, the Scheins concluded, better results depend far more on better relationships—on systems that emphasize interdependency over independence—where collaboration drives better outcomes.[14] This shift reflects the evolution from an agrarian and manufacturing-based economy to one centered on services and information, where value is increasingly created through shared knowledge and collective problem-solving.

This is harder than it sounds, because the basic tension between interdependency and independence plays out constantly. We might idealize the Adam II values of humility and deeper human connection, yet we still live in the transactional world of Adam I individualism. We say that we value teams, but at times we'd rather do without them. We invest in team building only when, as Schein pointed out, "it is pragmatically necessary to accomplish the task." We trumpet teamwork and winning teams, "but we don't for a minute believe that the team could have done it without the individual star, who usually receives much greater pay."[15] This is why, when we think of Apple, we think first of Steve Jobs, and secondarily about Steve Wozniak and then Tim Cook. Or lavish attention on Michael Jordan, hardly remembering Scottie Pippen. Or bestow awards on Commander Jim Lovell, forgetting any pats on the back that are due the Apollo 13 team who brought him and his astronauts safely home.

No doubt it's just human nature that we tend to place exceptional leaders on pedestals. This not only inflates their significance but can also magnify the sense of disillusionment when events upset our expectations. "The more we believe in leadership myths, the more we absolve ourselves of responsibility and action," wrote Margaret Heffernan.[16] She continued, "Believing that a company or a country succeeds or fails because of one mighty person is simple and alleviates our anxiety. It turns a complex world into a simple narrative. We have only to change the person to change the story."[17]

In cultures centered on individualism, we often see what's known as the "attribution error." This refers to a tendency to ascribe any success or failure to a single leader. In *The Romance of Leadership*, James Meindl and his coauthors argued that, as important as leadership might be, its effects are often exaggerated. Within their own sampling, leadership accounted for only about 15 percent of the variation in task performance.[18]

"By the excessive promotion of leadership," wrote management guru Henry Mintzberg, "we demote everyone else." The problem, he said, is that "We create clusters of followers who have to be driven to perform, instead of leveraging the natural propensity of people to cooperate in communities." Mintzberg argued that our way of idealizing leadership elevates style over substance and gives an inaccurate picture of the real dynamic within teams. Better, he said to stress mutuality among people at every level of an organization. He invited us to think of it this way, perhaps overstating the point to accentuate the value of mutuality: "There is no such thing as a good husband or a good wife, only a good couple."[19]

In the United States, it's odd that we so often identify commercial enterprises with a single name or personality. After all, these enterprises are called *companies*, a term referring to collections of employees and teams. In corporations, CEOs are elected and governed by boards that serve at the pleasure of shareholders. Yet for all this, we still focus on the man or woman who happens, for the moment, to hold the highest title, as if the contributions of the hundreds or thousands of others in a company were just a detail.

The Fellowship of a Team

To recognize the attribution error is not to overlook the enormous difference for the better that leaders can make. And it is certainly not to dismiss the urgency of developing awareness, agility, and other qualities that make for great leadership. The point is simply that in any enterprise, everyone on the team can make valuable contributions, and drawing out the strengths of others is part of what makes a leader.

Placing significant trust in his team, Jeff Miller, the unassuming CEO of Halliburton, one of the world's largest energy companies, practices what he calls "self-honesty"—an awareness of his ability, or inability, to solve every problem that arises. Quickly leveraging the expertise and capabilities of his team, "there are days when I lead, and others when I need to follow."[20]

Of course, there have always been leaders, like Jeff Miller, who understood the importance of collaboration, and they provide memorable illustrations in settings more demanding than most any we can imagine in business. During World War II, some of the Allies' best generals made a point of assembling diverse teams, knowing that a good team of soldiers would outperform the sum of its parts. With his aversion to yes-men, General George Marshall is said to have told General Omar Bradley and the rest of Marshall's staff, "Gentlemen, I'm disappointed in you. You haven't disagreed with a single decision I've made."[21]

For his part, Dwight Eisenhower observed that "Leadership consists of nothing but taking responsibility for everything that goes wrong and giving your subordinates credit for everything that goes well."[22] Anticipating our own era's appreciation of interdependency, these iconic military officers met immense responsibilities by seeking out talent and relying, at crucial turns, on the fellowship of teams.

The Elite Performers

Looking at the surprisingly small share of teams that rate as "high-performing" or "accelerating"—13 percent, according to Heidrick & Struggles research—what do they do differently? In the short of it, they excel in three distinct ways. After analyzing data from more than 2,500 teams, my Heidrick & Struggles colleagues Alice Breeden, Becky Friend, and T. A. Mitchell identified those factors as: *clarity in direction, discipline in decision-making,* and *a distributed leadership model.*

1. *Clarity in direction.* It's amazing how often this simple imperative is missing in the day-to-day work of teams and entire businesses. In the routine of any workplace, the spirit of joint effort and well-defined priorities can easily slip away. Accelerating teams don't let that happen. When teams are clear about where they are headed, how they relate to other teams and functions, and how they measure and reward performance, the results are as striking as you would expect—a very substantial improvement in performance.[23]

    I think again of the team at ExxonMobil. Under Darren Woods's leadership, that company is renowned in the industry for its accountability mindset and clear direction. Respected by Wall Street analysts for its highly disciplined planning, Darren's team starts with mission clarity: "to provide the products society needs that make modern living possible (energy and chemicals) while dramatically lowering emissions."[24] The company is equally intentional in how it measures and rewards performance. These strengths help explain why ExxonMobil meets or exceeds shareholder expectations nearly every quarter.

    The accountability culture of Hilcorp Energy, one of the largest private oil and gas companies in North America, is also noteworthy. Though not as well-known as ExxonMobil,

Hilcorp has a reputation for its nimble operating style, absence of bottlenecks, and absolute clarity of direction. The founder and chairman, Jeff Hildebrand, credits the success of this multi-billion-dollar company to an operating culture of "open-book management." Such transparency, Jeff told me, builds trust among employees and teams that "management has got their back." Jeff tries to keep a vibe of camaraderie throughout the organization so that everyone feels a sense of direction and purpose in a "culture of communication and transparency."[25]

His company, said Jeff, also benefits from a belief in "meritocracy," reflecting a prime value of his own upbringing. It's not easy to keep a sense of direction and purpose when you feel abandoned in life, but somehow Jeff did that as a teenager in Texas after the tragic loss of his mother in an airplane accident. She was a vibrant and daring personality, he told me, a kind of "Amelia Earhart figure" who pursued her dreams as a flyer and one day crashed and disappeared in the Sierra Madre Mountains. He remembers a lonely time in the years after his mom's death and his subsequent isolation from his father, during which he still managed to work his way through the University of Texas and eventually make his mark in an industry that prizes self-reliance, perseverance, and teamwork.

As we at Heidrick & Struggles were trying to zero in on what accelerating teams do differently, my colleagues were impressed by the example of a global car manufacturer that had been falling behind in performance. The company's ideas were unfocused, and probably no two people in management could have provided the same version of the overall strategy. They decided to go back to basics, with group sessions and workshops to produce a revised and compelling statement of purpose. From there, it was almost magically easy to align each division with its own part in the broader mission. A period of drift for the company ended. This suddenly more purposeful organization lowered cost, reduced plant opening times, and improved its product's pace to market.

Repeatedly at Heidrick & Struggles, we've seen how a sharper, clearer vision and sense of direction can build teams of excellence and lift a company out of mediocrity. The necessary condition of acceleration is always a team working in sync toward a defined common purpose, and far more than 13 percent of companies can make that happen.

2. *Discipline in decision-making.* Teams that make good decisions have at least three things in common: They share information seamlessly. They have streamlined processes, avoiding the cul-de-sacs and laborious rituals of bureaucracy. And they have clearly delineated rights and responsibilities.

You will not be surprised to find me pointing again to Wil VanLoh of Quantum Capital Group to illustrate an executive strength. In 2021, Wil saw that his company stood in need of streamlining in decision-making, especially when the deal flow was intense and time was at a premium. After an extensive organization and culture study, Wil put in place a coaching program to move investment professionals toward closer collaboration. He also pushed more authority down in the organization for quicker decision-making and clearer accountability. These changes, plus some new talent that Wil brought on, prevented Quantum from losing its edge.

A few blocks from Quantum, at Hilcorp Energy, Jeff Hildebrand likewise shows the value of disciplined decision-making. Having started out at a much larger company, he's always been wary of bottlenecks and bureaucracy—indeed, that's one of the reasons Jeff ventured out to build his own oil and gas company. His engineering mind is always at work to keep internal processes direct, disciplined, and data driven.

The model at Hilcorp checks off the three elements of disciplined decision-making. "Open-book management" allows a seamless sharing of information. There are no elaborate committees or approval processes to stand in the way of timely decisions. And at every level where decisions are made, responsibilities are clearly defined. Jeff has moved Hilcorp from a "founder-led" to a "manager-led" company, explaining the approach this way:

> We built the company on a team of the best engineers, geologists and accountants that were trying to make smart decisions. Together, we look at the data and make sound decisions. That is the trick of running a successful business. The best CEOs have the best teams, and they are the ones who can assimilate complex information and make the right decisions most of the time.[26]

Spend some time at Hilcorp and you'll quickly find that you're watching a team that possesses something extra. More than a collection of colleagues brought together by necessity, it's always a reminder to me that even amid the pressures of the business world, a corporate team can be a genuine fellowship. The word *discipline* can sometimes carry a harsh ring, but in practice the most disciplined teams are usually the most collegial.

3. *Promoting distributed leadership.* This third element of "what accelerating teams do better" refers to a model that ensures the full participation of all. "Distributed leadership" does not mean a diffusion of responsibility and decision by consensus; it simply means the careful placement of responsibilities in the right places. When teams get the distribution right, they operate

inclusively; everyone has a voice, and no one hesitates to share ideas or concerns. What underlies the distribution of responsibility is the assumption that every team member has the confidence of the others—that the whole enterprise is based on trust.

A good example here is the Denver-based Liberty Energy, founded by its former CEO Chris Wright. In the industry, Chris was known as his own man, and not one to be timid in expounding on the vast benefits to society that come from fossil fuels. When the outdoor-products company North Face refused to co-brand with and fulfill an order of four hundred jackets from an oil and gas company, Chris's team at Liberty demonstrated that as much as 90 percent of materials in North Face are petroleum based. With a perfect touch, Chris didn't answer their sanctimony with scorn; instead, he laughed it off and praised The North Face as "one of the best customers of the oil and gas industry." And only Chris would have answered criticism of fracking, as he once did, by going on a radio program and drinking a tall glass of fracking fluid just to show that it was harmless.

Self-confident maverick though he is, Chris is also aware of his limitations. He's wired more like a tech CEO in Palo Alto than an oil company CEO in Denver, and he has built his team and culture accordingly. Unlike the sprawling corporate campuses of his much larger rivals, Liberty hosts smaller industry get-togethers on Chris's modest spread. These have the feel of family gatherings, complete with ping-pong tables and craft beer on tap.

The distributed leadership model leans heavily on collaboration, and in Liberty's case it helps that the CEO is a talent magnet. His top priority, Chris told me, was to "get the best people with character and heart."[27] He believes in the kind of "team where they feel valued and empowered to make decisions at multi-levels in the company." (When Chris Wright was tapped for President Trump's cabinet, his groomed successor, Ron Gusek, smoothly stepped in.) By sharing authority and decision-making among talented leaders, and by retaining those leaders in a system of trust, Liberty has grown its market share significantly. As one analyst put it, the company has generated "some of the best if not the best full cycle returns in the business."[28] And those returns are just the most tangible dividends of teamwork in action.

The Collaboration Dividend

"It takes two flints to light a fire," to borrow a phrase from Louisa May Alcott.[29] Solitary achievements in business are rare; wherever we see innovative breakthroughs or big wins against the competition, we usually find successful teamwork.

When Steve Jobs was forced out of Apple in 1986, he didn't go off and try to build something on his own; instead, he sought out new collaborators. And when he founded Pixar, his priority was to form a winning collaborative culture. The various Pixar teams did their work in a single vast space with an atrium in the center. Inside the atrium were meeting rooms, a cafeteria, a coffee shop, and mailboxes. As his colleague Brad Bird, director of *The Incredibles* and *Ratatouille*, recalled, "Steve realized that when people run into each other and they make eye contact, things happen."[30]

Jobs understood that innovation and creative thinking require bringing people together around a common cause. And you have to wonder whether that kind of synergy is at risk of being lost today amid the trend toward more dispersed and more digital workplaces. It's nice to have the flexibility of working virtually, but it might sometimes come at the cost of creative energy. Teams have a harder time accelerating if they see one another only sporadically or on their computer screens.

An example from the automotive industry also points to the difference that direct, in-person teamwork can make. When Ford Motor Company needed to enhance the fuel efficiency of its popular F-150 pick-up truck, it created a highly confidential project that pulled together parallel teams. Ford managers recognized that only intense collaboration would keep the F-150 at the top. The result was a more efficient vehicle now in its forty-eighth year as the best-selling truck in the United States.[31]

Then there's the example of Heidrick & Struggles itself when the firm encountered some leadership challenges. It was our 2021 study that conclusively showed the connection between a company's culture and its bottom line. That broad survey of CEOs demonstrated that when a company's culture is strong on collaboration and trust, its revenues will likely far exceed those of comparable firms that lack those strengths.[32] Yet for all our focus on how to make organizations thrive, at one point we had issues of our own.

After the financial crisis of 2008, we had difficulty maintaining market share amid aggressive poaching of our top talent. It shook our confidence. At the same time, the executive recruiting field was changing, pressuring us to revise our business model. Profits fell almost 30 percent, revenue was stagnant, and leadership was slow to respond. The irony wasn't lost on industry analysts or even casual observers. At the height of it all, an article in a trade journal appeared under the title "Heidrick & Struggling."

With the board's heightened awareness of the organizational "blind spot," our CEO was replaced in 2013. After our own exhaustive executive search, the board hired a veteran Goldman Sachs executive, Tracy Wolstencroft. To the relief of all his new colleagues, Tracy reoriented the firm back to the collaborative and trusting mindset that had built Heidrick & Struggles's reputation. He focused as well on expanding our leadership and strategic consulting services worldwide.

The Fellowship of a Team

At one point, I am embarrassed to recall, after hosting an important call with a group of CEOs, Tracy noticed that I had neglected to involve my team. I had not been walking the walk when it came to teamwork, and he politely called me on it. Reminding me of one of our values, "We Win as One Firm," he said, "even if they didn't participate on the call, your team would still learn and grow from it." That was always Tracy's outlook—the more collaboration, the better.

When Tracy tried to explain the roots of his unique mix of bluntness and warmth and focus on collaboration, he took a reflective turn. He shared a deeply personal story about losing his father to cancer at just fifteen years old. Diagnosed in April, his father passed away that August—the same day Nixon resigned from office. Walking into his home to find family and neighbors gathered by the sad news, young Tracy did what any overwhelmed teenager might do: He bolted to the backyard for a few precious seconds of solitude. In that fleeting moment, he made a choice: "I could either soak in the pity . . . or pour it on—pour it on in the classroom, in sports, and in everything else."

His resolve was set. Even when his mother took him to see the parish priest for grief counseling, Tracy was already moving forward with a mindset of "pour it on" positivity. That decision became the hallmark of his life, fueling both his career as a senior banking executive at Goldman Sachs and later as our firm's CEO.

Tracy's sharp self-awareness, fierce determination, and collaborative spirit weren't just personal tools—they were professional game changers. Within weeks of stepping into his CEO role, he delivered a tough diagnosis: The firm was "personalizing the wins and institutionalizing the losses," a mentality that was draining its energy. But instead of just pointing out the cracks, Tracy offered a way forward, replacing the envy-fueled "my search, my win, my client" culture with a collective focus on "we" and "us."[33] With a mix of self-awareness, determination, and a vision for unity, Tracy didn't just "pour it on"—he poured it into others, leaving a legacy that transformed the firm.

Tracy also gave us our current purpose statement, "We Change the World, One Leadership Team at a Time." Frankly, at first, I thought it was a little too lofty, and kidded Tracy, "Change the world? You sound like Steve Jobs." But the motto grew on me and my colleagues, and he was clearly on to something. His insistence on collaboration, and his sense of larger purpose for the firm, had the intended effect of partners locking arms in service to clients as "one firm" rather than just a collection of individual partners.[34] That sense of direction and teamwork resulted in a Total Shareholder Return (TSR) of almost 120 percent as CEO and then as chairman, and rebuilding our consultants ranks from 325 to almost 400. It carried over into the tenure of Tracy's successor as CEO, Krishnan Rajagopalan, who would help turn Heidrick & Struggles into a global provider of leadership advisory and talent solutions—doubling revenues in seven years to more than $1 billion annually.[1]

That additional $500 million is certainly a tangible gain for a firm that looked to be in trouble a decade ago. But the intangible dividends have made a big difference too. Great leaders and organizations accelerate when they are most aware, brave, and agile. Going to work every day with a clear sense of purpose, knowing that your colleagues are not just a team in name only, makes work more meaningful and success more fulfilling. The feeling might never equal the Fellowship of the Ring, with those daring journeys and epic battles. But it's worth a lot, in whatever calling we pursue, to realize how much we depend on one another in the shared efforts that lead to lasting achievement.

---

1 Under Heidrick & Struggles CEO, Tom Monahan's first year in 2024, annual revenues increased almost 10 percent to $1.1 billion on margins of 10.1percent.

NINE

The Invisible Crown

*There is joy in self-forgetfulness. So, I try to make
the light in others' eyes my sun, the music
in others' ears my symphony,
the smile on others' lips my happiness.*
—Helen Keller, *The Story of My Life*

In more than thirty years of executive recruitment, I've met many highly confident men and women—accomplished professionals with plenty to be confident about. Three decades is also long enough to have noticed that a confident exterior can be misleading. On closer acquaintance, we sometimes find that a vivid, forceful personality is actually putting something less appealing on display. Dealing with people who seek prominence and power within organizations, you're going to meet more than a few narcissists.

Ambitious, independent, and talented leaders sometimes have an underside to their character. While they might say they value teamwork, what they want in reality are sycophants to praise and reinforce their views. In ego-driven environments like the banking sector, this can create a culture of self-deception, as happened during the financial crisis when a few unchecked narcissists brought down entire institutions and brought immense harm upon millions of people.

The word, of course, traces back to the mythical Narcissus, who saw his own reflection in a pond and fell in love with the image. Hopelessly entranced, he can do nothing else except keep staring, and in the end he dies. The flower that bears Narcissus' name may be beautiful and alluring, but brings madness and destruction. No better word has yet been coined for real-life leaders who have been undone by their own outsized egos.

In our day, it doesn't help that so many influences seem to encourage self-absorption, cultivating arrogance and devaluing modesty. The temptations of social media, with its endless opportunities for attention-seeking, only magnify the problem. It's a trap so easy to fall into, so difficult to escape, so far removed from the humility that comes with true self-knowledge. And when there's a narcissist in the corner office, exerting control and influence over an entire organization, you can safely predict that problems will multiply.

The Narcissistic Trap

People in executive search are familiar with narcissistic traits, although that hardly makes us immune from them ourselves. After all, when you make a career of assessing the qualities and credentials of others, it can be a short step from there to a sense of superiority. And even when we are put off by arrogance in executive candidates we encounter from time to time, that might mean we are seeing something not only distasteful but a little too familiar. As C. S. Lewis observed, "The more pride one has, the more one dislikes it in others."[1]

Years ago, while interviewing a recruiter from a rival firm, I encountered someone unforgettable—but for all the wrong reasons. He walked into the conference room impeccably dressed in a sharp Italian suit, with coordinated tie and handkerchief, his hair perfectly styled. But what really stood out was the overpowering scent of cologne and a manner suggesting he had an exaggerated opinion of himself. With me was a very bright colleague of mine who was there to help assess the candidate, and he had a similar air about him. The stage was set for a clash of egos, each man clearly repelled by what he saw in the other.

"Can you provide more than generalities of your success in building your book of business?" my colleague asked.

"Well," our candidate replied, "that's a smart-assy way of asking the question." This launched him into a series of boasts about how he, unaided by a team or anyone else, had built a multimillion-dollar client base.

When he was finished, my colleague said sarcastically, "And you did this all on your own. *Wow*."

It went on like this for a little longer, revealing two people who plainly didn't like each other and yet were so much alike. When one of these guys told the other he was being "too sensitive," that was my cue to separate them as quickly as possible and move on to the next meeting.

There is a reason why "check your ego at the door" is one of the stock lines in CEO job profiles. It's a given that anyone who seeks to oversee others is unlikely to be the meek and unassuming type. For leaders aspiring to grow in self-awareness, the key is to guard a healthy ego from the lures of narcissism. And it helps to know the two basic forms that narcissism can take, one of them far worse than the other.

Specialists in this area point to the "incredible pros" and "inevitable cons" of narcissists, to quote a *Harvard Business Review* article by Michael Maccoby. The author identified a certain type known as the "productive narcissist." Though overbearing at times, such people, Maccoby told us, can be described this way: "They are gifted and creative strategists who see the big picture and find meaning in the risky challenge of changing the world and leaving behind a legacy." They believe in themselves, but they are outward-looking and not given to self-absorption. In this category, we might place such figures as Steve Jobs, Ross Perot, and Jack Welch, and before them Henry Ford, Andrew Carnegie, John D. Rockefeller, and Thomas Edison. "Productive narcissists," argued Maccoby, "have the audacity to push through the massive transformations that society periodically undertakes."[2]

Narcissists take a much different turn when they isolate themselves, spiral into self-obsession, and, inevitably, steer their organizations off course. The mark of "destructive narcissists" is an utter lack of self-reflectiveness. At the extreme, they can descend into narcissistic personality disorder, a state in which, Maccoby explained, "They foster grandiose visions and cling to the belief that only external circumstances or enemies impede their success . . . even the most brilliant narcissists can be undermined by their self-absorption, unpredictability, and, in severe cases, paranoia."[3]

The destructive narcissists can be confident, but in truth they are fragile and don't take criticism well—like my colleague in that hostile candidate interview, who afterward was still so wound up and simmering that I decided I had to offer a little gentle coaching. I told him, "I know this guy was never going to work, but we might have been a bit more gracious and polite in representing the firm."

"Bullshit," he said. "If you aren't going to protect our culture and do your job to screen these guys out, I will."

"Honey attracts more flies than vinegar," was all I could think to say. But he wasn't in a listening mood.

The literature on destructive narcissism tends to stress the value of collaboration. This makes sense because, obviously, overcoming self-obsession cannot be a self-guided journey. The point of arrival in the journey is greater humility when a leader's hyperactive ego is finally tamed. For all of its self-preoccupation, narcissism is really the opposite of self-knowledge. It can be an exhausting, soul-depleting trap, and renewed awareness is the only way out.

The Freedom of Self-Forgetfulness

Some of the most impressive, balanced, and well-adjusted people I have come across in executive recruiting are those who seem to have found a larger purpose beyond adding more credentials and achievements to their résumés. Friendly, unpretentious, attentive to others—you can usually recognize the type the moment they walk through the door.

It was a set of qualities I often looked for but didn't think of giving a name until I came across a compact little book titled *The Freedom of Self-Forgetfulness*.[4] Written by the late Tim Keller, founder of Redeemer Church in New York City and a widely admired Christian apologist, this book became my recruiter's gospel in separating the true leaders from the inflated egos.

Writing in 2012, in the aftermath of the financial crisis, Keller zeroed in on contemporary culture's obsession with self-esteem, ascribing this to the view of modern psychology that many social problems arise from a lack of self-worth. Traditionally, in civilized cultures, people who displayed excessive self-regard were recognized as prideful and arrogant, needing corrective influences. With the self-esteem movement in psychology came a different attitude altogether. Now, suddenly, self-respect gave way to self-esteem, and all kinds of self-indulgent behavior was to be excused or even praised as long as it satisfied a need of the person doing it.

This trend was already evident years ago in the business world. At the height of the dot-com boom, when CEOs became rock stars and posed for magazine covers, they became far different from their less image-focused predecessors. This new breed of CEO, drawn to the spotlight, started showing up as well in our executive searches, and it was Keller's insights that gave me a deeper read on what was going on.

When people require constant attention, validation, and external approval, it reflects not the strengths they might see in themselves but, instead, a deep sense of inadequacy. Pride and self-assertion are an endless treadmill, an all-consuming drive for psychic rewards that will never seem enough. And, as Keller points out, excessive self-esteem has the same source as low self-esteem. When we fall into despair and see ourselves in a negative light, it often signifies an excessive focus on ourselves or a longing for validation. Both extremes come about when we are fixated on self-worth. "A superiority complex and an inferiority complex are basically the same," Keller wrote. "They are both results of being overinflated."[5]

In both cases, Keller's remedy is the freedom of self-forgetfulness that we find in the New Testament. The Apostle Paul told the Corinthians that it was a "very light matter" for him to be judged by them. In fact, he didn't even judge himself.[6] Paul not only didn't care what others thought, he didn't even care what he thought of himself. The tentmaker and church planter was well beyond all that, concerned with how his Creator saw him, and with nothing else. He took his place on the stage, performing solely for the audience of one.

The mark of "self-forgetfulness" is genuine humility, defined by C. S. Lewis as not thinking less of oneself, but as thinking of oneself less. A proper understanding of identity and self allows us to find true contentment, independent of worldly achievements or of the opinions of others. Those who walk this path and live by this virtue might be famous or might be obscure, but each wears an invisible crown.

> *A proper understanding of identity and self allows us to find true contentment, independent of worldly achievements or of the opinions of others. Those who walk this path and live by this virtue might be famous or might be obscure, but each wears an invisible crown.*

When we see humility on this order, it makes an impression. For me, the quality has never been more beautiful than in my mother, who thought so little of herself while always trying to help and advance me and others. And I've been lucky enough to encounter a few others who exemplify this virtue.

It is one of the main reasons I admired the late President George H. W. Bush. All his life, even at the summit of achievement, he stayed true to his mother Dorothy's teaching never to speak too much about himself. "Nobody likes a braggadocio, George," she would say. He was so considerate of others that, while in office, he never traveled home to Texas until the day after Christmas because he didn't want members of his Secret Service detail separated from their families on that holiday. When staff members moved on to higher jobs in government or the private sector, he encouraged their advancement and never took it as disloyalty.

President Bush attracted his own kind, and among them was my first boss, Chase Untermeyer. As director of presidential personnel, Chase was the picture of an intelligent, wise, and modest public servant. Although he was constantly receiving calls from all kinds of important figures, he had a rule he always adhered to. Calls from his own staff were answered first, and only then would he get back to members of Congress, governors, party leaders, CEOs, and the press. It was one of the many ways he showed his team he viewed us as equals.

A later role model for me is my friend Bob McClaren, the CEO of 44 Farms in Cameron, Texas. Bob, a highly accomplished attorney and businessman, is a big name in the cattle industry. He was president of the Houston Astros and was a major force in the revival of downtown Houston. I have known the man for many years, yet I cannot recall his ever once bringing up the subject of his own achievements. Friends are much more likely to hear him talk about his wife, Dana, and their two daughters.

Bob stands out for me as a case of self-belief without self-absorption. He is grounded in his roots, guided by his core values, and shaped by the highs and lows of his life. One of the lows came when Bob's father, a captain in the US Army's 82nd Airborne Division, was injured and paralyzed. Bob was just a teenager and put off going to college to help his mother care for his father. The patience and selflessness he showed in those days are not "small things," as he would call them. They clearly helped make him the very impressive man that he is.

I think as well of Alan Armstrong of the energy giant Williams Companies, who is one of America's longest-serving CEOs. He attributes his success to the example of his grandfather, Gene Armstrong, whom he remembers as a "salt-of-the-earth kind of guy—very simple and smart." There was a time in his career, Alan told me, when he was more "piss and vinegar" in his dealings with others—a little full of himself. "I remember looking down on people around me, but I am grateful for some early mentors who modeled humility and grace which brought me back to the roots of Granddad."

When Alan was fifteen, he and his grandfather started a small hay-hauling business. One day, before work, Alan was watching a TV interview of a woman who had won a million dollars. Seeing that Alan was impressed by the story, his grandfather said, "You think that is what success looks like?" As they drove out to the hayfield, Gene explained to his grandson that the boy's work ethic and ambition would very likely make him wealthy one day, but that he should focus instead on the things that bring true happiness. "I didn't think about it at the time," Alan recalled. "But that wisdom was foundational." It stayed with him.

The influence of his grandfather probably gave him the instinct he followed, decades later, in declining a lucrative position at Enron, a company that would soon become a synonym for corporate arrogance and ruin. At just the time when so many were trying to get on that money train, Alan responded to the job offer with a simple, modest, and very wise, "Thanks, but I'm out."[7]

The Advantages of Humility

Humility and self-forgetfulness are easy to illustrate in life experience, but what is their impact on the performance of an organization? The research, including our own at Heidrick & Struggles, finds marked improvement not only in performance, but also in relationships and in overall well-being.

Consider Jim Collins's study of "Level 5" leaders. His research showed that most CEOs who took their companies from good to great had managed to combine fierce resolve and understated humility.[8] Contrary to the misconception that humility is a sign of weakness, leaders less bound by their egos are more likely to show strength and resilience. They tend to inspire cooperation, which time and again have been proven to drive results.

In a recent study by Heidrick & Struggles, we tracked the various career paths of CEOs.[9] More often than you might expect, we found that the highest positions were occupied by modest, unexpected leaders rather than those driven by obvious ambition.

One of these is Vicki Hollub of Occidental Petroleum, who never set out to become CEO. Her focus was on a career in engineering and operations until then-CEO Steve Chazen encouraged her to aim higher. In time, Hollub was chosen, and under her leadership Occidental has flourished—earning even the investment attention of Warren Buffett.[10]

Likewise, Jeff Miller, the rodeo cowboy from McNeese State turned Halliburton CEO, never imagined riding the global energy circuit when he was dodging bulls for a living. But as one of his no-nonsense accounting professors once told him while he was still competing, "A competent accountant can always find a job—and trust me, you'll need one." With the hardiness of a rodeo rider and the humility of someone who knows what it's like to hit the dirt, Miller has weathered more industry slumps than most and steered Halliburton to become a trailblazer in powering the energy needs of the world.

Similarly, Bill Thomas didn't aspire to be CEO. A geoscientist at EOG Resources, Thomas—despite an unassuming nature—caught the attention of the EOG board as well as founder and director Mark Papa. From 2014 to 2022, this unlikely candidate for the top job led EOG to become the most successful shale oil company in North America, more than quadrupling its value during his eight-year tenure as CEO.

Advancements like these shouldn't really surprise us, researchers say. In the workplace, as Rob Nielsen and Jennifer Marrone noted, "humble individuals acknowledge their limitations alongside their strengths, seek diverse feedback and appreciate contributions from others without experiencing significant ego threat."[11] Still another study found that humility was a "unique predictor" of performance[12]—which makes me think yet again of my friend Chris Wright of Liberty Energy.

Chris has immense influence in the industry (and will now have even more as United States Secretary of Energy), but to meet him you would never know he was so important. When he was younger, Chris told me, he was prone to overconfidence and even arrogance. Growing up, he carried a chip on his shoulder, especially as a first-year high school student standing just four feet eleven and weighing only seventy pounds. He was very self-conscious about his size, and some problems at home with an alcoholic father left him with a hard and emotionally distant exterior. As Chris told me, "It was me against the world, man. And I was going to show the world how tough I was and not expose any of my weaknesses or flaws"[13]

A turning point came when Chris met two high school classmates who were both bigger and more athletic than he was. They were good-natured, self-effacing guys, and fun to be around. These two friends helped him lighten up and show more openness to others. Chris said:

When you are struggling, those friends respond to you with their own vulnerability. And it absolutely transformed me. What I learned was that when you let your guard down and admit your weaknesses, the ego no longer needs to be fed and the arrogance wears off.

Yogi Berra, a man also known for his self-awareness and humility, famously said, "You can observe a lot by watching." One of the great rewards in the recruiting business is observing leaders who have the rare gift of making others shine. Among all the CEOs I've known, Chris Wright truly stands out as such a leader—a man with self-belief that has taken him far, while remaining so impressively free of self- regard. His unassuming character and future dreams never got as far as one day serving in the president's cabinet, and where Chris has quickly become to energy policy what Dan Yergin has been to energy history.[1]

Another leader who never aspired to a CEO position, and yet excelled in the role, is Steve Reinemund of PepsiCo. Raised by a single mother whom Steve still calls "the hero in my life," he has strived ever since to be faithful to her example of godliness and integrity. Meeting this good and humble man, it's amazing to consider all of the high places where he has served in the corporate world—not only at the helm of an iconic American brand, but also on the boards of illustrious companies such as Marriott, Walmart, American Express, ExxonMobil, and Chick-fil-A. Throughout a long career, Steve told me, he made it his practice not to think of promotions and titles, but instead to focus on "doing the job before me." His years at PepsiCo were among the company's best ever. His reputation as a corporate executive is golden. But you have to hear all this from me. Steve is the last guy you'll ever hear reciting his many feats as a leader.[14]

---

1 Daniel Howard Yergin is an American author, economic historian, and consultant within the energy and economic sectors. Yergin is vice chairman of S&P Global and author of *The Prize*, among other best-selling energy history books.

Bench the Ego

Serving on the President's Commission on White House Fellowships from 2007–2008 was nothing short of exhilarating—and it kept me on my toes the entire time. This program, which has groomed leaders such as Generals Colin Powell, David Petraeus, and Stanley McChrystal, along with Doris Kearns Goodwin, Elaine Chao, Sanjay Gupta, and Senator Tim Scott, sets a bar so high you need a ladder just to glimpse it. Spending a weekend at the Naval Academy alongside fellow board members and powerhouses such as Judge Edith Jones, Myrna Blyth, and Governor Terry Branstad was inspiring enough, but the real test was selecting fourteen White House Fellows from thirty-two finalists who were all extraordinary in their own right. As the "headhunter" in the room, I was often called upon to parse the fine differences between candidates. But in the end, it came down to one simple, timeless quality: Did they have the self-awareness to keep their ego in check?

The freedom that comes in being outward-looking, instead of being wrapped up in ourselves, can't be gained by watching a YouTube video, hearing a popular podcast, or taking a leadership course at Harvard, Stanford, or even Rice University, where I studied coaching. It comes with adopting a wholly different mindset, and the best teachers are the people around us who show a genuine interest in others—friends and strangers alike. My son, Thomas, a singer and songwriter, has a simple lyric that expresses this mindset: "I want to sit next to a stranger and learn about his life."[15] In the same spirit, C. S. Lewis described the sort of humble person we meet in life as "a cheerful, intelligent chap who took a real interest in what you said to him."[16]

In leadership coaching, I always recommend the initiative-taking method, with emphasis on Phil Jackson's rule: "bench the ego."[17] How exactly do we bench the ego? There are doubtless as many ways of doing this as there are of inflating the ego. Here are some little habits and turns of mind that can keep the ego in its place:

1. *Embrace weakness.* When evaluating candidates in executive recruiting, one thing we want to know is whether a leader can reveal vulnerability. A mature, emotionally attuned person is aware that he or she has weaknesses and can frankly acknowledge them without feeling threatened or diminished. Humility in this way is being connected with reality, free of illusions about ourselves and our place in the world.

    The trouble is, in professional settings, vulnerability is usually the last thing we want to put on display. In my work, I've found that one effective way to bring it out in executive candidates is to show a bit of my own. Being open about my own challenges—such as people-pleasing and the discomfort I feel in having difficult conversations—helps to break down the interview's power dynamic and place us on a more equal footing. The approach makes interviews less rote and formal—and almost always more candid and productive.

    When Chris Wright candidly shared his past struggle to acknowledge defeat or vulnerability, he offered a profound life lesson that transformed his leadership and deepened his relationships. As he wisely observed, "People form true connections and friendships around their weaknesses, not their strengths." This self-awareness and emotional attunement have become cornerstones of his leadership, fostering trust, authenticity, and a stronger sense of followership among those he leads. In a similar way, when Steve Reinemund was asked about being in the top job today versus twenty years ago, he pointed to this difference: "In previous generations, the hierarchical nature of business allowed leaders to be isolated, and in some cases fake it. . . . people [today] want leaders who admit their weaknesses and demonstrate their strengths. Transparency can be a powerful advantage."[18]

2. *Practice gratitude.* When we bench the ego, we can also start showing up as the best versions of ourselves. Our research at Heidrick & Struggles confirms what you might expect intuitively—that people operate at their best when they are most grateful. In fact, "grateful" is at the top of the "Mood Elevator," a construct developed by my colleague Larry Senn, because it is impossible to be simultaneously depressed, angry, or self-absorbed while feeling grateful. The calm and joy that gratitude brings consistently outweigh feelings of frustration, anger, or self-centeredness. Shifting our focus to the blessings in our lives pulls our attention away from the ego.

   Human nature tends to isolate and compartmentalize, often reserving gratitude for special occasions like Thanksgiving, when we go around the table listing the reasons why we are thankful. "Man," as Dostoevsky observed, "only likes to count his troubles, but he does not count his joys."[19] Yet the most successful leaders are those who are fully aware of their blessings, including the gift of their colleagues and teammates, whom they are never reluctant to elevate and publicly praise. For such leaders, gratitude is a source of strength.

   I've seen this spirit in action many times in clients and candidates I've dealt with. A name that comes straight to mind is Clay Williams, who has served for ten years as the CEO of NOV Inc., a multibillion-dollar global oilfield services company. It's a demanding and highly uncertain sector of the energy industry, constantly putting executives like Clay to the test. Still, as he told me, "We always learn more going through the meat grinder of the downturns, and they actually give you more freedom to innovate and become better on the other side." It's a "tough industry," he said, "which is hard on everyone's ego. But I learned long ago to take my ego out of it, which makes the leading so much easier and more freeing." Clay credited the example of his father, a man of gentleness and humility whose character never changed even when illness forced an early retirement from his dental practice. Admired throughout his company for a calm, understated way of handling business, Clay told me, "I am more blessed than I ever thought I would be and pinch myself from time to time about our amazing people and our team."[20]

3. *Laugh at yourself.* When my first book on leadership came out and friends asked me to sign it, I liked to say "Sure . . . or else you could have one of the rare unsigned copies." It got a laugh, and frankly there was some truth to the line. The last thing I wanted to be was a first-time author who seemed to take himself too seriously.

But beginning to laugh at yourself, like every other argument in this book, requires a keen awareness of strengths and, especially, a vulnerable assessment of the flaws that might be holding you back. Such wisdom, I have learned, not only from leaders in the top job, but even at home. My eldest son, Will, is a sensitive, shy, and extremely thoughtful young man. Yet his quiet nature often masks a rich inner world where thoughts and feelings are deeply considered but seldom shared. He is also wryly self-aware. During the pandemic when staying at least six feet apart from others was all the mania, he remarked, "Not sure what the big deal is—I have been social distancing all my life!" Self-deprecation doesn't show weakness; usually it is a sure sign of confidence. A sense of humor helps anyone in the top job especially in challenging times. As Abraham Lincoln said during the Civil War, "If I did not laugh, then surely I would cry."

Lincoln figures into one of my favorite situations of laughing at yourself or the situation you might find yourself living through. One evening, the deputy clerk of the Interior

Department came with important papers for him to sign. As he did so, the President asked about the chief clerk, who normally brought the papers. The deputy said, "I'm sorry to tell you he died this morning." Lincoln expressed regret and went back to signing the papers. The deputy cleared his throat and said, "And, Mr. President, I would like to take his place." Lincoln looked up and said, "Well, that's all right with me, but you'll have to speak to the undertaker."

4. *Take the window seat.* Even though I can get as bored as the next guy from the often-forgettable magic of air flight, looking through the window provides perspective, and not only on the wonder of modern aviation. Years ago, I watched a clip from Conan O'Brien's show where a comedian highlighted how easily people get frustrated with slow cell phones or flight delays. With humor that struck a chord, he quipped, "Everything is amazing right now, and nobody's happy." He pointed out how people complain about their flight being twenty minutes late or sitting on the runway for forty minutes, then sarcastically asked, "Oh really, what happened next? Did you fly, like a bird? Did you experience the miracle of human flight?" The joke resonated deeply, garnering 1.5 million YouTube views because of its undeniable truth.[21]

    Being reminded of what we should be grateful for is often the first step toward cultivating more humility. But also, when sitting in the window seat and raising the shade, you're lifted into a world of mysterious clouds, drifting through formations of fluff, and witnessing some of the most breathtaking sunsets to be seen. Then, gazing below, it becomes a challenge to identify the glistening cities at night, to observe the patchwork of farms that feed the world, or, in the sky above Texas, to see the wells in the vast oil fields that provide the very energy fueling the plane.

As the aircraft descends and you can make out the tiny figures of people below, you begin to feel that "good shrinking feeling" that Pastor Louie Giglio talked about,[22] a sense of how vast the world is and how small we are in comparison. And then, in any seat on the plane, don't forget the figure sitting next to you. Some of the most interesting conversations I've had have been on planes, with strangers I never saw before or since. Maybe because you both have time to kill and because you're brief visitors in each other's lives, these exchanges can be wonderful, and they certainly take you out of yourself.

5. *Read the obituaries.* Aside from my mom, the most selfless person in my life is my wife of almost forty years. One of Anne's endearing habits, which our children often tease her about, is reading obituaries. It's her routine wherever we are in the world; she pulls up our hometown paper's obituaries on her iPad. This explains why friends and family are always amazed at how many people she knows and how easily she can trace connections among them. Many times, she has sat me down and, with pen and paper, illustrated for me these intricate webs of relationships.

As Anne will tell you, obituaries can be so engrossing because they trace the whole arc of a life in very few words. Published at the time of parting, they often hold a special poignancy, which connects with my wife's unfailing compassion for friends and strangers alike. Even in the most unheralded lives, Anne will note some great accomplishment or striking detail that other readers might overlook. For her these life stories are "the best news in the paper," affirming the good that anyone does in life and leaves behind. It's true that I have also seen Anne lingering over the *Wall Street Journal's* Friday "Mansion" section, but it's the obituaries that really hold her interest, for the best of reasons.

6. *Visit a cemetery.* Like another walk in the park, visiting a burial ground creates perspective and helps bench the ego. It will remind us of the Apostle James's answers to the question "what is your life?" but "a mist that appears for a little while and then vanishes."[23] On a frosty night, when you exhale and watch your breath disappear, that's the image James gives us of who we are. Self-forgetfulness deepens when we reflect on the fleeting nature of life. It's also a reminder to make the most of the time we have left—to contemplate the "dash" of your life, like the dashes between the years on the tombstones you pass by, symbolizing the lives lived in between.

I suppose all of us need reminding that we're fellow passengers on the same journey, and that we should make good use of the time that's been given to us. Reading the obituaries is one way to remember that; another is a walk through a cemetery. We've all done this in laying to rest someone we knew, but it can also be a good experience even when we don't have a specific person in mind. Surveying all the grave markers, one naturally reflects that these were all men, women, and children who were just as alive as we are—until their numbered days were over. It can be a very humbling and healthy experience. There's no place like a cemetery to stir our awareness of the most basic reality: There will come a time when our egos are not merely benched but buried.

TEN

Return to the Soil

*No one is useless in this world
who lightens the burdens of another.*
—Charles Dickens

*If you will think about what you ought to do for other people,
your character will take care of itself. Character is
a by-product, and any man who devotes himself to
its cultivation in his own case will become a selfish prig.*
—Woodrow Wilson

I'll never forget the polite but unexpected rejection I received from a CEO and friend when I presented a prime corporate board opportunity. The friend was Jeff Hildebrand, a name on the Forbes 400 list of America's wealthiest people. I had called to offer Jeff a chance at a spot that most anyone else would covet, but he wasn't in the least interested. On that and other occasions, his response has always been the same. "Nah, I'd rather focus on the nonprofit space, if you have something interesting." If it's not charitable, or maybe connected to somehow helping his beloved Texas Longhorns, I've learned to count Jeff out.

Jeff is the founder, Chairman, and former CEO of Hilcorp Energy and one of the most successful businesspeople I know. As his friends will tell you, however, there is much more to the man and his reputation than wealth. If there were a Forbes 400 list of America's most generous and self-giving people, I would expect to find Jeff's name somewhere near the top.

A quick story shows the kind of CEO he is. One year, Jeff organized an event for his Young President's Organization (YPO) chapter. Everyone was staying at the famous Hotel del Coronado in San Diego. To fill in "free time" on the group's schedule, Jeff had all the attendees and their families board buses early in the morning, all bound for an unnamed destination. Expecting the usual shopping or sightseeing expedition, the group crossed the border into Tijuana, Mexico, where they would all spend the rest of the day helping to renovate homes in a poor neighborhood. The outing turned out to be an unforgettable experience for all, and for Jeff such work has become a regular practice. He and his three children have taken time over the years to volunteer with a charity in Mexico called Homes for Hope.

This is a man who, like his mentor David Weekley, aspires to donate half of his income to charity. That's certainly beyond what even extremely generous people would give away. During an interview in his office, I asked Jeff what inspired charitable giving on that level. A devoted Catholic, Jeff immediately cited Jesus' words in the Gospel of Luke: "to whom much was given, of him much will be required."[1] Those blessed with talents, wealth, time, and resources are called to a higher standard of responsibility and service. Jeff's work supporting disadvantaged children and the poor, he said, helps keep him "centered and grateful." It also prevents him from becoming isolated in the bubble that could easily form around the life of a multibillionaire.

At sixty-five, with no plans to retire, Jeff described himself as a "work in progress." With enormous self-belief and determination, he is also self-aware enough to understand the importance of staying connected with his people, being grounded, and fighting off indifference. One way he does this is through the company's donor program. For each new hire at Hilcorp, Jeff creates a Donor Advised Fund in the person's name through the Greater Houston Community Foundation, starting with a $2,500 donation and matching yearly contributions. Since the program began, it has generated more than $80 million for Houston charities.

Character as a Life Mindset

If cultivating selfless character adds so much to a leader's effectiveness in business, shouldn't we give it more attention? If character yields such clear dividends for employees and for entire organizations, shouldn't we add to that moral capital?

Dostoyevsky, my old favorite, told us in *Crime and Punishment* that it is not the brains that matter most, but that which guides them—the character, the heart, and generous qualities. Leaders in every era have offered their own eloquent testimony to the central importance of character. The author of *Common Sense*, Thomas Paine, observed that "Character is more easily kept than recovered."[2] And the great evangelist Billy Graham used to say that "When wealth is lost, nothing is lost. When health is lost, something is lost. When character is lost, everything is lost."

If this is true, then the "generous qualities" of character will always matter in the end, no matter what life brings—wealth or poverty, sickness or health. Like Alfred Nobel, we should ask ourselves, "What did our lives amount to beyond ourselves?"

A word of caution as we focus on building character: It's a mindset, not a project, which starts with self-awareness to address our blind spots. As Dostoevsky said, "If you want to overcome the whole world, overcome yourself."[3] This begins with our Adam II nature examining our lives, confronting our core flaws, and battling to overcome them. Developing that leadership muscle is a daily effort, but it is well worth the grind. But, pursuing or displaying character just for others to see is a greediness of another kind. Machiavelli profited from the appearance of morality, the Pharisees prayed publicly for attention, and even Lucifer quoted Scripture for his own sinister purposes.

Woodrow Wilson's quote in the epigraph highlights the caution—we must guard against becoming a "selfish prig." Any deliberate attempt to cultivate or project one's character can backfire, leading to a reputation for self-centeredness and hypocrisy. The real question should be: If there's a leadership dividend in having strong character, shouldn't we focus on engaging in selfless acts that naturally strengthen it? As Jeff Hildebrand suggested, it's the kind of generosity that provides perspective and guards against indifference.

In history and literature, character is a universal theme. In *The Underground Man*, Dostoevsky described selfless character as a "return to the soil"—a return to essential values such as family, faith, personal responsibility, and brotherly love.[4] And yet it's striking how little the subject figures in modern life, even as so many are preoccupied with "self-improvement" in one form or another. In professional settings, everyone seems to be "working on" something—communication skills, financial fluency, social-media presence, sales and marketing prowess, agility, interpersonal skills, and whatever else they feel might need polishing. We tend to obsess as well about diets, appearance, attire, fitness routine, golf swing, and on and on. These can all be useful and important in their own way, of course, but we'd better make sure there is enough space and energy left over to keep working on character.

It takes a mindset that heeds our Adam II nature—examining our lives, and confronting and engaging core flaws. It has to be a quiet effort, because character building comes with its own temptations of moral self-display. The best advice I know is to seek out the company of people whose character we admire. When my children were growing up, I often told them, "You become the average of your five closest friends." A loftier authority, Warren Buffett, has an axiom along similar lines: "If you want to become a better person, you should surround yourself with better people."[5] And an even loftier source, the Old Testament, states, "He that walketh with wise men shall be wise."[6]

Our character is influenced by the choices we make. If we fill our minds with entertainment and literature that uplifts rather than degrades, it will enhance our character. When we recognize our blind spots, admit our mistakes, and stay vigilant against potential derailers, we grow as leaders. If we keep our promises and reduce the risks for those who choose to follow us, we build trust. When we show genuine interest in the lives of others and make them feel valued, empathy deepens. Sitting with a stranger, listening to his or her story, nurtures understanding and respect. Serving where the need is greatest, changing lives with generosity and compassion, changes us for the better too. Whenever we rise above calculated self-interest, we connect ourselves to others and help to fortify institutions larger than ourselves—teams, communities, and families.

The idea of selfless character as a "return to the soil" might leave us wondering about the basis for morality in the first place. Like so many literary greats, Dostoyevsky was steeped in the Judeo-Christian philosophical traditions of the West, and his readers took that moral foundation as a given. He spoke for a fundamentally theistic view that accepts it as our duty to live according to God's transcendent purposes for humanity and for each life. Without those purposes, there could be no moral rules at all. As the character of Smerdyakov says in *The Brothers Karamazov*, "If God does not exist, everything is permitted."[7]

> *Whenever we rise above calculated self-interest, we connect ourselves to others and help to fortify institutions larger than ourselves—teams, communities, and families.*

Modern philosophy offers alternative views on morality that attempt, in various ways, to supply moral imperatives in the absence of any belief in an ultimate, transcendent authority. The Kantian social-contract approach, for instance, posits that conventional moral codes are essential in allowing human beings to live peacefully with one another, even if they have no mandate beyond that. It's in everyone's self-interest to observe them, and without such conventional rules a society would quickly unravel—or never coalesce to begin with. Whether or not we actually feel called to love our neighbor, it pays, under contract theory, to act as though we do. Conventional morality requires that we at least respect the rights of others so that they will respect ours.

The problem with such approaches is that we're still acting on selfish motivations, and morality itself is just a practical arrangement of mutual self-interest. I leave the philosophical disputes and finer points to others, except to observe that social-contract theories offer little to inspire the best in us, and nothing at all to explain it. If morality is really just a set of pragmatic calculations, and if people of character are simply the best adapted to an elaborate scheme of self-preservation, we're entitled to wonder: Is that all there is?

Author David Brooks, who has written extensively on character building, regards Kantian ideas as sterile and impersonal, arguing that there must be more to the moral life than "simply adhering to abstract principles."[8] He discerns much grander purpose in life, adding his own practical observation—a thought especially relevant to leaders—that the truest mark of good character is to make others feel heard, seen, and valued. "No crueler punishment can be devised than to not see someone, to render them unimportant or invisible,"[9] wrote Brooks, citing the words of George Bernard Shaw: "The worst sin toward our fellow creatures is not to hate them, but to be indifferent to them; that's the essence of inhumanity."[10]

Brooks's bestseller *How to Know a Person* stresses the power of truly seeing others and making them feel seen. We can choose to be one of two types of people known in every workplace: "the diminisher" or "the illuminator." Diminishers make others feel small and invisible, while illuminators, driven by curiosity and concern, make people feel seen. In leadership, illuminators empower others, helping them attain their full potential.

I heard somewhere that the three most powerful things you can say to another person are: (1) "I was just thinking about you today," (2) "I'm glad you're in my life," and (3) "I love you." No stipulation of any social contract requires such fellow-feeling. No self-interested angle makes it necessary. But whenever you say any of these things to someone and mean it, you're an illuminator in that person's life, and they will feel it.

For Christians, of course, to treat others in this way is to reflect the light of the greatest of all illuminators, Jesus. But all of us, regardless of our ultimate beliefs, can be such a force in others' lives. And in lifting others, we lift ourselves, becoming the kind of person and leader we were meant to be.

I think of it as a kind of escalator, which at every point each of us is riding either up or down. As we think more of others and strive to overcome our flaws and blind spots, we rise and feel more fulfilled. When we obsess over ourselves, disregard the well-being of others, and follow no consistent moral rule, we're headed downward—further and further away from true happiness.

THE CHARACTER ESCALATOR

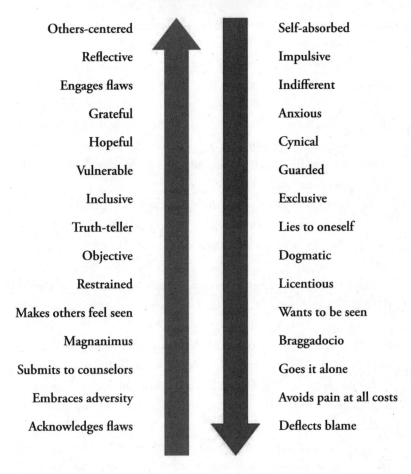

Others-centered	Self-absorbed
Reflective	Impulsive
Engages flaws	Indifferent
Grateful	Anxious
Hopeful	Cynical
Vulnerable	Guarded
Inclusive	Exclusive
Truth-teller	Lies to oneself
Objective	Dogmatic
Restrained	Licentious
Makes others feel seen	Wants to be seen
Magnanimus	Braggadocio
Submits to counselors	Goes it alone
Embraces adversity	Avoids pain at all costs
Acknowledges flaws	Deflects blame

The Self-Giving Spirit

An executive recruiter always wants to get a sense of what drives the leaders he interviews. What motivates them? What directs their moral compass? What experiences shaped their sense of right and wrong? Do they genuinely care for others? Are they diminishers or illuminators? Do they serve something bigger than their own ambitions? Which way are they going on the character escalator?

Without delving into the personal beliefs of job candidates, these are fair questions to explore. As a recruiter, I'm not looking just for a polished résumé, a charming presence, or financial expertise. I want to know about their character. I want to see if they're dedicated to something beyond self-interest. And often, the best way to assess character is to see who they are outside the office. What could be said about them if one knew nothing about their résumé and career? Beyond professional aims, what else do they serve?

When I think of leaders I know who are clearly riding the "up" escalator, a whole parade of names comes to mind. Consider Frank Tsuru, an engineer-turned-energy-entrepreneur who has built and sold companies worth billions of dollars. I've known Frank for some years and admired both his business success and his volunteer work mentoring young men in Houston's poorer neighborhoods. But my first real insight into the man's character came when I recruited him for the board of Diamondback Energy, a premier multibillion-dollar oil and gas company. There was a lot more to Frank Tsuru than his résumé, his wealth, or his title as one of Houston's "Best Dressed Men" could ever convey. Those who know him understand he's much more than just a suit.

Hearing his family history, I found myself wondering how it shaped such a generous and patriotic man. When his mother and father met in 1958, they discovered that they had both been in the same internment camp during World War II. Their families had been rounded up under the post–Pearl Harbor executive order requiring detention of Japanese Americans without due process. Talk about feeling "unseen": In that era, such families had only days to sell their homes and businesses before disappearing into train cars bound for internment camps.

After that experience of loss and injustice, Frank's mother and father could easily have felt bitter and resentful. Instead, they were determined to be good citizens and to show loyalty to their country. Frank recalled asking his mother if she was angry at the US government for their imprisonment. She answered, "We're not mad, just embarrassed for our country of origin." Frank's parents often told him, "Your life will prove the US government wrong," vowing that he would become the "most honorable American."[11]

And what better way to begin a boy's patriotic American journey than signing him up for the Boy Scouts? Frank excelled and rose to the rank of Eagle Scout, which set him on a lifetime path of service—including as president of the National Eagle Scout Association. One of Frank's most cherished possessions was his mother's high school graduation gift—a framed collection of his Boy Scout patches, which he carried with him throughout his career, from the dusty oil fields of Oklahoma, New Mexico, and Texas to the boardrooms, as a reminder of his family's love and his duty to a life of selfless service.

Frank's service also includes many nonprofit boards and his role as chairman of Yellowstone Academy, a faith-based school in Houston for children in extreme poverty. Beyond the millions of dollars he has donated to this school, Frank made himself a regular presence on campus and knows many students by name. This is a guy with billion-dollar deals on his mind, but he and his wife Stephanie somehow always find time for the kids at Yellowstone.

Perhaps the best testament to the kind of man Frank is, and to the influence he has on other lives, is a decision that his grown stepchildren made. As they were starting their own families, they told Frank they wanted to change their last names to his and asked his blessing. This brought him to tears in a beautiful and rewarding moment for a man who has brought nothing but credit to himself and his parents. "A good name is rather to be chosen than great riches," as Scripture tells us.[12] The name Tsuru, for those who know Frank, denotes great generosity and true character.

The same could certainly be said of another major player in energy, Stephen Beasley, whose friendship I consider one of the blessings of my career. When Stephen, a retired executive of El Paso Corporation, died of cancer in 2016, a lot of people felt the loss.

We first met when he interviewed for a corporate board position and quickly discovered our shared connection to Brookwood Community, a Houston residence for adults with special needs. It turned out that his sister-in-law and my brother-in-law were both citizens at Brookwood. Stephen and his wife Nancy were devoted to Brookwood and its mission. Brookwood "citizens," as they are empoweringly called, find real purpose through meaningful work—creating ceramics and pottery, managing a restaurant, waiting tables, and operating a nursery full of plants and vegetables. It's not only a nonprofit but also a thriving enterprise. As it is often said in Houston, if you're ever having a bad day, Brookwood is a good place to go, a place filled with sweetness and love.

Brookwood was founded in 1983 by Yvonne Streit after her daughter Vicki was left severely brain-damaged from encephalitis and meningitis. Yvonne's older daughter, Vivian Streit Shudde, served as CEO for two decades and has a son, Wilson, at Brookwood. The Brookwood citizens have a range of disabilities, from paralysis and blindness to autism and developmental challenges. What sets Brookwood apart is its focus on providing fulfilling lives for its residents, alongside their physical care.[13]

My brother-in-law, who has suffered from seizures and the resulting cognitive issues all his life, has been a citizen there for thirty years. Anne and I visit him often, and I never spend time at Brookwood without thinking of Stephen, whose business pulled him in a hundred different directions but who still gave so much of himself to this amazing place. He told me, "Its wonderful citizens, and the way they value each other, give me energy. As challenging as it has been for our family, I can't imagine life without Brookwood." The place lives on without Stephen Beasley, but not without the generous spirit of this exceptional man.

Like Stephen and Frank above, the self-giving spirit also extends to business leaders who are moved to act by community investments that endure decades beyond themselves. Perhaps one of the greatest disparities in wealth in recent years has been in the oil-rich region of the Permian Basin and its twin towns of Midland and Odessa. The communities in the epicenter, from which more billionaires have been created than perhaps even Wall Street in recent years, has woefully not been able to keep up. The third largest standalone oil play in the world, its towns, and residents, however, have been held back by shoddy and unsafe infrastructure, inadequate schools, and unexceptional healthcare.

Even before the longtime Midlander, Tim Leach, had sold his company (Concho Resources) to ConocoPhillips in 2021, he was already investing in the future of his community. A reclusive man, Tim has been louder in his deeds by investing in the schools, hospitals, parks, and infrastructure of his community that has nurtured many giants in the industry over the decades—including George H. W. Bush, who got his start in the oil industry in Midland in the 1950s before venturing into politics.

"We can't keep attracting businesses and families to our community if we don't invest in the future," said Tim, whose private sector initiatives include fixing roads, buildings schools, improving teacher pay, starting charter schools, and investing in modern healthcare.[14] Since Permian Strategic Partnership's founding in 2018, the twenty-nine energy companies that participate in the partnership have invested $153 million into communities across the region, contributing to investments that total $1.5 billion.[1]

Adam Smith, author of *The Wealth of Nations*, understood that the proper use of wealth always includes generosity. He wrote, "To feel much for others and little for ourselves; to restrain our selfishness and exercise our benevolent affections . . . constitute the perfection of human nature."[15] Contrary to the stereotype of greedy businesspeople, so often in my work I have witnessed the self-giving spirit that transforms lives. And for all the other qualities we expect in a business leader, there are none I would rate above compassion, generosity, and clear moral direction. To borrow a rule laid down by Norman Schwarzkopf, the four-star general who commanded coalition forces in the Persian Gulf War, "Leadership is a combination of strategy and character. If you must be without one, be without strategy."[16]

---

[1] Other founding partners or current members of the Permian Strategic Partnership in 2019 (https://permianpartnership.org/) include CEOs such as Ryan Lance of ConocoPhillips, Vicki Hollub of Occidental, David Hager and Rick Muncrief of Devon, John Christmann of Apache, Travis Stice of Diamondback, Jeff Miller of Halliburton and Tom Jordan of Coterra.

ELEVEN

Making Others Feel Seen

People will forget what you said.
People will forget what you did.
But people will never forget
how you made them feel.

—Maya Angelou

Just a few weeks ago, as I was preparing to write this chapter, some close friends of mine suffered a tragic loss. In a text that came through as Anne and I were driving and caused us to pull over, we learned that David and Kristi Lumpkins had lost their beautiful daughter Kathryn. For years this young lady had struggled with mental health issues, and now suddenly she was gone.

David is among the finest people I have met in the energy business. He was a senior energy banker with Morgan Stanley, and he later founded Petrologistics, a private equity-backed petrochemical manufacturing and logistics business, a portion of which he took public and later sold to Koch Industries for $2 billion. While building their wealth over the decades, David and Kristi found time to start Yellowstone Schools, a private Christian lower school and charter middle and high school.

Yellowstone has been serving kids in Houston's Third Ward for over twenty years, and I have been privileged to serve on the board since the beginning. Then their daughter's challenges opened their eyes to another unmet need—the lack of resources in Texas for families with a child with serious mental illness. So, even prior to their daughter's passing, the Lumpkins had determined to establish a residential treatment center for people with serious mental illness. In January of 2024 they acquired an under-resourced facility in Houston in collaboration with a major research hospital system. The goal for the rebranded Monarch Community is to create a nationally preeminent resource in Houston for families facing these challenges.

The Lumpkins's initiatives in urban education and mental health go beyond the notion of merely "giving back." The first arose from a recognized need of families living in our urban centers and the second from a major challenge experienced in their own family. One of David's favorite maxims is, "a lot of people have good ideas; the difference is that only a few actually act on them." That holds true both in business and the philanthropic world. And in fact, David views the latter as merely an extension of the former. Both are necessary and interrelated to fulfill our purpose to leave the world a better place than how we found it.

From Empathy to Compassion

Human empathy—an active, visible concern for the well-being of others—is the mark of a good person and a great leader. It hinges on awareness, not just of the need but of our capacity to care and move to action. It isn't just an emotion reserved for personal crises; it should be an everyday quality and attitude, in professional settings where people matter apart from their utility and status, where everyone is cared for, and where no one feels unseen.

Many companies have lately awakened to this need and look for qualities of openness and empathy in the executives they hire. Not surprisingly, strong, affirming cultures lead to all kinds of better results and to generally more successful companies.

> *Human empathy—an active, visible concern for the well-being of others—is the mark of a good person and a great leader. It hinges on awareness, not just of the need but of our capacity to care and move to action.*

Jamie Dimon considers empathy part of the "emotional intelligence" that the best leaders have. When Jamie interviews candidates, he told me, he asks himself, "Would I want my kid to work for this person?" He wants colleagues with enough awareness to notice when someone else is hurting, or worried, or fearful, and so might need extra attention. He is always looking for talent and smarts, but he also wants empathetic people who can see beyond themselves to the needs of others.

The epigraph of this chapter is widely known in business circles and is sometimes referred to as the Maya Angelou Rule—that whatever you say or do, people will never forget how you made them feel. This sentiment underscores the profound impact of emotional connection. Similarly, some of the most poignant words came from the late comedian Robin Williams, who once remarked playing the character Lance Clayton in the 2009 *World's Greatest Dad*, "I used to think the worst thing in life was to end up alone. It's not. The worst thing in life is to end up with people who make you feel alone." That is the essence of empathy—a real human connection—and it's got some leaders thinking as well about how to better connect with customers, even those they will never directly encounter.

My favorite example of practical empathy in business is Ford Motor Company's testing of vehicle seats to see how the ride feels for pregnant women. To accomplish this, male engineers wrap themselves in a pregnancy simulator and sit in the car so they experience driving as an expectant mother would. As one thing leads to another, auto companies also have begun testing their car designs with a view to the elderly and people with disabilities. As Adam Waytz observed in the *Harvard Business Review*, "if nothing more, these exercises are certainly an attempt to 'get the other person's point of view,' which Henry Ford once famously said was the key to success."[1]

As you might expect, the prolific cultural commentator David Brooks has a thoughtful take on the value of empathy. His 2023 *How to Know a Person* has been widely read in corporate America. In that book, Brooks reflected on his own growth in empathy. Raised in a Jewish intellectual household where ideas figured more in conversation than emotions, he described his upbringing this way: "think Yiddish and act British." Yet over time he felt a need to become less emotionally detached. As Brooks wrote, "Smart people know things and wise people know life."[2] He wanted to be a wiser man, more emotionally connected with others.

At a pivotal moment in his life, following a painful divorce, he took a hard look at himself and recognized his shortcomings—chief among them, his tendency to be aloof and lacking in empathy. He saw people around him who connected with others and made them feel seen, heard, and understood. Brooks wanted to become that kind of man.

In *How to Know a Person*, he cited a McKinsey study that asked CEOs why they thought employees left their companies. Most of the CEOs assumed it was because of better financial opportunities elsewhere. However, when the employees who had left were surveyed, the most common reason given was that "my manager didn't recognize me." Viewed in this light, it's easy to understand why employees in the survey had chosen to move on. We all need affirmation and recognition, as Brooks wrote, "there's nothing crueler than making somebody else feel invisible, feeling that you just don't get them."[3]

Of course, empathy without action isn't worth much, and it can easily become a posture among business leaders rather than a consistent and meaningful practice. If it does not shape conduct, then all this corporate talk about empathy is just a cliché. Indeed, in 2023, Ernst & Young conducted an "Empathy in Business" survey that offers a more nuanced look at what's actually happening. It found that more than half of employees believed that their company's efforts to be more empathetic were more for show than a reality. They heard the talk but had not seen much follow-through.[4]

So, while the trend in business to stress empathy is all to the good, clearly more is needed. In reality, empathy is an emotional response, a feeling, which does not necessarily lead to active moral concern shown in what one person does for another. Feelings might be praiseworthy, but they don't accomplish anything.

I find it interesting that the Greek word for compassion, *splanchna*, appears frequently in the Bible, and typically in connection with the conduct of Jesus. The term is the root of our own

English word *spleen* and denotes a visceral response causing one to be moved to action. To recall a few examples from Scripture, when Jesus saw the crowds, "he had compassion for them, because they were harassed and helpless, like sheep without a shepherd."[5] When he saw that they had not eaten, he had compassion for them and then fed them. When the blind man cried out to Jesus to be healed by Him, he had compassion, and touched his eyes and gave him sight. *Splanchna*, in the literal Greek, means "to be moved in your gut"—to feel so deeply that doing nothing becomes unthinkable.

As Brooks pointed out, empathy without a firm moral foundation can be hollow, showing no real fruit in the lives of others. All that changes when empathy awakens active compassion, and we no longer merely identify with the hurts and needs of others, but now feel called to step in and make a difference.

The Three Ls

As an example of dynamic compassion in a CEO's office, it is hard to do much better than Jay Brown, who for eight years led the Houston-based communications infrastructure company Crown Castle. This is an immense and complex enterprise, encompassing more than 40,000 cell towers and some 90,000 miles of fiber-optic cable. Before assuming his current post as CEO of David Weekley Homes, Jay took Crown Castle to new heights of success and share value.

Everyone who knows Jay will tell you that they admire the whole man, not just the superb executive, and that his personal qualities are what make him such a standout in the business world. To see him running a $95 billion enterprise, you would never have guessed that this is a man with a background far from privilege. He grew up in Texas with parents who wanted the best education for their son but could not afford it. Determined to enroll Jay in a private school, his father worked out an arrangement with the headmaster. In lieu of tuition payments, the father and son would take on odd jobs at the school on weekends and during the summer. So here was Jay in a prestigious prep school, studying with his classmates five days a week and cleaning up after them the other two.

It's the kind of life experience that stays with a person, no matter what highlights come later in a career. It taught him, he recalled, the dignity of hard work, the sacrifices that achievement requires, and the importance of meeting everyone in a workplace with respect and understanding. As Jay told me, "I just started feeling for others intuitively, recognizing the dedication and challenges of employees who, like my father, are striving to provide the best for their loved ones."

He summed up his general approach as the "Three Ls": *love well, learn well, lead well.*

In practice, to love well means showing that you genuinely care for each colleague as a person, allowing second chances and addressing performance issues with candid, direct, and supportive feedback.

To learn well means listening attentively, recognizing that you don't have all the answers, and valuing insights from all levels of the organization. Jay has found that "the best ideas often come from those closest to the customers, not from the top." To leverage your strengths, you also need to know your limits and defer to the knowledge and abilities of others. Jay himself is one of the self-aware leaders I have admired. He told me that sometimes, during meetings, "I will hear in my head, *Jay, that is not your strength*, so it's time to remain quiet."

Add the first and second elements and you get the third of the three Ls. As Jay put it, "If you love well and learn well, then you have the chance to lead well." And in moving an enterprise forward to its next goal and next level, "we should take everybody there." An old mentor once shared with Jay the time-worn wisdom that "it's lonely at the top," but it didn't square with Jay's outlook. "My view is that I would want to take my people to the top; and in fact, it should be clubby at the top, not lonely there."[6]

To give you a sense of how Jay ran Crown Castle, on one busy workday an employee suffered a seizure, and when an ambulance arrived the CEO was on the scene to meet it, having put everything else on hold until he knew his colleague was in good hands. At the ambulance, the employee insisted he was feeling better and didn't want to be taken to the hospital or even call his wife. But Jay insisted, a fortuitous sense, as the employee turned out to have had a more serious medical issue which wouldn't have been detected otherwise. Jay is not the type to hear about an employee in trouble and leave others to deal with it. As a Crown Castle executive told me, "'Empathy' falls short in describing Jay's leadership, because his empathy moved him to action."

Jay and his wife Ashley have two adopted children, in addition to their four biological children, who can further testify to his compassion. When he and Ashley traveled to Ethiopia to adopt an orphaned baby girl, they learned that she would be leaving behind a brother who was very ill. So the Browns adopted both.

When a guy like that runs a large corporation with thousands of employees, you can be sure that empathy will be more than a motto framed on the wall. As CEO, Jay recalled, he constantly asked himself, "Are your values authentic? Are they believable? Are they used in everyday processes like hiring? Do they resonate throughout all levels of the business, not just at the top?" Talk to anyone who has worked with or for this man, and they'll tell you that the answer was always yes.

Cultivating Compassion

There's a good reason why, in the business world, we now hear so much talk about empathetic leadership. Among CEOs, the Jay Browns are hard to come by. We clearly need more of them.

In 2023, my colleagues at Heidrick & Struggles did a vast analysis of more than 30,000 leadership surveys, zeroing in on how this one quality can set leaders apart. "Empathy," they concluded, "is a crucial part of leading with humility."[7] It strengthens relationships, humanizes a workplace, and lifts overall team performance.

David Brooks noted three key skills that can help leaders to grow in empathy: (1) *mirroring*, or reflecting the emotions of the other person; (2) *mentalizing*, or imagining the feelings and experiences of others and asking how we would feel in a given situation; and (3) *caring* enough to act in response to the feelings and needs of another, turning empathy into an active rather than a passive quality.

As an example, Brooks related the poignant story of a woman with a brain injury who frequently fell to the floor. She observed that while people often hurried to help her up, what she truly needed was for them to "get on the ground" with her.[8] This points to a deeper level of compassionate caring, not only helping in misfortune but, in a sense, sharing in it.

Like other admirable qualities, empathy has to be encouraged, cultivated, and reinforced. No doubt some people are especially empathetic by nature, and this can be a wonderful thing to see. But in my experience, most every executive can still stand to gain from a deliberate nurturing and practicing of empathetic conduct. Even for the naturally empathetic, it can take focus and effort. For myself, I keep three words in mind to guide me:

1. *Relating.* Empathy, as Oprah Winfrey put it, "is the ability to step outside of your own bubble and understand the realities of someone else's life." To really relate to them, we need our awareness to go where it might not want to go—to the wounds and suffering of others. And if we are where we should be, showing our solidarity, often words are not even necessary. When Anne and I rushed to the home of David and Kristi Lumpkins after the death of their daughter, we knew of course that nothing we could say could make things better. At such moments, in fact, I always rely more on Anne's awareness intelligence than on my own, so I just nodded when she told me on the drive, "We just need to show up and shut up!" Anne was living out the sentiment expressed by the Apostle Paul in his letter to the Hebrews: "Remember them that are in bonds, as bound with them; and them which suffer adversity, as being yourselves also in the body."[9]

    We can so easily detach ourselves from the suffering endured by others. It can take real effort to close that gap and make those experiences feel less abstract. This is why, when my eldest son turned thirteen, we took a trip that followed my father's path of escape from communist Hungary in 1956, and also took us to Dachau, the concentration camp outside Munich. Anne and I wanted our children to be where the victims had been, see what they saw, and imagine what it was like to face such a fate. My son has always seemed to be compassionate by nature, and this visit, like our trip years later to the Yad Vashem Holocaust Museum in Jerusalem, left a powerful impression on us all. Reading or hearing about sorrowful events doesn't always take your mind the full distance. Sometimes you have to be physically present to truly relate.

2. *Listening.* Of all the performance reviews I've conducted, one stands out, and not for reasons I'm happy to recall. After spending

about thirty minutes discussing an employee's midyear review, I thanked her for her time and swiveled back in my chair to my screen. A few moments later, seeing that she was still there, I suddenly sensed that something was wrong, and my colleague had more to say. "Are you okay?" I asked. With tears in her eyes, she opened up about troubles in her marriage and a divorce on the horizon. I offered a few words of support, but my real job now was to simply listen.

How could I have sat there for thirty minutes without realizing earlier that my colleague was passing through a terrible time in her life? I was just processing her along as one more performance review but not really hearing her or showing that I cared. She was right there in front of me, but she might as well have been in another room or on another floor of the building. She was present, but I wasn't fully present myself until I started paying attention.

When empathy is engaged, listening is more than information gathering. In coaching, I break the discipline of being a good listener into three parts. There is (1) *internal listening*, which centers on our own reactions; (2) *focused listening*, which is aimed at understanding others; and (3) *global listening*, which attunes us not just to words, but also to tone, context, and body language. The latter is what tells us the story behind the story. I've known a lot of executives who thought of themselves as good listeners until they discovered how much they had missed before making empathetic listening a regular practice.

The importance of learning to listen is beautifully illustrated by renowned horse whisperer Warwick Schiller, who found profound transformation through authentic presence. By cultivating deeper emotional connections with his horses, Schiller not only reshaped their behavior and impacted the lives of horse owners but also experienced a personal awakening. He realized that true listening begins with self-awareness—shifting from speaking *at* others to engaging *with* them.[10]

Inspired by the wisdom of legendary trainer Ray Hunt—"A horse knows when you know and knows when you don't know"—Schiller understood that effective leadership and connection, whether with horses or humans, hinge not on mere understanding but on the ability to be genuinely present. Listening, he discovered, is as much about fostering trust and safety as it is about hearing words or commands. "It's from horses that I learned to listen," Schiller reflected. "Listening instead of telling."[11]

3. *Doing.* The virtue of self-denial in leadership, for all its goodness, has its limits and ultimately must be replaced by the even sturdier virtue of unconditional love, which causes us to act. David and Kristi Lumpkins are selfless people but are emboldened by the stronger *splanchna* in their gut to act and serve. Sanctification, or true self-denial, has always been a community project.

Likewise, what David Brooks stressed as "moral action" means that empathy isn't just about understanding or sharing someone's feelings; it must prompt a caring and compassionate response. Moreover, once we really open our hearts to the hurts and needs of others, the scope of our empathy only expands. As with a mental skill or physical strength, exercise and repetition lead to growth. As often happens with virtues, if we try hard enough to act as though we have them, sooner or later we do.

On this score, I remember once hearing a blunt observation from a man named Denver Moore. A middle-aged homeless man who had served time in prison, Moore was saved from the streets by a family in Fort Worth. Moore and Ron Hall, the man who found him in a homeless shelter, wrote a bestseller together, titled *Same Kind of Different as Me*. Though a man without much formal education, he had his own way with words and a whole storehouse of folksy wisdom. I met Moore at a Christian school fundraiser where I was to introduce him, and we got to talking about Bible study groups. "You know what I've noticed traveling around the country doing all these talks?" he said. "There's a lot of Bible studyin', but not much Bible doin'."

For "Bible doin'," with moral action stirred by empathy, anyone can find inspiration in the World War II–era story of Sir Nicholas Winton, known as the "British Schindler." In late 1938, as the people of Prague braced for a German invasion, a friend urged Winton, a busy stockbroker at the time, to see the growing humanitarian crisis firsthand. Scrapping plans for a skiing vacation in Switzerland, Winton flew to Prague instead. Witnessing that dire situation, Winton felt compelled to act, especially for the children who would soon suffer under Nazi occupation.

What began as a small effort—collaborating with British authorities to secure the escape of a few children—soon became an all-consuming mission. By day, Winton continued his stockbroker duties; by night he coordinated efforts to rescue as many children as possible, arranging their placement with British families. His dedication grew into an obsession, as he and a team of volunteers in both Czechoslovakia and England worked fervently to move the children to safety. In the end, they saved 669 Czech boys and girls from the horrors of Nazi occupation.

For nearly fifty years, little was known of Winton's heroic rescue efforts, and he himself sought no recognition. The story was revealed in 1988 on an episode of the BBC show *That's Life!* It made for quite a scene, and you can watch on YouTube the moment when Winton realized he was seated in an auditorium filled with the very people who owed their lives to him—hundreds and hundreds of them.[12]

According to his daughter, who wrote *One Life*, which inspired a film featuring Anthony Hopkins as Winton, there are now some six thousand people alive today—the children he rescued and their descendants—who owe their existence to Winton.[13] Later knighted by Queen Elizabeth, Sir Nicholas passed away in 2015 at the age of 106.

It's true that most of us will never find ourselves in a position to make so great a difference in such desperate circumstances. The story reminds us, though, that when a virtue like compassion finds purpose and direction, it can touch other lives in ways we hardly realize, and there is no end to the good it can spread in the world.

TWELVE

From "Great" to Good

*If a thing is free to be good it is also free to be bad.
And free will is what has made evil possible.
Why, then, did God give them free will?
Because free will, though it makes evil possible,
is also the only thing that makes possible
any love or goodness or joy worth having.
A world of automata—of creatures that
worked like machines—would hardly be worth creating.*

—C. S. Lewis

Before leaders can be truly great, they must first be good. That's been my experience, anyway, in more than thirty years of observing men and women who aspired to reach the top. While greatness is often measured by results, influence, or achievements, it usually rests on practices like honest dealing, making others feel respected and valued, shaping future leaders rather than merely amassing followers, and so on. As Peter Drucker put it, "Management is doing things right; leadership is doing the right things."[1]

We have all seen ambitious people going fast in the business world without a moral compass, and we've all seen them come to grief. The finest leaders I have observed don't actively *pursue* greatness; instead, greatness can *ensue* from qualities they do strive for—not just professional excellence, but also empathy, loyalty, a sense of fairness, and other marks of personal goodness. Achievements reached in such a way have been aptly termed the "return on character."

Tracy Wolstencroft understood this when he arrived in 2014 to right the ship at Heidrick & Struggles. He saw that the firm had taken on a "Me Club" culture that didn't exactly match the core values we were supposed to stand for. We needed to be steered in a more purposeful direction, behaving more like the exceptional leaders and teams we're in the business of shaping. Tracy's vision of the firm—what it was and could be again—made all the difference, and his influence can still be felt in the way we treat one another and our clients.

Around that same time, Microsoft brought on a new CEO, Satya Nadella, who apparently had a similar effect. By 2014, Microsoft was struggling with internal rigidity and declining innovation, all while facing intense competition. Nadella led with an emphasis on collaboration, a spirit of mutual respect among colleagues, and personal growth at all levels of the company. "Empathy makes you a better innovator," he famously said, and proved this with a new growth mindset that allowed Microsoft to reinvent itself and once again become one of world's most valuable companies.

I think as well of examples from literature that show how simple goodness in individuals can help set the stage for greatness. *To Kill a Mockingbird* is the story of how one lawyer's uncompromising integrity will not allow him to let an innocent man go undefended, in disregard of his standing in the community and even of his own safety. Then there's the character of Samwise Gamgee in *The Lord of the Rings*, who begins as a humble gardener, fiercely loyal to

Frodo, and throughout their perilous journey together reveals a quiet strength that eventually grows into heroic courage.

If we hope to do great things, we can start by doing good things. No opportunity for doing what is right is beneath a true leader, and the most conscientious and upright leaders will never lack for the trust and loyalty of colleagues. What's more, virtue in this case is more than its own reward: Personal character can be the decisive factor in reaching lasting and meaningful success.

Where Greatness Begins

Nearly twenty-five years ago, Jim Collins's *Good to Great* gave us the image of the Level 5 leader—someone driven by ambition yet grounded in humility. It was a very useful framework, especially in light of the dot-com bust and corporate scandals like Enron and WorldCom. Selling more than four million copies, the book became a mainstay in the literature of business leadership, and "good to great" became a catchphrase of the era.

I spent a little time with Jim Collins in 2003, at a Heidrick & Struggles global partners conference, and later interviewed him for my first book, *Trust: The One Thing That Makes or Breaks a Leader*. While I admired his work, I had my doubts on one point. Collins argued that while successful companies must have specific core values, it's less important exactly what those values are. This didn't sound quite right to me. Obviously not all values are equal, and in business what could possibly matter more than integrity?

At the time, I saw this as a small quarrel about an otherwise outstanding book, but over the years it became increasingly significant to me. Thorough scholar that he is, Collins stressed in *Good to Great* that solid research often uncovers unexpected findings—and in the social sciences, sometimes unwelcome findings. Celebrated companies like GE, HP, Sony, Disney, and 3M all had distinct values, yet the research revealed no consistent set of values among them. As Collins explained,

> If you take a value like "respect for the individual," you will find that core value in HP as it became a great company, but you will not find it in Disney when it became a great company. Disney had different core values that had to do with imagination and fanatical consistency and attention to detail and the notion of wholesomeness and magic. These were all part of the Disney core values—not "respect for the individual."[2]

In his remarks at our conference, Collins drove home this same point, which, he stressed, only reflected what careful research had found. Still, I wasn't persuaded. It felt to me like he was avoiding any talk of a common and universal moral value, perhaps in deference to the "value-neutral" stance so trendy in academic circles. After his talk, I ran my difference past him. Assuming that business is inherently a moral activity, I asked Jim, couldn't we agree that integrity—always doing the right thing—should be a core value across all industries?

He saw what I was getting at but still stopped short of accepting that integrity is a value essential to any company. The research didn't go that far, Collins insisted. As he explained to me, "Integrity is the ability to act consistently and imaginatively over a long period of time with your core values. One can have core values," he said, "yet still lack integrity with those values."[3] I still wasn't sure about the logic of this position; after all, his own strict adherence to what research could validate was an example of intellectual integrity, which makes a thinker like Jim Collins so credible in the first place. In the abstract, he might reject integrity as an essential core value, but in practice he was demonstrating how essential it is.

In line with Drucker's moral view of business, one could argue that integrity is so intrinsic to every facet of an organization that to list it as a core value may undervalue its true importance. Yet considering recent instances where companies have pursued results at any cost, integrity should not be seen merely as a value to be claimed but as an inherent quality that guides a leader's actions and casts a luminous shadow over the entire organization. Modeling goodness and consistently doing the right thing must be at the heart of every strategic plan and business initiative.

As philosopher and humanist Albert Camus famously observed, "Integrity has no need of rules," implying that doing the right thing arises from an internal moral compass rather than from external laws or regulations.[4] This perspective underscores my skepticism toward the concept of teaching "business ethics," a notion that gained traction in business schools after corporate scandals like Enron and Arthur Andersen. There is no such thing as "business ethics"—there is only ethics.

Jim Collins, for instance, described ethics as staying true to one's core values, which he equated with integrity but perhaps more accurately reflects "fidelity." Fidelity is adherence to one's beliefs, but integrity goes beyond—it transcends fidelity by unifying those beliefs with actions across all aspects of life. True integrity represents a wholeness, much like its mathematical meaning: a state of being unified and indivisible, where ethical principles are seamlessly and consistently woven into the fabric of who we are.

There is a lot of common sense in *Good to Great*, although this has not spared Collins from criticism even a generation later. Business writer Margaret Heffernan, for one, found fault with Collins's basic framework; it assumes, she said, that executives somehow already possess the qualities necessary for greatness, having no need for transformational change. *Good to Great*, she also pointed out, rested on a belief that market valuation defined greatness, a measure that, in light of the many corporate disasters and scandals that occurred after the book came out, hasn't held up very well. As Heffernan wrote, "The belief on which the book relies, that stock price alone anoints the great, makes reading it today feel inadequate, ideological, and naïve. . . . Good in parts perhaps, but not great."[5]

Heffernan's argument resonates because she grasped a fundamental truth about leadership: Without a strong moral compass, leaders can easily fall prey to the temptations of power and wealth. There is the inherent common sense in *Good to Great*, she conceded, namely that the Level 5 leader is tenacious, focused, and smart. But we aren't just interested in kindness, but true goodness. Leaders should first pursue and operate out of their goodness, which always starts with awareness of blind spots and flaws, and the courage to engage them. The book assumes that the Level 5 leaders were already rooted in their goodness so the aim can be greatness.

It's true that *Good to Great* is very much of its time, an era when business literature was generally optimistic and, often, given to flattering the business audience. And it's certainly true that much has happened in twenty-five years to shatter any illusions about good character as a given in positions of corporate responsibility. Even so, there is a reason why Collins's book is still so widely read and well-known. It speaks to the aspirations of men and women who want to show their best and aim high for their companies and organizations. In a world that rewards commercial success and admires those who achieve it, they want to make their mark as standout leaders—an entirely worthy pursuit that Collins was right to encourage.

All these years later, it strikes me that Collins's ideal of Level 5 leadership presupposes the virtue of integrity, even if the author told us otherwise. The leaders he profiled weren't interested in self-aggrandizement; in fact, they often shunned the spotlight. Highly aware, they were simply committed to excelling in business while also always doing the right thing. Their obvious integrity is the "good" that allows the journey to greatness.

> *Leaders should first pursue and operate out of their goodness, which always starts with awareness of blind spots and flaws, and the courage to engage them.*

It helps to remember that goodness hardly means perfection. What matters is the pursuit of goodness, starting with heightened self-awareness and a commitment to personal growth. In every kind of work, in every setting, we should guard our integrity and set nothing above it. As Henry Kravis, the philanthropist and cofounder of the private-equity firm KKR, has observed: "If you don't have integrity, you have nothing."

Choosing and Persevering

Of course, when we compare pure ambition with moral aspiration, the relentless drive for achievement with the desire for personal growth, we're back in Adam I and Adam II territory. Adam I is the hard-charger, Adam II the more reflective type, and they both contend within us. The former always tends to dominate, and today, especially, we could use more of the thoughtful influence of the latter.

In our modern business landscape, where financial results are prized above all else, it's easy to lose sight of other priorities. A purely transactional mindset takes over, and as long as we're getting what we want everything else seems to fade in importance. We might not be noticing, but at the same time we're losing company morale, a team spirit, the respect and trust of colleagues, and many other of those "returns on character" that good people earn in business. When a leader focuses solely on the how of a business and never on the why, the first thing to go is the sense of purpose that every enterprise needs to stay cohesive and moving forward.

From one angle, leadership is the responsibility of constantly choosing between doing what is right rather than what is merely expedient. The more responsibility we have, the more we feel the weight of free will, and keeping Adams I and II in balance can be a tricky business. In the end, we can best fill out the role of a great leader by concentrating on the duties that make for a good person.

C. S. Lewis, in the chapter epigraph, emphasized the critical role of free will in the human experience, asserting that without choice, life would lack true meaning. In an Adam I world, where leaders are often programmed to chase greatness, there is little space for genuine connection, love, or moral development. As Lewis suggested, if humans merely follow predetermined paths, their actions cannot be truly virtuous because goodness derives its meaning from being chosen freely. A "world of automata," Lewis agued, would strip away the ability to choose goodness and build character.

Consider the experience of Travis Stice. A friendly acquaintance of long standing, Travis leads Diamondback Energy, a big producer in the Permian Basin that consistently outperforms peers. He is also the quintessential Adam II executive, although reaching that point took a great deal of intentional effort. And Travis can tell you exactly when he realized that goodness came first and that business greatness, if it ever came at all, would have to wait.

It was 1993, and he was a young engineer at Burlington Resources. He had worked hard and felt certain he was in line for a promotion. Instead, three of his peers moved up and he was left behind. The feedback on his job performance made for tough reading: Most everyone at the company seemed to think that Travis was using others on his team primarily for his own advancement. It had the ring of truth and got him thinking.

From then on, he resolved to be the opposite of the self-seeking person he had read about in that feedback summary. He made a conscious decision to be a servant leader. He would support others instead of seeking advantage or accolades. As Travis recalled, "That moment of heightened self-awareness was foundational and instrumental in my transformation." At that same time in his life, he was growing in his Christian faith and learning a lot from the motivational talks of Zig Ziglar. It all had the effect of getting him past a career setback and shaping him as a better man—even as he remained a very competitive player in the energy field, with a drive to excel and create value for shareholders, as Diamondback has done under his leadership.

He attributes his drive to the influence of his mother, who, said Travis, set high standards and gave him the confidence to meet them. If he brought home a test from school with a grade of 96, he told me, she would express approval but then encourage him to review the questions he missed. And, added Travis, he has leaned heavily on the steady influence of a wife who keeps him grounded. They have been through a lot together, Travis and Brenda, and one experience in particular changed their lives and perspective forever.

They had a son, Matthew, who was born with severe disabilities, and his care involved many health crises over the years. One day not long ago came the crisis that Matthew didn't survive. The boy's name, Travis reminds me, means "gift from God," and that's exactly how he and Brenda think of their son even with all the hardships and sorrows they faced together. As he explained, "There is no way I am who I am without that special child."[6] When a man has known loss like this, the stresses and trials of work can never weigh on him quite the same.

Staying grounded in today's business environment, staying

authentic, isn't easy—especially for those at the commanding heights of a business or industry. The money, the notoriety, the excesses, the pretensions—they've gotten the best of many leaders, but certainly not of Travis Stice. Like many of the best executives I've known, Travis has gained the wisdom and humility of Adam II, without losing the intensity and striving spirit of Adam I. He faced his weaknesses early on, corrected course, and decided what kind of person and leader he wanted to be. A life-changing loss only deepened his awareness and empathy. And from all this he emerged as a leader whom others naturally trust and follow. He's a very impressive man who shows us that when personal strength and goodness are the aim, sometimes greatness will take care of itself.

The Shadow of the Leader

My colleague Larry Senn has spent decades studying and writing about the dynamics of business organizations, along the way becoming known as the "Father of Corporate Culture." When Larry sought to identify the key driver behind successful cultural transformations, he found that nothing is more decisive than self-awareness and a personal sense of responsibility in a CEO.[7] This squared with Larry's research going back fifty years to his idea that organizations inevitably become "shadows of their leaders." Now in his ninetieth year of life, and with sixty-five sprint triathlons to his name, Larry has long been a friend and advisor to me at Heidrick & Struggles, and his insight about "shadows" has always proved useful and broadly applicable.

The idea is that people often adopt the traits of those who hold power or influence over them. For instance, children might not always follow the advice of their parents, but it's always a good bet that they will imitate their parents. You can often observe the same thing in business settings: Whatever the official line or message is, actions always resonate more. As the author Warren Bennis often said, leaders don't just communicate the message; they *are* the message.

If a leader rarely shows up at the office, is it any surprise when the team largely stays home? If the boss consistently arrives late, why expect others to arrive early? If leaders lack honesty, can they reasonably assume integrity in their people? And if leaders fail to acknowledge their own mistakes, what are the chances that others on the team will take ownership of theirs? As Tracy Wolstencroft used to remind us at the firm, "What you think, what you say, and what you do must align." This kind of consistency hardly adds up to greatness in a business leader. But it certainly shows part of the goodness that makes greatness possible.

Once we realize how much a single leader can influence an entire organization, the obvious key is to use that influence for the better. To help shift from a mindset of blame and excuses to one of ownership and responsibility, Larry devised an "Accountability Ladder." The image is self-explanatory, listing behaviors that either hinder or advance the performance of the business.

ACCOUNTABILITY LADDER

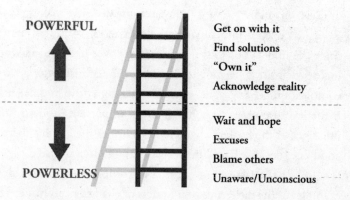

Source: Heidrick & Struggles (Culture-Shaping)

When leaders operate "below the line," they are reactive and adopt a victim-oriented mindset. They often blame others, make excuses, or avoid taking responsibility. These leaders may "wait and hope," expecting someone else to solve the problem, or else rationalize failures and poor performance. They tend to deflect accountability and can be unaware of, or oblivious to, critical issues.

Conversely, leaders who operate "above the line" take ownership and responsibility. They acknowledge reality with heightened awareness and take proactive steps to address challenges—in the manner of a CEO like John Christmann. After John's succession to the top job at the global energy company APA (formerly the Apache Corporation), he told me that a man in his position couldn't afford to have a bad day or operate below the line. Being in charge, John quickly realized, meant always being highly visible and having influence on everyone around him every day.[8]

By fostering a culture in which both leaders and employees consistently operate "above the line" on Larry Senn's ladder, organizations create an environment of accountability, problem-solving, and responsibility. This, in turn, enhances performance and contributes to a more positive and productive workplace culture.

The concept of the "shadow" that every leader casts, for good or ill, is only more relevant today, as more decision-making authority is pushed deeper into organizations. A recent study estimates that since the mid-1960s jobs requiring employee decision-making have increased from 8 percent to 34 percent.[9] As businesses grow more complex, quick, and agile, decision-making at the middle- management level becomes that much more important, and so does the influence of the leader's character. His or her shadow had better be a good one, because it will be pervasive, and often decisive.

Over the last several years, I've witnessed two rather dramatic examples of the difference that leaders of character can make. The first is my Heidrick & Struggles colleague Tatiana Furtseva, the managing partner of our firm's office in Kyiv, Ukraine. She's had to lead her team in just about the worst circumstances you can imagine, with her country under brutal attack. I've traveled to Ukraine several times during its war with Russia and seen for myself how Tatiana handles both her professional and personal responsibilities—including the care of her gravely ill son—under relentless pressure. As she told me, "I didn't realize the strength I had within me to lead and care for others."[10]

In April 2022, just two months after the Russian invasion, Heidrick & Struggles interviewed various Ukrainian CEOs leading large-scale businesses to better understand how they were navigating crisis leadership and how the experience had shaped them. The powerful common theme was that they had all but forgotten personal ambition and made the well-being of others their priority. As one Ukrainian leader poignantly put it on my visit to Kyiv in describing the shared spirit, "We all sleep under the same blanket."

The second example is Cheli Nachman, the partner-in-charge of Heidrick & Struggles's Tel Aviv office, who has also had to lead during a very dangerous time for her country and her family. She has a ten-year-old daughter, along with two sons who are nearing the age for Israel's mandatory military service. Cheli described her country feeling smaller than ever after the horrific attacks of October 7, 2023. We've stayed in close touch, and I recall one night when she texted me from a bomb shelter where, huddled with her family, she remained calm and positive even as Iranian missiles were hurtling toward Tel Aviv. In our conversations, Cheli has told me with great feeling about the bravery, resilience, and sheer goodness of the Israeli people—and I have certainly seen those qualities in this amazing woman.[11]

My Heidrick & Struggles colleagues and I can take special pride in Tatiana and Cheli, who amid crises have been standout leaders casting unmistakable shadows of goodness, resilience, optimism, and moral clarity. Their leadership not only boosts morale but has also kept their teams working and achieving at a time when everything could easily have fallen apart.

How do you show up to work feeling hopeful and grateful when the stresses are so great and there is so much to worry about? Knowing Tatiana and Cheli as I do, the answer is sheer determination, along with an ability to manage one's emotions regardless of external circumstances.

This is another leadership attribute—emotional self-awareness—that Larry Senn has examined and has explained with what he termed the "Mood Elevator." The simple idea is to show the various emotional states we might experience throughout the day, putting in plain language what a leader aims for and what a leader should avoid. The leader's mood will catch on, one way or another. The right attitude will be contagious; so will the wrong attitude. Whenever a leader is going up that elevator, or going down, many others are riding along.

MOOD ELEVATOR and AWARENESS and EQ

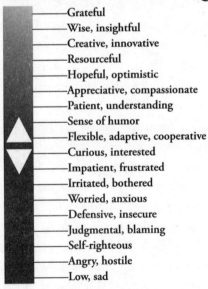

High awareness and high EQ when we're at our best
- Grateful
- Wise, insightful
- Creative, innovative
- Resourceful
- Hopeful, optimistic
- Appreciative, compassionate
- Patient, understanding
- Sense of humor
- Flexible, adaptive, cooperative
- Curious, interested

Low awareness and low EQ when we're not our best self
- Impatient, frustrated
- Irritated, bothered
- Worried, anxious
- Defensive, insecure
- Judgmental, blaming
- Self-righteous
- Angry, hostile
- Low, sad

Source: Heidrick & Struggles (Culture-Shaping)

Return on Character

To address a candid objection, some will argue that while character is important, when you're running a business it pales in comparison to other qualities like intelligence, drive, strategic acumen, and communication skills. For skeptics, a winning strategy and innovation are the true drivers of success. Leaders of character are nice to have, but hardly essential.

To the extent such matters can be quantified, however, the research clearly shows that the influence of good character is a business advantage. For instance, one Heidrick & Struggles study of five hundred CEOs worldwide found that when companies were intentional about their culture and values—putting people first, and so on—they achieved double the revenue growth of those that were not.[12] Companies with "culture-accelerator CEOs" generally have better financial performance to show for their efforts.[13]

Even before we did this research, there was ample evidence linking character to business performance. Fred Kiel's 2015 book *Return on Character* draws connections that square with my own experience with hundreds of leaders—that when they prioritized goodness, both individual and organizational performance flourished, and greatness often followed. After extensive research over seven years, Kiel concluded that leaders with strong character significantly outperformed their counterparts.[14] CEOs rated highly for character achieved an average ROA—return on assets—of 9.35 percent over a two-year period, compared to just 1.93 percent for those with low character ratings.[15] The key takeaway, Kiel told us, is that character is not just a moral ideal but a key driver of tangible business success.

Typically, this kind of character traces to early influences, and Kiel cited such factors as parental examples, mentors, adversity, and the kinds of episodes in a young life that instill perseverance, truth-telling, humility, empathy, and other values. Adversity, of course, is often a profound force in some of the greatest lives. And though no one ever welcomes hardship, it changes people in ways they are grateful for later in life.

The story of Joseph Pulitzer—who, as my father would quickly point out, was Hungarian—is an example of this. When Pulitzer was a child, he lost not only his father but also seven of his eight brothers and sisters—and the one surviving brother ended up committing suicide. That was the youth he left behind as an immigrant coming to America, where he rose above this sorrowful past and made his family name renowned to this day.

In Fred Kiel's quest to identify what sets the character-driven leader apart, he settled on four basic measures: integrity, responsibility, forgiveness, and compassion. He illustrated these by profiling ten standout executives, such "virtuoso CEOs" as Dale Larson, who expanded his family's storm-door business after inheriting it from his father, growing the company from thirty or so employees to more than 1,500 and capturing 55 percent of market share; Sally Jewell, the former CEO of REI, America's largest outdoor retailer; and Charles Sorensen, a surgeon who transitioned into management at Intermountain Healthcare and led the organization to substantial growth. In all the case studies, employees rated Kiel's virtuosos highest according to his four measures. These leaders were found to consistently stand up for what is right, prioritize the common good, let go of mistakes (both their own and others'), and show empathy. These virtues were central to their leadership and to the success of their organizations.[16]

"Return on character" brings to mind leaders I've long admired, up close or from afar. Like other prominent CEOs, Warren Buffett—to mention that storied name yet again—is a man of enormous gifts and confidence in himself. But was there ever a man so materially successful and yet so free of self-importance? He's a truly remarkable figure, so wealthy and still so little motivated by wealth.

From "Great" to Good

There is nothing Buffett couldn't buy, but he's content with what he has, happy in the same old house where he's lived for sixty-plus years, and in the end he plans to give away most of his money. All this surely speaks to a special modesty, humility, and goodness in a man universally admired in the business world as one of the greats.

Likewise, if asked to list my own "virtuoso" CEOs, Doug Lawler would be right near the top. I never walk away from Doug without thinking how lucky I am to know such a good man. His journey, which I've recounted earlier, from the grief of losing his young wife to his high-performing leadership in a demanding industry is a story of incredible grit and resilience—with returns on character evident to all. My colleagues Tatiana and Cheli also exemplify this virtuoso leadership. Their unwavering goodness continues to drive solid commercial success in Kyiv and Tel Aviv, despite the agony and cruelty of war. Then there's Travis Stice again, who changed himself, as described above, thereby changing his fortunes more than he could have imagined at the time.

Travis's determination to improve himself cast a large shadow for the better at Diamondback Energy. If you doubt how much impact one CEO's commitment to a healthy culture can have on performance, just look at Diamondback's increase in shareholder value since 2012: an incredible 940 percent. Goodness was the goal, greatness the result, and things only got better in 2024 with an acquisition that did not come about by chance.

Starting the year before, Diamondback was among several companies looking to combine with Endeavor Energy Resources, known in the industry as the "crown jewel" of the Permian Basin. The competition was intense, and Travis knew that his initial offer of $26 billion could well be topped by larger rivals. What kept Diamondback in the game was something about Travis that stood out to Endeavor's leadership, and especially to its founder, the legendary oilman Autry Stephens.

In Travis, Stephens saw a man who shared his unostentatious style of leadership, and who could be trusted to care for Endeavor and its people. There was an alignment in culture and values, not just in the financial angles of a single transaction. Stephens wasn't looking only for the right deal; he also wanted the right man to steward the company he had built with care over forty-five years. He knew Travis well because the two companies were literally across the street from each other in Midland, Texas, and decided in the end—and as it turned out, just before Stephens passed away—to sell to the good guy next door.

Travis himself wouldn't tell the story this way, but everyone in the know understood the rationale behind Autry Stephens's decision. In his last days, his main concern was finding a leader of clear decency who would look after Endeavor and its people. The deal nearly doubled the size of Diamondback, which continues to flourish, yielding returns on character that can hardly be counted.

THIRTEEN

Cracking the Interview Code

I'm a people person, very personable.
I absolutely insist on enjoying life. Not so task-oriented.
Not a work horse. If you're looking for a Clydesdale,
I'm probably not your man. Like I don't live to work,
it's more the other way around. I work to live.
Incidentally, what's your policy on Columbus Day?

—Owen Wilson, as Randy Dupree, *You, Me, and Dupree*

No matter how high we lift our sights professionally, no matter how well-equipped we might be to strengthen a team or even lead it, someone has to give us that chance. The first step is always the same: getting hired. And before the job offer comes a ritual there is usually no escaping: the job interview.

I've conducted roughly ten thousand interviews, for positions ranging from cabinet-level offices to senior executive roles in business, on corporate boards, and with nonprofits. Some have been courtesy meetings lasting thirty minutes; others have been hour-long interviews or half-day assessments focused on leadership competencies and behavior. Frankly, much of the experience is a blur, although some interviews stand out in vivid detail.

Decades ago, I found myself in a second-floor office of the West Wing, seated with a senior CIA official under consideration for the agency's deputy director. My boss, Connie Horner, director of presidential personnel, and I were conducting the interview at a moment of profound historical consequence. The Berlin Wall had just crumbled, German reunification teetered in uncertainty, and the Soviet Union stood on the brink of collapse. This appointment was far from routine; it carried the weight of a world in transition.

Within minutes of meeting this man, Connie and I were starstruck. He had glided into the room, given us each a firm handshake, and cooly taken a seat. He had quiet confidence and radiated gravitas. "Thank you for having me," he said, then smoothly took the lead by adding, "Now, how can I help you today?"

Though he showed a touch of deference, it was clear he was comfortable and in command of himself. Self-assurance without arrogance is an impressive sight in a job candidate, and this agent struck just the right balance. His words and entire manner conveyed competence and trustworthiness, leaving no need to say it outright. In the way of credentials, he was a decorated Navy veteran of the Vietnam War and had already served as deputy under three consecutive CIA directors in both Republican and Democratic administrations.

After the interview, Connie said to me, "Wow, talk about presence and demeanor." There was no missing it—this guy knew how to carry himself. First impressions are powerful, and they are formed far less by credentials on paper than by a person's appearance, manner, attitude, and tone. It's "the way about you" that others remember.

We have all heard the standard advice, before an interview, to just be yourself. But if you're naturally anxious, fidgety, or overly gregarious, then of course you need to be aware of that and be mindful of your demeanor. More than anything else, your presence—your "way"—shapes the impression you make. Those first five minutes of an interview are the most critical. As any executive recruiter will attest, there's a lot of truth in the saying that you get just one chance to make a good first impression.

Face-to-Face

In any interview, it helps an applicant to try to see things from the standpoint of the employer or recruiter asking the questions. What are they really looking for? What do they really want to know about you?

If you didn't have certain strengths and qualifications, it's a safe bet you would not have advanced to the interview stage in the first place. Yet in the interview, you are not just expected to showcase your strengths. Employers and recruiters want a grounded, mature person who is self-aware enough to acknowledge room for growth. Few traits are more off-putting in a job candidate than a surplus of self-regard. Interviewers want to see someone who is still striving to be better. Self-confidence in an interview is great, but it means more than just pretending you have no faults.

Likewise, even basic people skills and good habits of speech can be prized assets these days because, frankly, they're getting more rare. Somehow these abilities just aren't naturally cultivated in the way they used to be. If a candidate has them, he or she will stand out. Indeed, PayPal founder Peter Thiel believes that as technology and AI transform the economy, the verbally adept—"word people"—will be harder to find and replace than those with math-based skills.

It's true that the hiring process is getting more complicated—for example, with the use of AI to predict performance through skillsets and psychometric assessments—and this has led some to discount the personal interview. But my experience tells me the opposite. As much as ever, there is simply no substitute for the impression one person makes on others, speaking face-to-face. No matter how impressive a candidate's profile might be, as a recruiter I could never confidently make the final recommendation of any prospective employee—much less a company's new leader—unless I had personally interviewed that man or woman.

Interview standards have evolved dramatically over the past two decades, particularly in a culture increasingly shaped by digital tools like AI. Some hiring managers, too, have begun to dismiss interviews, citing research that suggests their predictive power is limited, often reflecting little more than whether the interviewer likes the candidate. After all, interviewers tend to favor candidates who remind them of someone familiar: themselves![1]

To counteract affinity bias, interviews must delve deeper, probing beyond surface impressions to reveal who a candidate truly is—not just how they wish to be perceived. As Yale Professor Gautam Mukunda, an expert on leadership selection, put it, "Interviews must be structured carefully" to ensure they provide an authentic and reliable portrait of a leader's potential.[2]

Even if I had not myself noticed a decline in people skills in interview settings, I'd have heard about it from my clients. It's something that employers talk about and that surveys have described. Asked to characterize their job interviews with recent college graduates, employers report that 53 percent of candidates struggled with making eye contact, 50 percent expected unreasonable compensation, 47 percent dressed inappropriately, 27 percent used coarse language, and 21 percent of those interviewed virtually didn't even turn on their cameras. Oh, and 19 percent thought it was a good idea to bring Mom or Dad to the interview.[3]

This kind of conduct in a job interview is going to make an impression, alright—in exactly the wrong way. And I suppose it's all of a piece with an era of "quiet quitting," "bare-minimum

Mondays," and an entitlement mindset toward virtual work. It can feel at times as though employees hold the upper hand in today's competitive talent market, in a position to sometimes dictate the terms. Yet the advantage will eventually shift back to employers—trust me, it always does. In fact, that same survey cited above found that some 60 percent of employers are willing to offer more benefits and higher salaries to attract older, more experienced workers rather than recent college graduates.[4] The simple reality is that just about everybody in the business world, sooner or later, and especially if they want to advance in a career, will have to sit down for a job interview, and it will pay to be prepared.

The Five Ps

In one of my most memorable interviews, the roles seemed to be reversed. At least, that's how it began. The candidate was Jerry Thompson, the COO of CITGO Petroleum. This was some years ago, back when showing up looking your best was a given, and Jerry arrived impeccably dressed and fully prepared.

His credentials were outstanding, and he knew how to manage an interview. Though the meeting was set for him to discuss the CEO role at TEPPCO Energy Partners, a pipeline company based in Houston, from the outset it felt as if I was the one being interviewed. Which was fine by me: In a good interview, it can comfortably work both ways.

Before I could dive into his background, Jerry wanted to know about mine. He had read my bio and was genuinely interested in my parents' story as refugees from the Hungarian Revolution of 1956, and how their experience had shaped me. His interpersonal skills and ability to make others feel seen were on full display. I found myself thinking, *Enough about me, what about you?*

As I attempted to steer the conversation, Jerry shifted to discuss the client company, offering sharp observations and thoughtful, respectful questions. "How does Mr. Duncan's refined products strategy fit into his overall plan?" he asked, referring to Dan Duncan, the founder of Enterprise Products. "Do you think the company has the appetite and balance sheet for acquisitive growth in this pricey environment?"

I thought, *This guy sure does his homework*, which led me to ask him, "So, what *don't* you know about the company?"

In the two hours we spoke, Jerry was pretty candid about both his strengths and his concerns—explaining why he might not be the right fit for the job. When he admitted to being somewhat risk-averse toward acquisitive growth, I liked that sign of self-awareness and humility. I even pressed the point that his cautious instincts might perfectly complement Dan Duncan's more aggressive style. It's always a good sign when a recruiter starts selling the role, as I was doing, and you won't be surprised to learn that Jerry Thompson became the new CEO of TEPPCO.

Jack Welch always liked to ask candidates how they had prepared for interviews. The answer told him something about their seriousness and their approach to challenges. Interview preparation, in my experience on the other side of the table, can set the tone for the entire conversation. It almost always makes for a more interesting, useful, and relaxed exchange.

Preparation extends to etiquette and personal appearance. In general, for men and women alike, interviews are not the time to be experimental, edgy, or daring in dress. Attire should align with company culture, and where there's doubt it's best to err on the side of formality. The interview itself can have a formal feel, although you'll be more yourself if you think of it as a conversation instead of a test or Q&A. And on the day of the interview, do whatever calculations are necessary to make sure you arrive with time to spare—so you can breathe easy and collect yourself before going in. The last thing you want is to be flustered and angry with yourself over some delay you could easily have avoided.

Interviews are like every other aspect of professional life: Failure and panic are far more likely when you haven't really prepared. Having prepared, you'll feel more focused and confident, and that shows too.

You can take similar advice from a truly eminent authority. Few figures today are more accomplished than James A. Baker III. Former secretary of state, secretary of the treasury, White House chief of staff, manager of national campaigns—this man has been around and has operated in situations that demand everyone's best. Baker has an alliterative maxim—which my children have heard often: "Proper Preparation Prevents Poor Performance." Whether it's school homework or global diplomacy, good outcomes usually reflect focused effort.

The same applies to interviews. How much preparation have you done? Are you well-informed about the role, the company, the interviewer? Have you considered what the company might already know about you, based on Internet searches and your social-media footprint? Have you thought about people in your life who might have good advice, and spoken to them? What real value would you bring to the position, and do you have in mind a concise and compelling way to express it?

Without weighing down a conversation with some long, canned pitch for yourself, you should have some basic talking points to make sure that everything is said that should be said. Naturally, these should cover career highlights and competencies, conveyed with self-assurance but with no hint of boasting. You should also come into an interview with smart questions of your own, remembering that you're not there merely as a supplicant awaiting the judgment of others; you're there to learn more about them and about the company as they learn about you.

Controlled Energy

In an interview, a candidate's energy level can be unmistakable as well. You want to show readiness and enthusiasm, but people will sense right away if it is forced or overdone. I've had candidates so excited and jumpy that I have actually wondered how many cups of coffee it took to get that way, or even whether they got their boost from something stronger. One fellow came in with his personalized coffee mug, decorated with family photos, and could be heard slurping from it throughout the interview. Even so, being too lively is better than being the opposite. A slightly overenthusiastic candidate might need settling down, but it beats coming off as disengaged or half-hearted. I once presented to executives of a TV sports network a CEO candidate who, for all his merits, had an extremely subdued and tedious way about him. His monotone delivery caused one of the executives to nod off. He left my clients with a good story to tell, and still searching for a CEO.

One of the biggest turnoffs in any interview is someone who comes across as a know-it-all. It is better to presume ignorance, and invite learning, as Dr. Jordan Peterson argued, than to assume sufficient knowledge and risk the consequent blindness. The interviewers want to know that they're dealing with a good listener, who is there to learn and not just to hold forth. I've come across more than a few executives who thought they could win me over with demonstrations of their boundless knowledge and brilliance. But it doesn't play well, and in the interview setting it can leave others feeling exhausted and ready to hear from the next candidate. Serious, self-aware people know better than to monopolize the conversation, as if no one in the room could have anything interesting to contribute.

The best leaders in any room are by no means the ones who always do the most talking. I've sat in interviews sometimes, as candidates were going on and on, and wondered whether they had any idea how they were coming across. As a favor—a classic "courtesy interview"—I once met with a man who wanted to serve on the board of a billion-dollar public company. He was determined to convince me that he was qualified, despite having no board or senior executive experience, and he was relentless in pushing his case. As tactfully as I could, I kept explaining the typical criteria for such posts, none of which he met, and he kept insisting otherwise. Having gotten nowhere with me, he finally blurted out, "Well, I suppose if I were a woman or minority, I'd have a better shot, but I'm not . . ." As if his arrogance weren't enough to take, I got a dose of his self-pity, too, and I didn't need to hear more.

> *Serious, self-aware people know better than to monopolize the conversation, as if no one in the room could have anything interesting to contribute.*

Of course, sometimes the moment is right for selling yourself in an interview. You just have to recognize the difference between selling and overhyping. Confident, capable people have no need to push too hard or overstate accomplishments and credentials. Even a hint of exaggeration can be a warning sign to a recruiter or prospective employer, suggesting an inflated sense of self that doesn't convey a healthy spirit of service and teamwork.

While honesty with a headhunter or hiring manager is crucial, being too self-revelatory carries a risk. You obviously don't want to be like the Randy Dupree character in *You, Me, and Dupree*, who says plainly that he's just not into hard work, or confess to other faults an employer is entitled to wonder about. Showing vulnerability is one thing; oversharing is quite another. Yet you'd be amazed how many candidates, out of nervousness perhaps, end up spilling too much information and undermining their prospects.

I recall one candidate who, on the morning of his interview, phoned our office in a panic. Having just realized we were on the sixty-eighth floor of Houston's tallest office tower, he explained that he had a fear of heights and was breathing heavily. When I assured him that he wouldn't be near any windows or have to look out, he came over and everything went fine from there. In fact, I knew he'd fit the role since the client's office in this case was in Enid, Oklahoma, where the tallest building barely reaches ten stories. It all worked out well for him, and he was right to tell us of his fears. It could've been worse—another colleague had a candidate ask to meet outdoors because he felt uneasy indoors.

Others, however, don't know when to stop. Brené Brown shared a story of founders unsure if they were up to the job. She asked if they should confess their fears to colleagues, noting that while it would be authentic, it would also be "a terrible idea." Brown clarified that real vulnerability isn't about spilling everything to everyone—it requires discernment. "Vulnerability minus boundaries is not vulnerability," she explained.[5] True vulnerability involves sharing with the right people, at the right time, for the right reasons—not using others as an emotional dumping ground.

Once, a female senior executive, in her interview with me, wanted me to know that she was a victim of sexual harassment. Naturally, I listened and was impressed with her candor. I asked how she had handled this awful ordeal and how it might have shaped her outlook as a corporate leader. When it seemed the subject had been covered, I tried to move on. "So, let's shift to your views of corporate governance." But she wouldn't let it go and insisted on recounting all the details of the incidents, and of the negotiations and legal settlement that followed, as if I were a lawyer and she was in a deposition. And that's how we spent the next half hour. It was an appalling story, and I was her sympathetic ally. Yet she would speak of nothing else, to the point that we hadn't covered other relevant interview topics, leaving me unable to recommend her for the role.

Sometimes in job interviews, you might be asked for an opinion on one or another provocative issue, and my advice is not to be too guarded or fearful of inviting disagreement. Peter Thiel has a favorite question for job candidates: "What very important truth do very few people agree with you on?" In his book *Zero to One*, Thiel explained that this question can draw out a candidate's independence from groupthink, which is one of the strengths he's looking for. If you're asked some similar question in an interview, within sensible boundaries, be candid. I remember one CEO candidate who didn't hesitate to push back on the DEI agenda at the height of its wave through corporate America. Without deference to ideological fashion, he explained why it was contrary to the pursuit of racial equality and opportunity. He spoke his mind, reasonably and calmly, and we were impressed by a man who clearly did his own thinking.

Reflectiveness, Resiliency, and Red Flags

One of my favorite questions to ask in interviews is this: "If you were the one hiring for this position, what qualities would you look for in the role—what would your criteria be?" The answer tells me how much thought the person has actually given to the assignment. A good response indicates a capacity to think objectively about what the position demands and what the company needs, apart from the candidate's own wish to be hired.

Having covered the needs of the position, I then ask: "Can you give me your own self-assessment, your own 360? What are your strengths and areas for development? Where do you see opportunities for growth?" I prefer the terms *development* and *opportunity* instead of *weakness* because they elicit candor rather than defensiveness. When such questions are cast in aspirational terms instead of corrective ones, candidates give thoughtful answers. And remember: If you're being interviewed for a job, you can usually give your answers an aspirational ring regardless of how the questions are framed.

Leaders with a balanced view of both their capabilities and areas for growth always make a better impression. Being forthright about professional or personal struggles—short of oversharing—is also a plus. One of the most memorable responses I've heard came from a single mother who shared how she had once taken a leave of absence to care for her autistic child. With obvious, heartfelt sincerity, she spoke of her difficulties, worries, and decision to put her child's needs ahead of anything else. She wasn't trying to make any particular impression; she was showing us who she was and what she cared about most. Her directness and authenticity made it a standout interview.

Another candidate I recall interviewing was equally candid in saying that he felt he had neglected family responsibilities. He had been "married to his work," with harmful consequences to his real marriage and to his family. He and his wife had separated, and this man realized that a good career should not come at the cost of a neglected family. We liked his frank way of acknowledging a fault and being determined to repair it—which he did, I'm happy to relate, by reconciling with his wife.

Most everyone "carries the reminders of every glove that laid him down," to recall a lyric from Paul Simon's "The Boxer."[6] We've all taken a few knocks. Times like those can come up in interviews, and they needn't cause any awkwardness at all. When they're sizing up leadership qualities, your interviewers want to see a reflective side. They want to know what you've learned from the challenges that life throws at everyone.

In an interview, I look for a candidate's ability to roll with the punches, as well as for agility and selflessness. The sum of these qualities is a certain resiliency that every enterprise wants in a leader—in someone who can rise to the moment when things get tough. Mere stubbornness, on the other hand, is not what anyone is looking for. This latter trait doesn't always appear in interviews but can reveal itself later, for instance during offer negotiations. If a candidate fixates on his or her own wants in compensation, title, and so on, it feels to employers as if they're suddenly seeing the true person. And the sooner that's identified, the better.

Having backbone is essential for leadership, especially in negotiating contracts, managing costs, and delivering on budgets. But rigidity is something very different, and in an interview it causes misgivings about hiring or recommending a candidate. One case in which I ignored a red flag was an interview for a senior executive role at Halliburton, the global oil-services company then led by CEO Dick Cheney. The finalist had all the right qualifications and experience but spent much of the interview obsessing on such details as the company's travel policy, business expenses, and perks like tickets to Astros and Rockets games.

Under pressure to expedite the process, and because the client was impressed by the guy, I dismissed all this as a minor annoyance. He was hired, but only three months later I got the dreaded call from my client. The verdict was, "Good guy, but just too high maintenance." He had spent more time continuing to negotiate first-class travel, expense allowances, and his relocation package than he did applying himself to the work. Halliburton was glad to see him go, and I resolved not to make the same mistake again.

A clear sign of self-absorption in a candidate is the overuse of *I, me, my, mine,* and the like. It's a common blind spot, and interviewers will always notice with approval when candidates speak of what they have accomplished with others as a team. Take a cue from golfer Jordan Spieth, who, after a round, always mentions his caddy and recounts how "we managed the round."

In the same way, it doesn't enhance the impression a candidate makes when the person is constantly describing him- or herself. In one recent interview I conducted, the candidate told me no fewer than six or seven times, "I'm a frank person." Another kept mentioning his humility, apparently fearing that I might overlook this quality unless again and again reminded. As a general rule, it's best not to cite one's virtues, as if they had been certified by an accredited institution. You don't need to tell me how frank, humble, or genuine you are—just show those traits in what you say and how you act. Whenever I hear people extolling their own humility, I recall a line attributed to Golda Meir: "Don't be humble, you're not that great."

Last Impressions

A parting impression can be every bit as consequential as a first impression. In fact, it can help make up for any awkwardness at the outset. An uneven start can be overcome by a strong finish, especially if you have a few closing questions in mind. This can be one more tool in cracking the interview code.

Here, for instance, are some of the smarter questions I've heard from candidates at the end of their interviews:

- *How do you define success in the first year of this role?* This shrewd question shows that the candidate is thinking in tangible terms of measurable accomplishment, and also makes it feel as if he or she is already visualizing goals as part of the team.

- *Do you have any doubts about my qualifications or experience?* This one is bold, forthrightly inviting any concerns the candidate can address.

- *Is there anything I could clarify, to ensure I'm the best fit for the role?* Instead of the candidate holding forth about his or her qualifications, this question shows a nice balancing of humility and confidence. It is also cast in terms of the interests of the organization and of how those interests can be well served.

After all this, most people walk away from interviews with a sense of relief. All the more if the encounter went well, it feels great to have it over with. It used to be standard practice to follow up with an appreciative note to the interviewer, and though that's not as common anymore I still recommend it. Keep the note short, and make it stand out in the pile by being handwritten. It's a way of stressing your interest and getting remembered—if not for the job you sought, then maybe for the next one. Here, too, there are limits you don't want to stretch. I once had a candidate who was so enthusiastic she sent me a poem that she had composed after the interview. No need for you to go that far, as long as you've said thanks and done your best—which is the measure that counts the most.

FOURTEEN

The Power of Your Story

In recent years, social scientists have come to appreciate that stories (narratives, myths, or fables) constitute a uniquely powerful currency in human relationships. It is stories—narratives that help individuals think about and feel who they are, where they come from and where they are headed—that constitute the single most powerful weapon in the leader's arsenal.

—Professor Howard Gardner
Leading Minds: An Anatomy of Leadership

At some point, we have all faced a tough moral dilemma that put character to the test. In business, this can happen when you're caught between two choices: doing the wrong thing and being rewarded, and doing the right thing but risking your job. You want to act with honesty and integrity, but the incentives—perhaps even the expectations—are pointing the other way.

The Enron fiasco, now a generation ago, gave us an example of men finding themselves in this situation. In a big way, each was writing the story of his career, mostly for the worse. But one Enron executive's story took a turn very different from the others. His name was Rod Gray, and the choices he made should always be remembered in the otherwise shameful undoing of that company.

Rod was CFO and Vice Chairman of Azurix, an Enron subsidiary. As executives prepared for a key conference call with Wall Street analysts, he urged Enron's top leaders, Ken Lay and Jeff Skilling, to be candid about the company's deteriorating financial situation.

For months, Enron had been playing up the supposedly robust performance of Azurix. But it was an illusion; in reality, Azurix was in trouble. Rod, who knew the financials better than anyone, was determined to set the record straight. He recommended providing "guidance" to investors and analysts to manage expectations. Lay and Skilling, however—men he had worked with for years—insisted that Rod stick to their upbeat growth narrative when his turn came on the conference call. He should highlight new growth opportunities along with other promising projects to attract more capital and investment and leave it at that.

Deciding that he could not in good conscience do as they expected, Rod instead spoke forthrightly to the analysts about where things really stood at Enron. The next day, Enron's stock fell by 40 percent. You can guess where Enron's leadership assigned the blame. As quickly as possible, Rod was dismissed.

All that followed was his vindication. He was watching from a safe distance when, three years later, Enron collapsed in a $63 billion bankruptcy—the largest ever up to that point. "Enron" became a shorthand term for corporate malfeasance, scandal, and criminality. Rod, meanwhile, his reputation unstained, continued on with a highly successful career with leading energy companies.

It could all have been otherwise, different choices adding up to a different story. But here was a man who understood that with some choices we make, we decide who we are. Whatever the titles of his ill-fated colleagues at Enron might have been, it's clear now that Rod Gray was the only true leader in the room.

That kind of character-driven leadership—a sense of who you aspire to be and the story you are living out—is a powerful weapon against the pressures and temptations that most every career brings. A leader needs to stay true to a vision of him- or herself, refusing compromise when integrity is at stake and accepting the hardships that can come with that choice. Recruiters and hiring managers, when they listen to a job candidate, want to hear more than a litany of credentials. We always hope to see candidates who stand apart like Rod, because they have high standards and can't be dragged down by others.

Knowing Your Story

To really know someone, when you think about it, means to know their story. Often, there's a period of pain and growth that shapes your character and story. As Viktor Frankl said, "what is to give light must endure burning."[1] Growing from the heat may be the most revealing aspect of who you are.

You could read in the business pages about the CEO who kept ExxonMobil on track when the going was rough. But you can't really know Darren Woods until you appreciate the resilience of a man who started out as a military kid bullied in school. Doug Lawler's résumé would impress anyone, but nothing in his story says more about him than the grief he suffered and overcame in the tragic loss of his wife. Or I think of my old friend, the legendary chairman of Heidrick & Struggles, Gerry Roche, who stepped in to help care for his daughter's children after her husband was killed in New York on 9/11. And it's the same with many names in this book—Jamie Dimon, Jeff Hildebrand, Frank Tsuru, Elaine Chao, and others. Professional achievements are often the least compelling thing about them.

Even so, many aspiring leaders struggle to convey their own stories to prospective employers. For whatever reason, they've never distilled their lives and career paths into a narrative about who they are, where they've been, or where they're bound. As they seek to move forward professionally, they are not making the most of what Howard Gardner, in *Leading Minds*, called the "powerful currency" of the personal story.[2]

Like a blind spot, an untold story can become an unbearable burden. In solitude, liberation comes with the realization of your own story. As you reflect, you begin to master the art of self-awareness—your story starts to unfold. But can you share it with others? Can you convey it to a hiring manager, an executive team, or a board of directors? Will you model it for your followers so it can inspire and be reflected in them?

Today's real competition in the marketplace is for leaders, not customers. Before companies can innovate, develop products, gain market share, or raise capital, they must first win the battle for talent. Corporate America is focused on recruiting and developing the next generation of leaders—not just brilliant minds, but good hearts. A leader cannot be virtuous without being effective, and true greatness requires goodness. That's where you and your story come in.

It is true, of course, that there are times in life when we're so busy, so occupied with our day-to-day responsibilities, that self-reflection feels like a luxury better left for another day. There is so much to do that we have to stay focused on the here and now. What I mean by the story that everyone can tell, even when the pace of life and work is fastest, is a sense of the larger purposes we're trying to serve, the kind of person we're trying to become, and the gifts we hope to develop and contribute to some overall mission.

There's a legend about the construction of St. Paul's Cathedral in the 1600s, after the Great Fire of London. The architect, Sir Christopher Wren, was walking about the worksite and spoke to three stone masons. He asked each what his particular job was. The first replied, "I'm a bricklayer." The second told him, "I'm putting up a wall." When he came to the third, and asked what he did, the man answered, "I am building a great cathedral for the Almighty." That man knew his story.

Like this tale about the stone masons, stories can get a point across more memorably, and in fewer words, than pages of general instruction, advice, or argument. A long list of famed leaders known for their storytelling comes to mind, starting with Abraham Lincoln. Even a story of two or three sentences can stay with listeners like nothing else. Consider these closing words from a speech by President John F. Kennedy, meant to convey a sense of urgency:

> [W]e must think and act not only for the moment but for our time. I am reminded of the story of the great French Marshal Lyautey, who once asked his gardener to plant a tree. The gardener objected that the tree was slow-growing and would not reach maturity for a hundred years. The Marshal replied, "In that case, there is no time to lose, plant it this afternoon."
>
> Today a world of knowledge—a world of cooperation—a just and lasting peace—may be years away. But we have no time to lose. Let us plant our trees this afternoon.[3]

Stories with a touch of self-deprecation can be especially effective when leaders share them. Gerry Roche, still a legendary figure at Heidrick & Struggles, always had a knack for this. Named "Headhunter of the Century" in 2000—a title he always downplayed—Gerry was known for leading through stories that inspired partners like me. Many of his tales were not only insightful but also fun. As a man still on the job into his eighties, Gerry once described the arc of his career in this way: "First, it's 'Who is Gerry Roche?' Then, 'Get me Gerry Roche.' Third, 'Get me another Gerry Roche.' Fourth, 'Get me a younger Gerry Roche.' And now, I'm at the fifth stage: 'Who is Gerry Roche?'"

As I near my own "Get me a younger" man stage, I guess I appreciate other people's career stories all the more and try to draw them out in my interviews with executive candidates. After the résumé has been reviewed and the usual questions covered, I wait to hear more. What are the highs and the lows, the hardships, and the victories, that don't appear on paper? I want to know about those.

You know your own story better than anyone. So why, when an executive recruiter or hiring manager calls, would you rely on a dry résumé listing your positions and roles? Sometimes you have to forget the paper and share your heart. Put aside your list of accomplishments and tell me who you are becoming.

> *Sometimes you have to forget the paper and share your heart. Put aside your list of accomplishments and tell me who you are becoming.*

Just as auditors sift through financial data, recruiters examine résumés, recommendations, and references, searching for the narrative that reveals whether we've found a leader. As we assess a résumé, we read between the lines in search of the story that sets a candidate apart. What path has this person been following? Does this person connect well with colleagues and generally make people feel seen, appreciated, respected?

Telling Your Story

One of the techniques I've picked up over the years is to help candidates share their real story by offering a bit of my own. If I want to explore how someone else has overcome adversity and built resilience, I might share a moment of vulnerability in that area to encourage them to open up. To understand how they've grown as a leader, I'll tell them a quick story about my own journey. It takes the burden off the other person, breaks the ice, and establishes an atmosphere of trust.

Of course I'm not talking here about excessive self-revelation, but just the ability to assess and speak candidly about yourself. Hiring managers today expect this, along with other qualities that didn't come into play in other times. They are more focused on "softer" factors like interpersonal and communication skills, and even personal chemistry, more than on academic credentials or financial achievements. As AI transforms the future workforce, these and other "meta-skills"—agility, resilience, and empathy—will be even more in demand.

If a leader's story can be both shared (when seeking leadership) and lived (when practicing leadership), that leader will guide their followers toward a virtuous goal. As Sue Monk Kidd wrote, "Stories have to be told or they die, and when they die, we can't remember who we are or why we're here."[4]

The great film director Alfred Hitchcock said that "drama is real life with the dull bits cut out," and that's worth remembering as you think about the story you share in interviews. The best advice I can offer is to *show* your story, not just tell it. Use vivid and concise ways to describe your journey—it makes all the difference. Remember, in every great story there's a hero and a guide. As a leader, in recounting where you've been and what you've done, it comes across as more real and effective to position yourself as the guide, not as the hero.

Donald Miller, the author and founder of StoryBrand, stresses the "guide" archetype. In his research, he found that guides are often the most influential characters in stories. Think of Sam Gamgee or Gandalf guiding Frodo in *The Lord of the Rings*; Yoda or Obi-Wan Kenobi in *Star Wars*; Lionel Lougue in *The King's Speech*; Mr. Keating in *Dead Poets Society*; or the figure of Virgil in Dante's classic epic poem, *The Divine Comedy*. What this means in practice is that, in your own story, you're the judicious observer of events and by no means always the star player. It's impressive when a person recounts his or her own experiences with the detachment and objectivity to see everything that happened and not just their own part.

Warren Buffett himself, for all of his investment genius, seems to regard himself in this way. He once said, "If each of us hires people who are smaller than we are, we shall become a company of dwarfs. But if each of us hires people who are bigger than we are, we shall become a company of giants."[5] The "Oracle from Omaha" doesn't view himself as some all-knowing figure, but more as a studious observer skilled at drawing on the talents of others and offering sensible advice. Steve Jobs, likewise, managed to cast Apple customers themselves as rebellious freethinkers in a world of conformists, and himself and his colleagues merely as guides offering them the chance to break free. And lately, Elon Musk has accomplished something similar, as a champion of free expression and enabler of human ingenuity.

In recruiting interviews, we meet plenty of candidates who have never given much thought at all to framing their stories—whether as lead figures, guides, or anything else. In their careers, some have been turnaround artists, cost-cutters, entrepreneurs, innovators, dealmakers, and the like—all of which should be good material for a compelling story. But so often, that's not what we hear in interviews, unless we are able to draw it out ourselves with prompts and questions. The times of testing, the obstacles that candidates have overcome, the values and standards that matter most to them, who and what inspires them—all of this tells us who they are, and that's what we want to know.

I remember an especially bright and talented executive who was competing for a COO position at a Fortune 1000 company. Given his impressive credentials and stellar references, I had high expectations for him. Yet the client still had doubts about the man's leadership abilities. He would list his accomplishments and talk about "leadership" and "managing teams," but could provide no specifics beyond that. There might have been a story that illustrated what made him a leader, but we never heard it. The résumé wasn't enough, and in the end he came in second—which is the same as last place when you're looking to get hired.

Job interviews can determine so much in a career—opportunities opened or closed, roads taken and not taken. And the outcome of an interview should not depend on whatever you happen to think of at the moment. Go in, instead, with a well-considered account of the experiences and beliefs that have shaped your life and career so far. Conducting ten thousand interviews has taught me a thing or two, so, to summarize, here are some basic pointers on sharing your story:

- *Above all, be truthful:* The least exaggeration can cast doubt on trustworthiness. And candor, even when it's not flattering to the candidate, establishes credibility. Get all of your facts straight and be vulnerable enough to acknowledge failures and blind spots. Honesty always makes the best impression, and it shows the real-life journey that you're on.

- *Make it compelling*: They've seen your résumé, so don't just lay out a chronology. The highs and lows of your career, the disappointments, the surprising turns, the lessons learned—these are what will keep them paying attention.

- *Keep it brief*: Enough said.

- *Keep it simple*: As Don Miller said, "If you confuse, you lose." If you know what you want to say, you'll know what you don't need to say. You can't afford clutter and too much context. The aim is a concise story with a clear meaning.

- *Be the guide, not the hero*: You might be the center of the interview, but there is no surer way to sound off-key than to make yourself the center of all action everywhere you have worked.

- *Summarize your story*: If you could compress all that you want an interviewer to know about you into one sentence, what would it be? That sentence should feel natural, genuine, and true to your heart.

The Apostle Paul told us that we are "known and read by all,"[6] wisdom that carries over into our quest to find opportunities and advance in the world. And often, to get where you want to be, you have to show who you are. Knowing yourself, having awareness of assets and flaws alike, and being ready with the story that only you can tell—these are real advantages to have on your side in a job interview. Make them your own and you are far more likely to be the candidate who comes in first.

EPILOGUE

Consider the Raven

Consider the ravens: they neither sow nor reap, they have neither storehouse nor barn, and yet God feeds them. Of how much more value are you than the birds! And which of you by being anxious can add a single hour to his span of life? If then you are not able to do as small a thing as that, why are you anxious about the rest?

—Luke 12:24–26 ESV[1]

Perhaps the most impressive member of the raven family is the magpie, known for its sleek, black-and-white feathers and that flashy green shimmer on its wings and tail. Magpies are overachievers even compared to many other very smart birds. They're highly versatile, self-aware, and adaptable, and in behavioral tests they have been observed studying themselves in mirrors. We would, too, if we looked that good.

On many summer mornings in Colorado, my dog Liesl and I are often joined by these beautiful, clever creatures. At first, they play it cool, hiding in the trees and keeping a quiet, watchful eye. Then they come swooping down, bursting with curiosity and a little mischief, as if they're in on our routine. But for all their smarts, even magpies have their blind spots. After years of taunting and dive-bombing the dogs with impunity, one bold magpie misjudged its timing and, unfortunately for it, Liesl's vertical leap. In one swift move, Liesl caught the bird mid-flight, her hunter instincts fully engaged. Despite my best efforts to intervene, she trotted back home triumphantly, magpie in mouth, and proudly deposited her prize on the porch—much to my wife's annoyance. The magpies, on the other hand, learned a valuable lesson about overconfidence that day.

This story isn't about Liesl's athletic agility—though I can't imagine a finer dog; the German Shorthaired Pointer is also known for its keen intelligence and awareness. It's really a reminder that even the most self-aware creatures can still be blindsided. And so can we. Even with a solid grasp of our strengths and weaknesses, we sometimes misjudge, letting pride, ego, or an overreliance on independence lead us into trouble. Like magpies straying too far from the safety of their flock, we often try to go it alone when sticking with the group might be the smarter move.

For centuries, ravens have made frequent appearances in literature, sometimes shrouded in mystery, as harbingers of doom or else as symbols of wisdom. After the Great Flood in the Old Testament, Noah sent a raven from the ark to test whether the floodwaters have receded, making that creature the first to survey a new world.

In the New Testament, Jesus used the raven to remind us not to burden ourselves with worry but instead to have confidence in divine providence. The birds, in their way, trust that they will be provided for, and we're assured that we are too: "And which of you by being anxious can add a single hour to his span of life?"[2] In contrast, Edgar Allan Poe's raven serves as a darker mirror, reflecting excessive self-reflection untethered from hope. The narrator, ensnared by the bird's haunting refrain of "Nevermore," succumbs to despair, a cautionary tale of emotions overwhelming reason. When my friend David Lumpkins faced the sudden and devastating loss of his daughter, he chose a path of renewed awareness, strength, and hope, rather than despair. Grounded in faith and surrounded by love, he embraced the assurance of Jesus' teaching: "Fear not, for how much more valuable are you than the birds!"

In today's fast-paced Adam I world, where chasing approval and accomplishments feels like a full-time job, it's easy to forget about the quieter, more important work: shaping our inner selves. We get so immersed in the hustle that we often overlook humility, empathy, faith, and self-awareness—the real building blocks of character. As we prioritize worldly success, we may become passive in addressing our flaws or brokenness, sacrificing essential qualities like vulnerability and self-reflection on the altar of productivity.

Unlike ravens, we humans have a leg up in the self-reflection department—our abilities go way beyond basic instinct. We can develop what's essentially a superpower: *awareness intelligence*. Think of it as human AI (but way less robotic), giving us the tools for self-actualization, clarity, and purpose. Of course, unlocking this superpower doesn't just happen overnight. It takes harnessing personal agency to keep our ambitious, go-getter Adam I nature in check, while leaning into the deeper wisdom of Adam II.

But self-awareness, as I use the term in this book, also involves an acceptance of things not always within our power to control or even to comprehend. For me, at least, this attitude can help dispel anxiety and bring peace of mind. Ravens never burn out, and I suppose there's a lesson for all of us in their lovely example. (Some of the rules I share in Appendix A below are inspired by ravens, so I decided to call them my Raven Rules.)

If the advice in this book has a personal ring at times, that is because striving to become a better leader so often means striving to become a better person. We can get so caught up in the outward signs of success as to lose sight of inner qualities that are the true measure. To be aware, as a leader, is to prize honesty, humility, empathy, vulnerability, and other qualities that would be admirable even if they did us and our careers no practical good at all.

I find much wisdom in the Adam I / Adam II framework that I've turned to often in the book. We each have different temperaments and natures, and we will usually tend toward one or the other type. One of the great challenges for a leader is to draw on the best of both, allowing the ambitious go-getter side to do its part while also cultivating the gentler and deeper qualities of the other side. It can take long, concentrated effort, but the man or woman who gets that far can fairly be termed too aware to fail.

Self-Awareness—The Ultimate Superpower

A leader's sharp self-awareness—knowing exactly how they're perceived by peers, supervisors, and subordinates—has always been a cornerstone of success in business. Sure, buzzwords like agility, empathy, and emotional intelligence come and go in leadership trends, drifting in and out of boardroom discussions. But with an increasingly uncertain and complex future, leaders who can cultivate heightened self-awareness and muster the courage to face their flaws head-on will have a skillset that's not just trendy—it's indispensable.

As a recruiter, I've seen firsthand—and have the data to back it up—that self-awareness is the ultimate performance accelerator. Without it, other qualities, no matter how flashy, tend to wither away, much like grapes on a vine that's gone too long without water. Or, as Erma Bombeck once joked, "I would never go to a doctor whose office plants have died."[3] Great leaders don't just nurture others—they pay attention to their own "garden," like self-aware horticulturists attuned to subtle clues using them as feedback to adapt care practices, such as watering, feeding, or pruning strategies.

Trust, I still believe, is the ultimate dealbreaker for leaders. Think of it like crystal: Once it's shattered, good luck gluing it back together without a ton of effort and a few awkward cracks.[4] That's where self-awareness swoops in as the hero—it's the preemptive shield that guards against trust-destroying pitfalls like greed, hubris, inflated egos, fake empathy, and so many other delusions that can drag us down.

Studies have shown that as leaders rise in their careers, they tend to believe more in their own hype. Add a dose of isolation at the top, and getting honest feedback becomes about as rare as a unicorn sighting. In fact, a study of over 3,600 leaders found that the higher up you go, the more you're likely to overestimate your abilities—particularly in areas like empathy, trustworthiness, and emotional self-awareness.[5] In nineteen out of twenty competencies measured, leaders scored way higher in their own minds than in everyone else's reality.

That's why self-awareness is the ultimate leadership superpower—it's the awareness intelligence or "AI" leader skillset for the next decade and beyond. It's like having x-ray vision—not to see through walls, but to see through *yourself*. With it, leaders can cut through their own blind spots, missteps, and habits, ensuring they don't just keep climbing but do so with trust intact and their team still behind them.

Gautam Mukunda, a leadership scholar at the Yale School of Management, has a knack for spotlighting the one thing too many leaders are missing: self-awareness. As someone who's spent years shadowing top CEOs and senior military officials, Gautam has some insider intel: "Most top leaders truly lack self-awareness," he told me.[6] And yet, it's this very trait that's key to peak performance—and avoiding the kind of missteps that make headlines.

> *That's why self-awareness is the ultimate leadership superpower—it's the awareness intelligence or "AI" leader skillset for the next decade and beyond. It's like having x-ray vision—not to see through walls, but to see through yourself.*

For example, consider his time spent advising Volkswagen during its diesel emissions scandal. Gautam warned the board early on that the management team's self-awareness levels were dangerously low—a red flag that came back to haunt them when CEO Matthias Müller was booted by the same board in 2018. It's proof that a little reflective work can save a lot of headaches later.

Day to day, self-awareness can mean simply hitting the mental pause button and asking yourself such questions as, "Why did I say that?" "Why did I hold back on giving an honest opinion?" "Did I really have to raise my voice?" "Do I speak to others, or do I speak *at* them?" "Am I doing my part on the team, and am I sharing the credit?" "Do I deflect blame, or do I take responsibility?" "Am I treating all my coworkers well, or just the ones who can do me good?" "Am I trying to advance the organization in everything I do, or sometimes just promoting myself?" "Am I giving in to fear and worry over things that are outside my control?" The questions keep going on like that once you're really in the mode of self-awareness. You will not always meet every standard you have set for yourself, but those standards will at least stay clear in the mind of the self-aware leader.

I began this book prompted by one basic observation over many years: The most successful leaders I've seen in action all display a heightened awareness of their blind spots, and also the courage to confront those blind spots. My interviews and research have only reinforced this view. The CEOs I spoke with collectively lead companies worth trillions, employ hundreds of thousands of people worldwide, and provide products and services that make modern life tick. Yet the kind of self-awareness they have attained can make a difference for those of us who will never have such outsized influence. Surely what works for them is worth giving a try in our own lives, even if the enterprises we lead are just our families, teams, or communities.

When I introduced the idea that self-awareness, paired with courage and leading to self-mastery, is a key ingredient for top-performing leaders, many CEOs nodded along—some even had light-bulb moments during our conversations. Jamie Dimon, for example, didn't just agree with the concept; he added his own twist: Self-awareness is great, but it's what you *do* with that awareness that counts.

When I sat down with Darren Woods, he didn't exactly roll out the red carpet for the self-awareness conversation. But when I casually mentioned that one of the prevailing blind spots in corporate America is people-pleasing, he immediately interrupted with a grin: "Well, no one's ever accused me of being a people-pleaser!" We both laughed. "See, Darren, you're more self-aware than you give yourself credit for," I said. It was a light moment that perfectly captured his direct, no-nonsense style—a hallmark of Exxon's accountability culture—but also revealed an insight he hadn't fully embraced: His self-awareness was a quiet strength.

When I chatted with Chris Wright, our talk about self-awareness took an unexpectedly emotional turn. He traced his leadership style back to the selflessness and quiet strength of his mother. As he reflected on her influence, along with the support of two loyal high school friends who had his back despite him being an undersized kid, tears of gratitude welled up. It was a powerful moment that caught me by surprise and showed just how deeply personal leadership can be.

These CEOs hadn't always thought of self-awareness as the secret sauce of leadership. It's not usually the first thing that comes to mind—not unlike quiet strengths like analytical thinking, resilience, or good old-fashioned integrity. So often there had been a formative period of adversity that each had to overcome. Rarely had there been a single moment of epiphany. The striking common theme was that, in one way or another, life had forced each one of them to look inward. There's no one method to follow, no one manual or fixed set of instructions for growing in self-awareness. From my conversations with leaders, what I know for sure is that it usually began with an attitude of openness, humility, or personal determination that changed them and redirected their paths.

And recall how self-aware leaders can influence and shape the paths of others, in ways that can take us beyond tension, division, and avoidable conflict. Just before the contentious 2024 presidential election, Heidrick & Struggles surveyed more than 250 corporate CEOs and directors to see how they were handling leadership in an increasingly polarized world. The study showed broad agreement on one key point: "Leaders must be self-aware to lead effectively in divisive settings."[7] Self-aware leaders tend to be more objective, easygoing, and mature in dealing with political and other differences that naturally arise in free societies. Being mindful, measured, and balanced themselves, they draw out those qualities in others.

The call to become the best version of ourselves resonates deeply—whether at work, in the community, or at home. Perhaps that's why you've chosen to read this book. Cultivating the protective armor of self-awareness does more than shield us from failure—it unlocks the potential to guide others toward meaningful destinations. In today's age of anxiety—where comfort too often eclipses sacrifice—self-aware leaders have the power to shape organizations that value purpose and depth over superficiality and complacency.

So, are we truly ready to face our reflection and accept Isaiah's challenge to "look to the rock from which you were hewn, and to the quarry from which you were dug"?[8] Reflection is not just an exercise in nostalgia; it is a journey into our origins, our purpose, and the lessons carved from both triumph and hardship. These moments of introspection reveal the people and experiences that shaped us, inviting us to honor them with gratitude. From that gratitude comes the strength to climb higher still and to pour into others, helping them ascend alongside us.

The other question we must ask ourselves is this: Will we continue to fuel the Adam I drive for success, and also embrace the selflessness and steadiness of Adam II? Do we aim to be the leaders we've admired from afar, or will we strive to become the ones people would willingly follow? This shift from self-focus to selfless action transforms not only our leadership but the lives of those who depend on it.

Taking New Flight

Willie Nelson famously quipped, "The early bird gets the worm, but the second mouse gets the cheese." While the early bird seizes opportunity, it's worth considering the risks of acting without awareness, much like the first mouse falling victim to the trap. The second mouse, reflecting the contemplative Adam II, approaches with patience and foresight, ultimately reaping the reward while avoiding unnecessary harm.

This principle aligns with the lesson to "consider the raven," a parable that beautifully complements the theme of cultivating deeper awareness. The raven, and intelligent animals like the German Shorthaired Pointer, direct our attention outward to the natural world, reminding us of the wisdom inherent in simplicity. Birds live free from the burdens we impose on ourselves—no titles to chase, no social pressures to meet, no relentless pursuit of recognition. They exist in a state of natural awareness, guided by instinct rather than by the weight of constant striving. In observing such creatures, we're reminded to embrace a more thoughtful, purposeful approach—one rooted in both clarity and foresight, where awareness becomes our guide.

And serious though the effort is, leaders on this journey typically take themselves less seriously and consider others more thoughtfully. There's a freedom that always comes as we escape self-centeredness. This is what G. K. Chesterton was getting at when he described excessive seriousness as a kind of weight that constrains us. "The swiftest things are the softest things," he wrote,

> A bird is active because a bird is soft. A stone is helpless because a stone is hard. The stone must by its own nature go downwards because hardness is weakness. The bird can of its nature go upwards because fragility is force. In perfect force, there is a kind of frivolity, an airiness that can maintain itself in the air. . . . Angels can fly because they can take themselves lightly.[9]

Take the challenge to grow in self-awareness, then, not as some heavy new task or onerous exercise in self-correction, but as a chance to take flight and always reach higher. Take it as the wonderful opportunity it is to add your share of wisdom and grace, in a world that always needs more of both. The destination is never quite assured, but simply to begin marks a victory, and no one making the journey has ever regretted trying.

APPENDIX A

The Raven Rules

---

1. Consider the raven who is unfettered and free in flight—enjoy the journey, not just the destination.

2. Reflecting on your flaws is seeing what others see already. Keep working on them until there is nothing left to notice.

3. Vulnerability and weakness can lift you up, just as the raven rises upwards, because fragility is force.

4. As you pursue personal goals, remember to give yourself an occasional leadership checkup—for awareness, agility, empathy, interdependence, self-forgetfulness, and courage.

5. Self-belief is a mark of great leadership. Goals are essential; selfless goals are superior because they leave footprints long after you've moved on.

6. Leadership sometimes requires recalculating. Stay flexible and ready to pivot when the compass points somewhere new.

7. Before greatness, pursue goodness: Character influences performance.

8. Goodness isn't about perfection; it's about aiming for it—starting with self-awareness, accountability, and personal growth.

9. Never grant yourself a moral license—a free pass to do something that's wrong because you've done so many things that are right.

10. Balance ambition with reflection. Let your Adam I side set the pace and your Adam II side set the course.

11. Great leaders don't just collect followers—they build more leaders, like ravens looking out for the flock.

12. Treat everyone with respect and dignity, without exception and regardless of whether they can do anything for you.

13. Give work your best but keep your priorities straight. As my wife (and the late John Candy) would say, "Like your work, love your wife."

14. Like the raven in Edgar Allan Poe's famous poem, stay steady and keep things calm—"never flitting, still sitting."[1]

15. Have the courage to let hard truths replace polite lies and turn tough moments into real change.

16. Don't avoid hard conversations. People-pleasing only makes problems worse down the road.

17. To stay grounded in your life and career, it helps to hit the refresh button now and then. Take time to quietly reflect and survey the big picture.

18. With false humility, we put ourselves down; with real humility, we lift up others.

19. FOMO—the fear of missing out—can be an obstacle to awareness and clarity, and those are developed away from the crowd.

20. Leadership is self-giving, never purely self-serving. If you're looking only to advance yourself, you're not leading.

21. To make others feel seen and heard, empathy isn't enough—it takes active compassion.

22. Self-denial is praiseworthy, but far greater is unconditional love that puts others first. Sanctification, or true self-denial, is more a community project.

23. Ask yourself what kind of leader you would choose to follow and strive to be that leader.

24. To strengthen your team, don't just hire people who mirror your own talents. Look for the ones who fill in the gaps.

25. Listen to the truth-tellers, not the yes-men. When you find yourself in an echo chamber of flattery, get out.

26. The hourly decision we make is where to focus our thoughts. Keeping our minds on the positive lifts the spirit and energizes those around us.

27. The leader doesn't have to be the first or loudest to speak. Listen to others first and be the one who says more by talking less.

28. Never skip class on *you*. Self-learning is essential to personal growth.

29. We can't help others without being our best selves, and we can't be our best selves without self-care and discovery.

30. Even superpowers, such as empathy, can be overplayed and become toxic. If you're too soft to hold someone accountable, you're not helping them.

31. Always be honest, especially with yourself.

32. Interdependency doesn't diminish us; it can instill fellowship and connect us to something bigger than ourselves.

33. If a leader feels "lonely at the top," he or she might be missing the camaraderie that comes with real teamwork and its rewards.

34. While self-discovery is healthy, too much of it can become self-absorption, making the cure worse than the disease.

35. In thinking about the "art" of your life, don't freeze up and worry how it looks to others. Just keep painting and fill the canvas with your best.

36. The tough, resourceful raven finds what he needs even in the roughest environments. Take adversity as free training in resilience.

37. Do not be weary in well doing, as Scripture tells us. Building character is not easy, but the rewards are endless.

38. Everyone feels despair, but a leader never gives in to it because he or she understands that to quit is worse than to fail.

39. Anxiety is often a needless burden. Birds go about their business without fearing what tomorrow might or might not bring. We can learn from them.

40. God is with those who persevere. So persevere in knowing God.

AUTHOR'S NOTE

A Last Word on Awareness

One of the profound influences on my understanding of self-awareness has been Anthony de Mello, a Jesuit priest and psychotherapist, who said, "You can change only what you understand."[1] De Mello passed away in 1987, yet his teachings have continued to resonate with readers worldwide, with his books—most notably *Awareness: The Perils and Opportunities of Reality*—selling more than two million copies. He challenged readers to illuminate the light within us and to recognize that we are more capable and extraordinary than we often realize.

De Mello's theory of self-awareness deeply resonated with me because I had observed that the most successful leaders—the ones who were truly alive and thriving—shared a common trait: heightened self-awareness. Their ability to understand themselves and the world around them enabled them to achieve remarkable things.

But de Mello's tough-love invitation to self-observation is not for the fainthearted or the closed-minded. It is for those who are willing to confront themselves honestly and seek transformation, whether as individuals or leaders. De Mello's stark observation is that most of us are asleep, even though we may believe we are awake.

"We are born asleep, we live asleep, marry in our sleep, breed children in our sleep, work in our sleep"—and as I would add, we *lead* in our sleep—"and then we die in our sleep without ever waking up."[2] His call is not to follow a prescribed method or formula but to engage in the lifelong practice of self-observation, finding your own path to waking up and discovering the truth of who you are.

Along the journey of waking up, de Mello offered an implicit disclaimer that the pursuit of self-awareness is not a comfortable or easy path. Why?

Awareness is unsettling. Awareness demands honesty and courage. It requires you to see the world—and yourself—as they truly are, not as you wish them to be. This can lead to profound discomfort, as it forces you to confront painful truths, challenge long-held beliefs, and let go of comforting illusions. The most difficult thing in the world is to listen and to see, de Mello said.[3] Awareness dismantles the filters through which we view life, often revealing a stark reality that we might otherwise avoid.

It's a solitary journey. Awareness is a deeply personal journey, one that each individual must walk alone. While no one can do it for you, and it cannot be imposed or taught by others, its solitary nature holds profound potential for influence. As de Mello observed, the tragedy of an awakened person is that they cannot make someone else see.[4] Yet, an awakened person's clarity, authenticity, and actions can inspire others to embark on their own path to self-awareness. Your transformation has the power to ripple outward, encouraging others to reflect, question, and awaken in their own time.

Awareness disrupts attachment. One of de Mello's recurring themes is the recognition that attachment—to people, possessions,

Author's Note

ideas, and even religion—hinders awareness. Letting go of them can feel like a profound loss, but it ultimately leads to liberation. People don't want to change; they want relief, he wrote. A person who really wants to change must be ready to give up all attachments and securities and, as de Mello argued, start from scratch.[5]

Awakening is liberating but comes at a cost. The journey toward awareness leads to joy, peace, and freedom, but it also entails the "death" of the ego and a redefinition of identity. This process can be unsettling, as it feels like losing a part of yourself—one that may have shaped your worldview for years. De Mello was said to have famously quipped, "You will know the truth, and the truth will make you free. But first, it will make you miserable."[6] For many, the discomfort of shedding old identities and facing the unknown is what makes the path to awareness so daunting.

While the journey of self-awareness may be challenging, it is also profoundly liberating, enabling us to soar to heights we never imagined possible.

Several of the themes in Anthony de Mello's work have challenged my own thinking and warrant clarification or caution. For instance, on the "renunciation" of our flaws or weaknesses, de Mello cautioned against the very act of "renouncing." He warned, "When you renounce something, you're stuck to it forever. And as long as you are fighting it, you are giving it power. You give as much power as you are using to fight it."[7] Similarly, Carl Jung echoed this wisdom: "What you resist not only persists but will grow in size."[8]

While I contend in chapter five that part of the journey to mastering oneself involves both awareness and the courage to confront our flaws—whether it be people-pleasing, temperament, being easily distracted, or unchecked emotion—de Mello's insight is a valuable reminder. The key is not to battle these flaws blindly but to understand them more deeply. The energy we expend fighting against our weaknesses often strengthens their hold over us. Awareness, again, is key. As de Mello put it, "Don't renounce it; see through it. Understand its true value, and you won't need to renounce it; it will just drop from your hands." The act of seeing, understanding, and waking up to the nature of these flaws allows them to lose their grip. "If you woke up," he argued, "you'd simply drop the desire for it."[9]

When writing about selfishness in chapter nine, I was mindful of de Mello's equally provocative perspective. He identified two forms of selfishness: the first, deriving pleasure from self-gratification, and the second, where you derive pleasure from pleasing others. This latter, what de Mello called a "more refined kind of selfishness," is more subtle, hidden, and, for that reason, more dangerous.[10] This is the trap I, and many leaders, often fall into. The caution here is that even in the pursuit of self-forgetfulness, we must remain vigilant and aware. Our clever minds may disguise our motives, tempting us to seek human praise or the reward of being known as "humble," which is another form of self-regard.

Finally, as I write about the first step of becoming "good" before striving to be "great" in chapter twelve, de Mello's emphasis on awareness once again emerges as fundamental. Doing good is never as good as when you have awareness that you're doing good, he argued.[11] This distinction is subtle but profound. True awareness does not mean being self-conscious or premeditated in doing good—it means acting from a place of clarity and authenticity. Yet, this level of awareness is rare, a lofty and almost extra-human effort.

So, De Mello asked provocatively, "Is this growing in awareness a gradual thing, or is it a 'whammo' kind of thing?"[12] He suggested that while the lucky ones may experience an instantaneous awakening, for most of us, awareness is a slow, gradual process—a journey we grow into over time.

De Mello illustrated this point with the famous proverb of the "Sheep-Lion."

Author's Note

There was a lion who came upon a flock of sheep and, to his astonishment, found a lion among them. This lion had been raised by the sheep since he was a cub. He bleated like a sheep, ran like a sheep, and thought he was a sheep. The lion approached him and asked, "What are you doing among these sheep?" The sheep-lion trembled and replied, "I am a sheep."

The lion said, "Oh no, you're not. Come with me." He led the sheep-lion to a pool and said, "Look!" When the sheep-lion gazed at his reflection in the water, he let out a mighty roar. In that moment, he was transformed. He was never the same again.[13]

Many of us live like the sheep-lion, unaware of the true greatness within us because we have been conditioned to see ourselves as small, limited, or defined by our surroundings.

The reason for this "last word" or disclaimer is to make clear that the journey to awareness is arduous. It will require courage, persistence, and the willingness to see clearly—looking into the "pool" of self-reflection—and awakening to the truth of who we are. Such transformation begins through the realization of our inherent potential. Yet, as I have argued throughout this book, this awakening requires the voice of another—someone willing (a leader, for instance) to guide us to the water and help us see our true reflection—one lion helping another roar.

Acknowledgments

It's often said that we're rarely unhappy because of what we lack, but rather because we fail to appreciate what we already have. If that's true, then authoring a book is the ultimate exercise in gratitude—because it quickly reveals just how much we rely on the wisdom, patience, and generosity of others.

This book would not exist without the CEOs, leaders, and visionaries who, despite their packed schedules and far more pressing matters, took the time to share their leadership journeys and reflections on self-awareness. Their honesty and vulnerability made this book far richer and more insightful than anything I could have produced alone.

It also wouldn't be nearly as readable without the tireless editorial guidance of Matthew Scully and John McConnell, who graciously (and repeatedly) reminded me that dressing up thoughts in long words does not, in fact, make for better writing. Their patience in resisting a full-scale intervention is worthy of its own acknowledgment.

A special thanks to Don Miller, whose generosity, clarity, and excellence have been an example to me. To Wes Yoder and Jonathan Merkh, for leading me toward the most author-friendly publisher at Forefront Books; to Kia Harris and Amanda Bauch, for their invaluable editing and warm spirit; and to Matt Baugher at HarperCollins,

Acknowledgments

for his steady guidance and counsel. To the many friends who generously read and improved this book in its various stages—David Lumpkins, Tracy Wolstencroft, Jeremy Hanson, Tim Holt, Doug Orr, and my pastor, West Brazelton—your feedback and encouragement kept me going.

I also want to honor and remember my friend Greg Kennedy, who walked alongside me through the final stages of this process and, heartbreakingly, passed away just as I was making last edits. As his wife, Victoria Reese, so beautifully said in her eulogy, Greg was truly "one of the good ones."

Writing a book is a team effort, and my Heidrick & Struggles team—Ali Van Norman, Claire Deaust, and Kyla Thompson—are simply the best. Special thanks to Kate Malter McLean and Karen West of HeidrickLabs for their research and data analysis, and to Josselyn Simpson for her literary advice. Tom Monahan, Heidrick & Struggles's CEO, took a keen interest in this topic and helped me sharpen my thinking along the way.

But the deepest thanks belong to my family: my children Will, Avery, Molly, and Thomas; my sons-in-law Francis and Travis, my daughter-in-law Alex, and the seven grandchildren who make me more aware of how truly fortunate I am. And, of course, my wife Anne, whose reassurance, patience, humor, and well-timed eye rolls kept me grounded throughout this journey.

And as always, my thanks to God, who continues to teach me that true awareness—of ourselves, of others, and of the sacredness of every moment—always leads back to gratitude.

Interviews

Alan Armstrong, President and Chief Executive Officer, Williams Companies, August 2, 2024.

James A. Baker, former United States Secretary of State, Correspondence, December 17, 2024.

Arthur Brooks, Parker Gilbert Montgomery Professor of the Practice of Public Leadership, Harvard Kennedy School, Correspondence, July 26, 2024.

Jay Brown, former President and Chief Executive Officer, Crown Castle International Corp., and current CEO, David Weekley Homes, September 10, 2024.

Elaine Chao, former United States Secretary of Labor, July 19, 2024.

John Christmann, President and Chief Executive Officer, APA Corporation, October 17, 2024.

Jim Collins, Author of *Good to Great*, June 14, 2003 (from *TRUST: The One Thing that Makes or Breaks a Leader*, 2004).

Jamie Dimon, Chairman of the Board and Chief Executive Officer, JPMorgan Chase & Co., July 25, 2024.

Ann Fox, Chief Executive Officer, Nine Energy Services, September 24, 2024.

Tatiana Furtseva, Partner-in-Charge, Heidrick & Struggles, Kyiv, Ukraine, August 14th, 2024.

Jeffrey Hildebrand, Founder, Chairman, and Chief Executive Officer, Hilcorp Energy Company, August 26, 2024.

Larry Kellner, former CEO of Continental Airlines and former Chairman of Boeing Corporation, October 17, 2024.

John Krenicki Jr., Vice Chairman, Clayton, Dubilier & Rice LLC, July 23, 2024.

Timothy Leach, former Chairman and CEO of Concho Resources and current Director, ConocoPhillips, November 22, 2024.

Robert Doug Lawler, President and Chief Executive Officer, Continental Resources, August 26, 2024.

Jeffrey Miller, Chairman and CEO, Halliburton, December 14, 2024.

Tom Monahan, CEO, Heidrick & Struggles Inc., December 4, 2024.

Gautam Mukunda, Professor, Yale School of Management, October 31, 2024.

Interviews

Cheli Nachman, Partner-in-Charge, Heidrick & Struggles, Tel Aviv, Israel, August 15, 2024.

David Petraeus, Retired General, United States Marine Corps, Correspondence, December 11, 2024.

Steven Reinemund, former Chairman and CEO of PepsiCo, from my interview with him for *TRUST, The One Thing that Makes or Breaks a Leader*, 2004.

Travis Stice, Chairman and CEO, Diamondback Energy, September 24, 2024.

Frank Tsuru, Cofounder and Chief Executive Officer, Momentum Midstream, September 4, 2024.

Chase Untermeyer, former Ambassador of the United States to Qatar, August 21, 2024.

Wil VanLoh, Founder and Chief Executive Officer, Quantum Capital Group, July 17, 2024.

Clay Williams, Chairman, President and Chief Executive Officer, National Oilwell Varco, September 12, 2024.

Tracy Wolstencroft, Senior Advisor, TPG and former CEO of Heidrick & Struggles Inc., September 22, 2024.

Darren Woods, Chairman and Chief Executive Officer, Exxon Mobil Corporation, August 2, 2024.

AWARE

Chris Wright, United States Secretary of Energy, and former Chairman and Chief Executive Officer, Liberty Energy, July 25, 2024.

Studies

Achieving Greater Agility, Forbes Insight, The Project Management Institute, 2017.

"Aligning Culture with the Bottom Line: How Companies Can Accelerate Progress," By Rose Gailey, Ian Johnston, and Andrew LeSeuer, Heidrick & Struggles, 2021.

"Bringing Your Organization up to Speed," Alice Breeden, Becky Friend, T. A. Mitchell, Heidrick & Struggles, quoting James Manyika et al., in their piece, *Jobs Lost, Jobs Gained; What the Future of Work Will Mean for Jobs, Skills and Wages*, McKinsey Global Institute, November 2017.

"Inclusive Leadership: Finding the Right Balance," by Paul Gibson, Karen Rosa West, PhD, and Ryan Pastrovich, Heidrick & Struggles, 2020.

Insight: Why We're Not as Self-Aware as We Think, and How Seeing Ourselves Clearly Helps Us Succeed at Work and in Life, by Tasha Eurich, (Crown Business, 2017). Dr. Tasha Eurich, an organizational psychologist, discovered that 95 percent of people think they are self-aware, but only about 15 percent really are.

Leadership and Dark-Side Derailers: The Risks and Rewards of Extreme Personalities, by Dr. Robert Kaiser, Oxford Academic, May 2022.

"Putting META into Action," by Steven Krupp, Heidrick & Struggles. This study provides more on Heidrick & Struggles's META (mobilize, execute, and transform with agility) framework for leadership. This article is drawn from posts previously published on LinkedIn. The thinking is adapted from Colin Price and Sharon Toye's book, *Accelerating Performance: How Organizations Can Mobilize, Execute, and Transform with Agility* (Wiley & Sons, January 2017).

"Research: We're Not Very Self-Aware, Especially at Work," by Erich C. Dierdorff and Robert S. Rubin, *Harvard Business Review*, March 12, 2015.

"Route to the Top: Today's CEO: The Growing Importance of Character, Learning and Leading in a Contested World," principally written by Jeremy Hanson, contributions from Les Csorba, Marie-Hélène De Coster, Jonathan McBride, and Atif Sheikh, Heidrick & Struggles, February 28, 2024.

"Too Aware to Fail," Karen West, PhD, and Kate Malter McLean, PhD, Heidrick & Struggles Digital Labs, August 1, 2024. A Heidrick & Struggles analysis of the assessments of 2,268 executives conducted February 14 to June 2, 2024 found that only 13 percent of leaders are truly self-aware. The survey found that leaders who are self-aware have strengths in four critical areas: reflectiveness, openness, inquisitiveness, and objectivity. Additionally, our research of 75,000 leaders and 3,500 teams highlights how rare self-awareness is. It also allowed us to pinpoint specific strengths, development areas, and potential derailers for individual leaders, teams, and organizations. In the course of this work, we identified

Studies

forty-four major blind spots that may cause derailment and, at times, destruction.

"Turning Capabilities into Superpowers," Drawing on data from thousands of executive assessments at Heidrick & Struggles, this research also suggests some basic steps that turn capabilities and strengths into something even greater, accelerating performance all around. A review of our data was conducted by Dr. Kate Malter McLean, Director of Psychology, Product Research & Science, Heidrick & Struggles Digital Labs, July 23, 2024.

"Understanding Self-Other Agreement: A Look at Rater and Ratee Characteristics, Context, and Outcomes," *Personnel Psychology, The Study of People at Work*, Cheri Ostroff, Leanne E. Atwater, Barbara J. Feinberg. , July 30, 2017. This study of over 3,600 leaders found that the higher up you go, the more you're likely to overestimate your abilities—particularly in areas like empathy, trustworthiness, and emotional self-awareness.

"Vulnerability in Leadership: The Power of the Courage to Descend," by Stephanie O. Lopez, Seattle Pacific University, January 1, 2018. Lopez surveyed 2,517 individuals in the study's online leadership development system, with 296 specifically meeting the strict criteria of being a formal leader in their organizations and who had completed all assessments.

"We Are Different," Heidrick & Struggles, November 5, 2024. Heidrick & Struggles surveyed more than 250 CEOs and directors of US-based companies on how they are handling leadership in today's increasingly polarized world. The study revealed broad agreement on one key point: "Leaders must be self-aware to lead effectively in divisive settings."

"What Accelerating Teams Do Better," T. A. Mitchell and Becky Friend, Heidrick & Struggles, 2021.

"When Ethical Leader Behavior Breaks Bad: How Ethical Behavior Can Turn Abusive via Ego Depletion and Moral Licensing," conducted by researchers at Michigan State University, published in the *Journal of Applied Psychology*, 2016.

"YouGov Survey on People-Pleasing." In one survey of 1,000 Americans, half self-identified as people-pleasers. Women (56 percent) are more likely than men (42 percent) to see themselves this way. And by far most Americans recognize some of this tendency in themselves. YouGov Poll, Jamie Ballard, Data Journalist, August 22, 2022.

The Author

Les T. Csorba is an author, CEO coach, and partner at Heidrick & Struggles, the world's premier executive search and leadership advisory firm. He previously served as Special Assistant to the President in the White House under George H. W. Bush, working in Presidential Personnel, and is a former member of the President's Commission on White House Fellowships. Les is also the author of *Trust: The One Thing That Makes or Breaks a Leader* (Thomas Nelson Business, 2004). He also serves on the Board of Directors of the Bettering Human Lives Foundation, which provides clean cooking fuel to families in extreme poverty in Africa. A graduate of the University of California, Davis, Les is the son of 1956 Hungarian refugees. He and his wife, Anne, have been married for thirty-eight years and have four children and seven grandchildren. They make their home in Houston, Texas.

For more information, visit www.lescsorba.com.

Notes

Preface

1. James Baker III, former United States Secretary of State, email correspondence to the author, December 17, 2024.
2. Epictetus, Enchiridion, trans. Elizabeth Carter, in *The Discourses of Epictetus with the Enchiridion and Fragments* (London: George Bell and Sons, 1890), 33.
3. Bill Murphy Jr., "With 11 Short Words, Elon Musk Just Showed a Tiny Glimpse of Self-Awareness and Humility. (This Needs to Stop Right Now)," June 15, 2019, https://www.inc.com/bill-murphy-jr/with-11-short-words-elon-musk-just-showed-a-tiny-glimpse-of-self-awareness-humility-this-needs-to-stop-right-now.html.
4. Elon Musk, remarks at Tesla Investor Day, *Markets Insider*, March 1, 2023, https://markets.businessinsider.com/news/stocks/elon-musk-warren-buffett-tesla-spacex-munger-optimism-insurance-billionaires-2023-5.
5. Ruth Umoh, "Warren Buffet Calls This Trait His 'Clear Weak Point,'" *CNBC*, June 29, 2018, https://www.cnbc.com/2018/06/28/heres-warren-buffetts-biggest-weakness.html#:~:text=%E2%80%9CA%20clear%20weak%20point%20of,means%20we%5D%20miss%20something.%E2%80%9D.
6. David Brooks, *The Road to Character* (Random House, 2015), 61.
7. W. E. Buffett, (2024), "2023 Annual Letter to Berkshire Hathaway Shareholders. Berkshire Hathaway Inc.," retrieved from https://www.berkshirehathaway.com/letters/2023ltr.pdf.
8. Marcus Tullius Cicero, *De Officiis*, translated by Walter Miller, (Harvard University Press, 1913), Book I, Section 22.

ONE: Subprime Leadership

1. Lilah Raptopoulos, "Weathering the Financial Crisis: How Seven Lives Were Changed," *Financial Times*, September 11, 2018, https://ig.ft.com/financial-crisis-voices/.
2. Ibid.
3. "London suicide connects Lehman lesson missed by Hong Kong woman," *The Sydney Morning Herald*, published on September 10, 2009.
4. Landon Thomas, Jr., "Losses Mount, Fears Overwhelm, and a Life-Ending Decision Is Made," *The New York Times*, November 6, 2008.

Notes

5. Ernest Hemingway, *A Farewell to Arms* (Scribner, 1997), 226.
6. Peggy Noonan, "Trump and the Rise of the Unprotected," *The Wall Street Journal*, February 25, 2016, https://www.wsj.com/articles/trump-and-the-rise-of-the-unprotected-1456448550.
7. Thomas Jr., "Losses Mount, Fears Overwhelm, and a Life-Ending Decision Is Made."
8. Bill George, "A Crisis of Leadership," The Wall Street Journal, October 29, 2009, https://www.wsj.com/articles/SB10001424052748703363704574503452362482292.
9. Nick Gass, "Lehman Brothers Ex-CEO Blames Everyone Else for Financial Crisis," *Politico*, May 28, 2015, https://www.politico.com/story/2015/05/richard-dick-fuld-lehman-brothers-financial-crisis-118374.
10. Milton Friedman, "A Friedman Doctrine: The Social Responsibility of Business is to Increase Its Profits," *New York Times Magazine*, September 13, 1970.
11. Charlie Munger, remarks at the Daily Journal Corporation Annual Meeting, 2022, quoted in Observer, "Charlie Munger's Top 10 Quotes On Life, Business and Morality," November 29, 2023.
12. Thomas Barrabi, "'Big Short' Investor Michael Burry Blames SVB Crisis on 'Hubris and Greed,'" New York Post, March 13, 2023, https://nypost.com/2023/03/13/investor-michael-burry-blames-svb-crisis-on-hubris-and-greed/.
13. Triston Bone, "Silicon Valley's Hubris Nearly Ruined the US Economy," *Fortune*, Triston Bone, March 18, 2023.
14. Proverbs 27:17 Berean Standard Bible.
15. Margaret Heffernan, *Willful Blindness* (Walker, 2011).
16. Margaret Heffernan, "The Three Problems of Power," *Medium*, January 12, 2021, https://m-heffernan.medium.com/three-problems-of-power-471deb905fb.
17. Jamie Dimon, board chairman and CEO of JPMorgan Chase & Co., interview with the author, July 27, 2024.
18. Ibid.
19. Tasha Eurich, *Insight: The Surprising Truth About How Others See Us, How We See Ourselves, and Why the Answers Matter More Than We Think*, (Crown Business, 2017).
20. Karen West, PhD, and Kate Walter McLean, PhD, "Too Aware to Fail," Heidrick & Struggles Digital Labs, August 1, 2024. This Heidrick & Struggles analysis of the assessments of 2,268 executives conducted February 14 to June 2, 2024 found that only 13 percent of leaders are truly self-aware. The survey found that leaders who are self-aware have strengths in four critical areas: reflectiveness, openness, inquisitiveness, and objectivity. Additionally, our research of 75,000 leaders and 3,500 teams highlights how rare self-awareness is. It also allowed us to pinpoint specific strengths, development areas, and potential derailers for individual leaders, teams, and organizations. In the course of this work, we identified forty-four major blind spots that may cause derailment and, at times, destruction. For more on our META (mobilize, execute, and transform with agility) framework for leadership and our ongoing work and research, see Steven Krupp, "Putting META into Action," Heidrick & Struggles, https://www.heidrick.com/en/insights/leadership-development/putting-meta-into-action. This study draws on posts previously published on LinkedIn. The thinking is adapted from Colin Price and Sharon Toye's book, *Accelerating Performance: How Organizations Can Mobilize, Execute, and Transform with Agility* (Wiley & Sons, January 2017).
21. Proverbs 16:32, paraphrased.

NOTES

TWO: The Other Man in Me

1. Fyodor Dostoevsky, *The Brothers Karamazov*, translated by Richard Pevear and Larissa Volokhonsky (Farrar, Straus, and Giroux, 2002), 292.
2. Isaiah 51:1, THE VOICE.
3. Brittany Wong, "The Most Damaging Things to Say to a People-Pleaser," HuffPost, January 26, 202 , https://www.huffpost.com/entry/most-damaging-things-you-can-say-to-people-pleaser_l_65b035f8e4b0f55c6e314ccb.
4. Jamie Ballard, "Women Are More Likely Than Men to Say They're a People-Pleaser, and Many Dislike Being Seen as One," YouGov, August 22, 2022, https://today.yougov.com/society/articles/43498-women-more-likely-men-people-pleasing-poll.
5. *Everybody Loves Raymond*, season 7, episode 13, "Somebody Hates Raymond," directed by Jerry Zaks, aired January 27, 2003, on CBS, https://www.imdb.com/title/tt0574157/.
6. Brené Brown, *Dare to Lead: Brave Work, Tough Conversations, Whole Hearts* (Random House, 2018), 48.
7. Ibid.

THREE: The Other Leader in You

1. Robert Louis Stevenson, *The Strange Case of Dr. Jekyll and Mr. Hyde* (Longmans, Green & Co., 1886), 107.
2. Ibid.
3. Robert Kaiser, *Leadership and Dark-Side Derailers: The Risks and Rewards of Extreme Personalities* (Oxford Academic, 2022), 399.
4. Ibid.
5. Ibid.
6. Szu-Han Joanna Lin, et al., "When Ethical Leader Behavior Breaks Bad: How Ethical Behavior Can Turn Abusive via Ego Depletion and Moral Licensing," *Journal of Applied Psychology* 101, no. 6 (2016): 815–30, https://www.doi.10.1037/apl0000098.
7. Joseph B. Soloveitchik, *The Lonely Man of Faith* (Doubleday, 1965), 10.
8. Edgar H. Schein, *Humble Inquiry: The Gentle Art of Asking Instead of Telling* (Berrett-Koehler Publishers, 2013), 53–54.
9. Schein, *Humble Inquiry*, 55.
10. David Brooks, *The Road to Character* (Random House, 2015), 12.
11. Soloveitchik, *The Lonely Man of Faith*, 64.
12. Charlie Munger, remarks at the Daily Journal Corporation Annual Meeting, 2016, quoted in Noah Buhayar, "Buffett's Empty Calendar Offers Billionaire Path to Bigger Ideas," *Bloomberg*, February 26, 2016, https://www.bloomberg.com/news/articles/2016-02-26/buffett-s-empty-calendar-offers-billionaire-path-to-bigger-ideas.
13. Ecclesiastes 3:7, ESV.
14. Ryan Holiday, *Stillness is the Key* (Portfolio, 2019), 215.
15. Anthony de Mello, *Awareness: The Perils and Opportunities of Reality* (Image, 1992), 5.
16. Fifty-five percent of all Fortune 100 Companies claim integrity as a core value. Patrick Lencioni, "Make Your Values Mean Something," *Harvard Business Review*, July 2002.

Notes

FOUR: To Find Your Blindspot

1. Lawrence G. McDonald and Patrick Robinson, *A Colossal Failure of Common Sense: The Inside Story of the Fall of Lehman Brothers* (Random House, 2009), 2.
2. Ibid.
3. Brian Wesbury (@wesbury), Twitter (now X), "Bernanke's use of QE for US Fed policy in 2008-2015, and Powell's use of it during COVID, was sold as a way to make 'the US banking system safer.,'" May 17, 2024, https://x.com/wesbury/status/1791521933604913362.
4. Margaret Heffernan, *Willful Blindness: Why We Ignore the Obvious at Our Peril* (Bloomsbury USA, 2011), 175.
5. United States of America v. Kenneth L. Lay, in the United States District Court for the Southern District of Texas, Houston Division (2006), https://www.justice.gov/sites/default/files/criminal-vns/legacy/2014/11/07/05-25-06lay.pdf.
6. A reference to the calamity of the Great Recession in what Andrew Ross Sorkin coined "Too Big to Fail."
7. Luke 6:39, KJV.
8. Gert Hofmann, *The Parable of the Blind*, translated by Christopher Middleton (Fromm International, 1989), 45.
9. Heffernan, *Willful Blindness: Why We Ignore the Obvious at Our Peril*, 201 and 222.
10. Schein, *Humble Inquiry*, 40.
11. Ibid.
12. Ken Olsen, of Digital Equipment on "Reflections of the Revolution," in an interview with Daniel Scrivner, 2003.
13. Bethany McLean, "I Can't Get Enough: The Legacy of a Fracking Billionaire Who Fed on Risk," *Yahoo Finance*, September 12, 2028.
14. Ibid.
15. Ibid.
16. Larry McDonald, *A Colossal Failure of Common Sense: The Inside of the Fall of Lehman Brothers* (Random House, 2010), quoted in Stephen Foley, "Crash of a Titan: The Inside Story of the Fall of Lehman Brothers," *The Independent*, September 7, 2009, https://www.independent.co.uk/news/business/analysis-and-features/crash-of-a-titan-the-inside-story-of-the-fall-of-lehman-brothers-1782714.html.
17. Susan Lucia Annunzio, "Five CEO Blind Spots That Put the Company at Risk," *Chief Executive*, April 2, 2024, https://chiefexecutive.net/five-ceo-blind-spots-that-put-the-company-at-risk/.
18. Maureen Farrell, "Inside the Collapse of Silicon Valley Bank," *New York Times*, March 14, 2023, https://www.nytimes.com/2023/03/14/business/silicon-valley-bank-gregory-becker.html.
19. Tasha Eurich, an organizational psychologist, discovered that 95 percent of people think they are self-aware, but only about 15 percent really are. Eurich's research on self-awareness, as outlined in her book *Insight: Why We're Not as Self-Aware as We Think, and How Seeing Ourselves Clearly Helps Us Succeed at Work and in Life* (Crown Business, 2017) and related studies identify "objective criteria" for determining self-awareness that is based on two core dimensions: (1) *Internal Self-Awareness*, which refers to how

well leaders understand their own values, passions, aspirations, reactions, and impact on others, and (2) *External Self-Awareness*, which focuses on how accurately individuals perceive the way others see them. It includes understanding how their behavior affects others, how they are perceived in social or professional contexts, and how aligned their self-perceptions are with external feedback. Such criteria can be measured through *Surveys and Self-Assessments, Feedback from Others, Alignment Between Perceptions and Reality, and Behavioral and Situational Tests*, and *Consistency over Time*. At Heidrick & Struggles, such "objective criteria" would include a thorough 360 feedback report with at least ten raters or references who work with the leader daily, including a superior, peers, and subordinates, and then annual or semi-annual 360 refreshment assessments.

20. Tasha Eurich, *Insight: The Surprising Truth About How Others See Us, How We See Ourselves, and Why the Answers Matter More Than We Think*, (Crown Business, 2017), 5.
21. Jonathan Haidt, *The Anxious Generation: How the Great Rewiring of Childhood Is Causing an Epidemic of Mental Illness* (Penguin Press, 2024), 112–115.
22. Zoe Williams, "Me! Me! Me! Are We Living Through a Narcissism Epidemic?" *The Guardian*, March 2, 201 , https://www.theguardian.com/lifeandstyle/2016/mar/02/narcissism-epidemic-self-obsession-attention-seeking-oversharing.
23. Tasha Eurich, Insight: *Why We're Not as Self-Aware as We Think, and How Seeing Ourselves Clearly Helps Us Succeed at Work and in Life* (Crown Business, 2017), 35.
24. General David Petraeus, in email correspondence with the author, December 10, 2024. General Petraeus is a United States Army (Ret.), Partner, KKR; Chairman, KKR Global Institute; and author of *Conflict: The Evolution of Warfare from 1945 to Gaza* (Harper, 2024).

FIVE: The Leader with Backbone

1. Jim Collins, "The 10 Greatest CEOs of All Time," *Fortune*, July 21, 2003.
2. Joseph L. Badaracco Jr. and Richard R. Ellsworth, *Leadership, and the Quest for Integrity* (Harvard Business School Press, 1989), 76–77; 82.
3. John Amaechi OBE and Nick Studer, "5 Big-Win Ways to Be Brave in the Workplace," Oliver Wyman, April 2023, https://www.oliverwyman.com/our-expertise/insights/2023/apr/john-amaechi-workplace-bravery-wins-and-tips.html.
4. Stephanie O. Lopez, "Vulnerability in Leadership: The Power of the Courage to Descend" (PhD diss., Seattle Pacific University, 2018). A total of 2,517 individuals were surveyed in the study's online leadership development system with 296 specifically meeting the strict criteria of being a formal leader in their organizations and who had completed all assessments.
5. "George + West: A Quest for Truth," Respect and Rebellion, accessed March 7, 2025, https://respectandrebellion.com/stories/west-george/.
6. Robert George and Cornel West, *Truth Matters: A Dialogue on Fruitful Disagreement in an Age of Division* (Simon & Schuster, 2025).
7. Edmund Morris, *The Rise of Theodore Roosevelt* (Coward, McCann & Geoghegan, 1979), 610
8. Herman Melville, *Moby-Dick* (Modern Library, 1926), 347–348.
9. Alex Jackson not only returned to his role at the firm but was then promoted to partner in December of 2024.
10. Ann Fox, CEO of Nine Energy Services, in an interview with the author, September 12, 2024.

NOTES

11. General David Petraeus, in email correspondence with the author, December 11, 2024.
12. Matthew 7:3, ESV.
13. Ariel Zilber, "MillerKnoll CEO Scolds Workers Complaining About Bonuses—Although She Made $1.2 Million in Extra Compensation Last Year," *New York Post*, April 18, 2023, https://nypost.com/2023/04/18/millerknoll-ceo-andi-owen-scolds-workers-over-bonus-complaints/.
14. Joan Halifax, *Standing at the Edge: Finding Freedom Where Fear and Courage Meet* (Flatiron Books, 2018).
15. Brené Brown, "Dare to Lead Hub: Developing Brave Leaders and Courageous Cultures," accessed March 7, 2025, https://brenebrown.com/hubs/dare-to-lead/.
16. Michael Lewis, *The Big Short: Inside the Doomsday Machine* (W. W. Norton & Company, 2010), 32.
17. Ibid.

SIX: Your Superpower

1. Jeremiah 29:11, NIV.
2. Arthur Brooks, Parker Gilbert Montgomery Professor of the Practice of Public Leadership, Harvard Kennedy School, in email correspondence with the author, July 29, 2024.
3. Charles Dickens, *A Christmas Carol* (Chapman & Hall, 1843).
4. Elon Musk, "Interview with Elon Musk on Chinese Television (2015)," November 30, 2015, https://elon-musk-interviews.com/2021/03/15/interview-with-elon-musk-on-chinese-television-2015-english/.
5. Chris Wright, United States Secretary of Energy and former chairman and CEO of Liberty Energy, interview with the author, Denver, Colorado, July 26, 2024.
6. Claire O'Connor, "Starbucks Billionaire Howard Schultz to Oprah: It's OK for Men to Cry (Even CEOs)," *Forbes*, December 4, 2013, https://www.forbes.com/sites/clareoconnor/2013/12/04/starbucks-billionaire-howard-schultz-to-oprah-its-ok-for-men-to-cry-even-ceos/.
7. John Krenicki, vice Chairman of Clayton, Dubilier & Rice LLC, interview with the author, July 23, 2024.
8. Governor Jared Polis, interview with CNN's Dana Bash, July 22, 2024.
9. Kate Malter McLean, PhD, is the Director of Psychology, Product Research & Science, Heidrick & Struggles Digital Labs.
10. Benjamin Franklin, *Poor Richard's Almanack*, October, 1750.
11. Steve Jobs, "You've got to find what you love," commencement address, Stanford University, June 12, 2005, https://news.stanford.edu/stories/2005/06/youve-got-find-love-jobs-says.
12. Chase Untermeyer, former ambassador of the United States to Qatar, interview with the author, August 21, 2024.
13. Charlie Munger, "Charlie Munger on How Warren Buffett and Berkshire Hathaway Succeeded," *Value Investing World*, November 2013, https://www.valueinvestingworld.com/2013/11/charlie-munger-on-how-warren-buffett.html.:contentReference{index=26}.

14. For more on J. D. Rockefeller's unrelenting self-belief and love for work, see G. Ng, *The 38 Letters from J. D. Rockefeller to His Son: Perspectives, Ideology, and Wisdom*, ed. M. Tan (independently published, 2021).
15. Ron Chernow, *Titan: The Life of John D. Rockefeller, Sr.* (Random House, 1998), 90.
16. Elaine Chao, interview with the author, July 19, 2024.
17. Susanna Wu-Pong Calvert, "Turning Your Strengths into Superpowers," *Psychology Today*, November 29, 2022, https://www.psychologytoday.com/us/blog/the-heart-healing/202211/turning-your-strengths-superpowers#:~:text=In%20addition%20to%20discovering%20hidden,to%20you%20through%20inner%20work.
18. Will Durant, *The Story of Philosophy: The Lives and Opinions of the World's Greatest Philosophers* (Simon & Schuster, 1926), 87.
19. Friedrich Nietzsche, *Beyond Good and Evil: Prelude to a Philosophy of the Future*, trans. Walter Kaufmann (Vintage Books, 1989), 201.
20. Gareth Hughes, "The Personality Trait That Was Steve Jobs' Superpower: This Is a Trait You Can Adopt Too," *Medium*, April 1, 2024, https://medium.com/change-your-mind/the-personality-trait-that-was-steve-jobs-superpower-24f980e07b0d#:~:text=He%20freely%20admitted%20himself%20that,his%20other%20gifts%20were%20leveraged.

SEVEN: The Captain of Your Soul

1. Alfred Bernhard Nobel, *Full Text of Alfred Nobel's Will*, November 27, 1895, NobelPrize.org, https://www.nobelprize.org/alfred-nobel/full-text-of-alfred-nobels-will-2/.
2. John F. Kennedy, "Address in the Assembly Hall at the Paulskirche in Frankfurt," June 25, 1963, in *Public Papers of the Presidents of the United States: John F. Kennedy*, 1963 (Washington, D.C.: U.S. Government Printing Office, 1964), 519.
3. Nassim Nicholas Taleb, *The Bed of Procrustes: Philosophical and Practical Aphorisms* (Random House, 2010), 45.
4. Michael Liedtke, "Delta Sues Cybersecurity Firm CrowdStrike Over Botched Update That Led to Global Tech Outage," *Associated Press*, October 2, 2024, https://apnews.com/article/43bb230d2edf235bb9f7928c4279fec2.
5. Alice Breeden et al., "Bringing Your Organization up to Speed," Heidrick & Struggles, quoting James Manyika et al., *Jobs Lost, Jobs Gained: What the Future of Work Will Mean for Jobs, Skills and Wages*, McKinsey Global Institute, November 28, 2017, https://www.mckinsey.com/featured-insights/future-of-work/jobs-lost-jobs-gained-what-the-future-of-work-will-mean-for-jobs-skills-and-wages.
6. *Achieving Greater Agility: The Essential Influence of the C-Suite*, Forbes Insight, The Project Management Institute, 2017, https://www.pmi.org/-/media/pmi/documents/public/pdf/learning/thought-leadership/achieving-greater-agility-series/essential-influence-c-suite.pdf?sc_lang_temp=en.
7. Jerome Powell, "Monetary Policy in an Uncertain Economy," speech delivered at the Jackson Hole Economic Symposium, August 25, 2023.
8. "Potential" refers to a set of psychometric and cognitive properties that form the basis for what might prompt or enable agile behaviors.
9. For more on Heidrick & Struggles Agile Leadership Potential Methodology, see Agile Leader Potential (ALP).

NOTES

10. Kate Malter McLean, PhD, HeidrickLabs, Director of Psychology, Product Research & Science, HLabs, March 7, 2025.
11. Based on Wil VanLoh's LAQ 360 assessment report on March 24, 2022.
12. Wil VanLoh, founder and CEO of Quantum Capital Group, interview with the author July 17, 2024.
13. "Powerful, Eye-Opening Quotes by Elon Musk," *Medium*, August 5, 2023, https://medium.com/r-blogs/powerful-eye-opening-quotes-by-elon-musk-892c4e039196.
14. Jim Collins, "The 10 Greatest CEOs of All Time," *Fortune*, July 21, 2003, https://www.jimcollins.com/article_topics/articles/10-greatest.html.
15. Matthew J.C. Partridge, "The Measure of Intelligence Is the Ability to Change – Albert Einstein," *Medium*, March 18, 2021, https://matthewjcpartridge.medium.com/the-measure-of-intelligence-is-the-ability-to-change-albert-einstein-f116ad70eeb5.
16. Jamie Dimon, 2024 Annual Letter to JPMorgan Chase Shareholders, April 8, 2024.
17. Sam Gustin, "Chesapeake Energy Bows to Raider Carl Icahn, Will Shake up Board," *Time Magazine*, June 4, 2012, https://business.time.com/2012/06/04/chesapeake-energy-bows-to-raider-carl-icahn-will-shake-up-board/.
18. Emily Moser, "After Past Excesses, CEO Lawler Reshapes Chesapeake," *Hart Energy*, April 23, 2015, https://www.hartenergy.com/exclusives/after-past-excesses-ceo-lawler-reshapes-chesapeake-26818.
19. Robert Doug Lawler, president and CEO of Continental Resources, interview with the author, August 30, 2024.
20. Ibid.
21. Jack Hough, "How Exxon Mobil Envisions Its Environmental Role," *Barron's*, July 9, 2022, https://www.barrons.com/articles/exxon-mobil-darren-woods-51657330334.
22. Darren Woods, chairman and CEO of Exxon Mobil Corporation, interview with the author, August 2, 2024.
23. "CEOs of the Year," *Barrons*, 2022 and 2024.
24. Jack Hough, "Darren Woods' Investments Have Given Exxon Mobil a Financial Edge," *Barron's*, June 21, 2024, https://www.barrons.com/articles/exxon-mobil-darren-woods-top-ceo-stock-price-eaa58346.
25. Larry Kellner, former CEO of Continental Airlines, former board chairman of Boeing Corporation, and former lead director of the Marriott Corporation, correspondence with the author, October 17, 2024.

EIGHT: The Fellowship of a Team

1. T. A. Mitchell and Becky Friend, "What Accelerating Teams Do Better," Heidrick & Struggles, 2021, https://www.heidrick.com/en/insights/team-effectiveness/what_accelerating_teams_do_better.
2. John Wooden and Jay Carty, *Coach Wooden One-On-One* (Revell, 2009), 65.
3. "The Fight," *The Office*, season 2, episode 6, directed by Ken Kwapis, written by Gene Stupnitsky and Lee Eisenberg, aired November 1, 2005, on NBC.
4. "The Return," *The Office*, season 3, episode 14, directed by Greg Daniels, written by Michael Schur, aired January 18, 2007, on NBC.

Notes

5. Gustavo Razzetti, "The Power of Self-Awareness: How to Build Successful Teams," July 5, 2018, *Fearless Culture*, https://www.fearlessculture.design/blog-posts/the-power-of-self-awareness-how-to-build-successful-teams.
6. Erich C. Dierdorff and Robert S. Rubin, "Research: We're Not Very Self-Aware, Especially at Work," *Harvard Business Review*, March 12, 2015, https://hbr.org/2015/03/research-were-not-very-self-aware-especially-at-work.
7. Breeden, Hogan, and Mitchell, "What Accelerating Teams Do Better."
8. Ibid.
9. "The Distillation of Phil Jackson" is an article and video by Sean DeLaney, published on January 31, 2022, on whatgotyouthere.com and YouTube.
10. Schein, *Humble Inquiry*, 53.
11. Schein, *Humble Inquiry*, 55.
12. Ed Schein and Peter Schein, "Culture Shift with Ed and Peter Schein," interview by Michael Canning, Duke Corporate Education, December 2020.
13. Ibid.
14. Ibid.
15. Edgar Schein, *Humble Inquiry*, 54.
16. Margaret Heffernan, "Three Problems of Power: Distance and Dehumanization," *Medium*, accessed March 14, 2025, https://m-heffernan.medium.com/three-problems-of-power-distance-and-dehumanization-1ecee4a1f113.
17. Heffernan, "Three Problems of Power."
18. James R. Meindl, S. B. Ehrlich, and J. M. Dukerich, "The Romance of Leadership," *Administrative Science Quarterly* 30, no. 1 (1985): 78–102.
19. Henry Mintzberg, *Managing* (Berrett-Koehler Publishers, 2009), 235. Mintzberg, Managing, 222 (as quoted in a piece by Colleen Sharen, "Leadership is Over-Rated," WordPress.com, October 31, 2011.
20. Jeffrey Miller, chairman and CEO of Halliburton, interview with the author, December 14, 2024.
21. Don Higginbotham, George Washington and George Marshall: "Some Reflections on the American Military Tradition," *The Washington Papers*, accessed March 14, 2025, https://washingtonpapers.org/resources/articles/george-washington-and-george-marshall/.
22. Edgar F. Puryear Jr., Nineteen Stars: *A Study in Military Character and Leadership* (Presidio Press, 1971), 289.
23. Jeff Hildebrand, founder, chairman, and CEO of Hilcorp Energy Company, interview with the author, August 30, 2024.
24. Exxon Mobil Corporation, 2024 *Advancing Climate Solutions Progress Report* (Irving, TX: Exxon Mobil Corporation, 2024), 5, https://corporate.exxonmobil.com/-/media/global/files/sustainability-report/publication/2024-advancing-climate-solutions-progress-report.pdf.
25. Hildebrand, interview with the author.
26. Ibid.
27. Chris Wright, United States Secretary of Energy and former chairman and CEO of Liberty Energy, interview with the author, Denver, Colorado, July 25, 2024.

Notes

28. James West, a senior managing director at investment firm Evercore ISI, quoted in Liz Hampton, "Can Liberty Oil Maverick's Corporate Culture Survive the U.S. Shale Bust?" *Reuters,* October 29, 2020, https://www.reuters.com/article/business/can-liberty-oil-mavericks-corporate-culture-survive-the-us-shale-bust-idUSKBN27D2SU/.
29. Louisa May Alcott, *Little Women,* (Roberts Brothers, 1869).
30. "5 Examples of Amazing Teamwork," *All One Health,* January 30, 2024, https://allonehealth.com/5-examples-of-amazing-teamwork/.
31. Dora Mekouar, "This is America's Best-Selling Vehicle for 42 Years Running," *Voice of America,* April 2, 2024, https://www.voanews.com/a/7549251.html.
32. Rose Gailey, et al., "Aligning Culture with the Bottom Line: How Companies Can Accelerate Progress," Heidrick & Struggles Inc., 2021, https://www.heidrick.com/en/insights/culture-shaping/aligning-culture-with-the-bottom-line-how-companies-can-accelerate-progress.
33. Tracy Wolstencroft, former CEO and chairman of Heidrick & Struggles, Senior Advisor, TPG Rise Climate LP, interview with the author, September 22, 2024.
34. Steve Job's Mission Statement for Apple was, "To make a contribution to the world by making tools for the mind that advance humankind," to which Jobs said, "Wow; that's something I would get out of bed in the morning for." Jim Schleckser, "Apple's Boring Mission Statement and What We Can Learn From It," Inc., August 16, 2016.

NINE: The Invisible Crown

1. C. S. Lewis, *Mere Christianity* (HarperCollins, 2001), 122.
2. Michael Maccoby, "Narcissistic Leaders: The Incredible Pros, the Inevitable Cons," *HBR Magazine,* January 2004, https://hbr.org/2004/01/narcissistic-leaders-the-incredible-pros-the-inevitable-cons.
3. Maccoby, "Narcissistic Leaders."
4. Timothy Keller, *The Freedom of Self-Forgetfulness: The Path to True Christian Joy* (10Publishing, 2012).
5. Keller, *The Freedom of Self-Forgetfulness,* 21.
6. 1 Corinthians 4:3–4, ESV.
7. Alan Armstrong, president and CEO of Williams Companies, interview with the author, August 2, 2024.
8. Jim Collins, *Good to Great: Why Some Companies Make the Leap . . . and Others Don't* (HarperCollins, 2001). Collins found that the Level 5 leaders "never wanted to become larger-than-life heroes. They were ordinary people quietly producing extraordinary results. . . . It is important to grasp that Level 5 leadership is not just about humility and modesty. It is equally about ferocious resolve, an almost stoic determination to do whatever needs to be done to make the company great."
9. Jeremy Hanson, et al., "Route to the Top: Today's CEO: The Growing Importance of Character, Learning and Leading in a Contested World," Heidrick & Struggles, February 28, 2024, https://www.heidrick.com/en/insights/chief-executive-officer/todays-ceo-the-growing-importance-of-character-learning-and-leading-in-a-contested-world.
10. Alan Murray and Ellen McGirt, "Occidental's Vicki Hollub on What Future CEOs

Notes

Need to Know Before Moving into the C-suite," *Leadership Next*, podcast, Fortune, April 5, 2023, https://fortune.com/2023/04/05/occidental-petroleum-vicki-hollub-what-future-ceos-need-to-know/.

11. Rob Nielsen and Jennifer Marrone, "Humility: Our Current Understanding of the Construct and Its Role in Organizations," *International Journal of Management Reviews* 20, no. 4 (2018): 805–24, https://doi.org/10.1111/ijmr.12160.

12. Megan K. Johnson, Wade C. Rowatt, and Leo Petrini, "A New Trait on the Market: Honesty–Humility as a Unique Predictor of Job Performance Ratings," *Personality and Individual Differences* 50, no. 6 (2011): 857–62, https://doi.org/10.1016/j.paid.2011.01.011.

13. Chris Wright, interview with author, July 26, 2024.

14. Steven Reinemund, former chairman and CEO of PepsiCo, from an interview with the author for Trust: *The One Thing that Makes or Breaks a Leader*, 2004.

15. Thomas Csorba, "I Want," *The Thomas Csorba Album*, September 25, 2020.

16. C. S. Lewis, *Mere Christianity* (HarperOne, 2001), 128.

17. Phil Jackson and Hugh Delehanty, *Eleven Rings: The Soul of Success* (Penguin Press, 2013), 12.

18. Celeste Smith, "Retired PepsiCo CEO: Leadership 'Starts with Understanding Yourself,'" *Charlotte Observer*, December 17, 2015 https://www.charlotteobserver.com/news/business/article50299410.html.

19. Fyodor Dostoevsky, *Notes from Underground*, translated by Boris Jakim (Eerdmans Publishing Company, 2009) 87.

20. Clay Williams, chairman and CEO of NOV Inc., interview with the author, September 12, 2024.

21. *The Conan O'Brien Show*, "Everything is Amazing and Nobody Is Happy," July 20, 2011.

22. Louie Giglio has often used this phrase "good shrinking feeling" in his talks and sermons to describe the difference between how big God and the universe is and how tiny we really are. https://louiegiglio.com/.

23. James 4:14, NIV.

TEN: Return to the Soil

1. Luke 12:48, ESV.
2. Thomas Paine, *The American Crisis*, No. 13, April 19, 1783
3. Fyodor Dostoevsky, *Demons*, translated by Richard Pevear and Larissa Volokhonsky (Vintage Classics, 1994), 123.
4. Fyodor Dostoevsky, *Notes from Underground*, trans. Richard Pevear and Larissa Volokhonsky (Vintage Classics, 1993).
5. Warren Buffett, quoted in Alice Schroeder, *The Snowball: Warren Buffett and the Business of Life* (Bantam Books, 2008), 133.
6. Proverbs 13:20, KJV.
7. Fyodor Dostoevsky, *The Brothers Karamazov*, translated by Richard Pevear and Larissa Volokhonsky (Farrar, Straus and Giroux, 1990), 69.

8. David Brooks, *How to Know a Person: The Art of Seeing Others Deeply and Being Deeply Seen* (Random House, 2023), 37.
9. Brooks, *How to Know a Person*, 9.
10. Ibid.
11. Frank Tsuru, cofounder and CEO of Momentum Midstream, interview with the author, September 2, 2024.
12. Proverbs 22:1, KJV.
13. Cheryl Ursin, "Brookwood Community: Where There's Opportunity for All," *The Buzz Magazines*, November 1, 2014, https://thebuzzmagazines.com/articles/2023/02/brookwood-story.
14. Timothy Leach, former chairman and CEO of Concho Resources and current Director of ConocoPhillips, interview with the author, November 22, 2024.
15. Adam Smith, *The Theory of Moral Sentiments*, ed. D. D. Raphael and A. L. Macfie (Indianapolis: Liberty Fund, 1982), 25.
16. H. Norman Schwarzkopf, quoted in Rod J. Rohrich, "Taking Charge and Doing the Right Thing," *Plastic and Reconstructive Surgery* 109, no. 5 (April 15, 2002): 1597.

ELEVEN: Making Others Feel Seen

1. Adam Waytz, "The Limits of Empathy," *Harvard Business Review*, January–February 2016.
2. David Brooks, *How to Know a Person: The Art of Seeing Others Deeply and Being Deeply Seen* (Random House, 2023).
3. Ibid.
4. Waytz, "The Limits of Empathy."
5. Matthew 9:35–38, ESV.
6. Jay Brown, former president and CEO of Crown Castle International Corp. and current CEO of David Weekley Homes, interview with the author, September 13, 2024.
7. Paul Gibson, et al., "Inclusive Leadership: Finding the Right Balance," Heidrick & Struggles., 2020, https://www.heidrick.com/en/insights/diversity-inclusion/inclusive-leadership-finding-the-right-balance.
8. David Brooks, in Katie Couric, "Katie Explores Empathy, Curiosity, and Vulnerability with David Brooks," Katie Couric Media, November 2, 202 , https://katiecouric.com/podcast/next-question/katie-explores-empathy-curiosity-and-vulnerability-with-david-brooks/.
9. Hebrews 13:3, KJV.
10. Sterry Butcher, "He Thought He Knew Horses. Then He Learned to Really Listen," *The New York Times*, November 18, 2024, https://www.nytimes.com/2024/11/12/magazine/warwick-schiller-horses.html.
11. Ibid.
12. BBC Archive, "1988: That's Life: Sir Nicholas Winton," Facebook, 2019, https://www.facebook.com/BBCArchive/videos/1988-thats-life-sir-nicholas-winton/524868598192459/.
13. Barbara Winton, *One Life: The True Story of Sir Nicholas Winton*, (Robinson, 2014).

NOTES

TWELVE: From "Great" to Good

1. Peter F. Drucker, *The Essential Drucker: The Best of Sixty Years of Peter Drucker's Essential Writings on Management* (HarperCollins, 2001), 45.
2. Jim Collins, audio commentary, 2017 https://www.jimcollins.com/media_topics/ItReallyMatters.html.
3. Jim Collins, author of *Good to Great*, interview with the author.
4. Albert Camus, "The Absurd Man," in *The Myth of Sisyphus and Other Essays*, trans. Justin O'Brien (Vintage International, 1991), 66.
5. Margaret Heffernan, "Books that shook the business world: Good to Great by Jim Collins," *The Conversation*, September 9, 2024, https://theconversation.com/books-that-shook-the-business-world-good-to-great-by-jim-collins-237049.
6. Travis Stice, chairman and CEO of Diamondback Energy, interview with the author, September 24, 2024.
7. Larry Senn, interview with the author, October 2, 2024.
8. John Christmann, CEO of APA Corporation, interview with the author, October 17, 2024.
9. "Measuring the Return on Character," *Harvard Business Review*, April 2015, https://hbr.org/2015/04/measuring-the-return-on-character.
10. Tatiana Furtseva, partner-in-charge, Heidrick & Struggles, Kyiv, Ukraine, interview with the author, August 14, 2024.
11. Cheli Nachman, partner-in-charge, Heidrick & Struggles, Tel Aviv, Israel, interview with the author, August 15, 2024.
12. Rose Gailey and Ian Johnston, "Aligning Culture with the Bottom Line: How Companies Accelerate Progress," Heidrick & Struggles, 2021, https://www.heidrick.com/en/insights/culture-shaping/aligning-culture-with-the-bottom-line-how-companies-can-accelerate-progress.
13. Gailey and Johnston, "Aligning Culture with the Bottom Line." Heidrick & Struggles's analysis of financial data on the publicly held companies responding to the survey, which was collected and anonymized by a third party and provided to Heidrick & Struggles.
14. Fred Kiel, *Return on Character: The Real Reason Leaders and Their Companies Win* (Harvard Book Review Press, 2015).
15. Kiel, *Return on Character*.
16. "Measuring the Return on Character."

THIRTEEN: Cracking the Interview Code

1. Gautum Mukunda, professor at Yale School of Management Practice of Management, Yale University, interview with the author, October 31, 2024.
2. Ibid.
3. "Nearly 4 in 10 Employers Avoid Hiring Recent College Grads in Favor of Older Workers," Intelligent.com, December 12, 2023, https://www.intelligent.com/nearly-4-in-10-employers-avoid-hiring-recent-college-grads-in-favor-of-older-workers/.
4. Ibid.

5. Jessica Stillman, "How Much Vulnerability is Too Much? Brené Brown Just Explained in 6 Words," Inc., March 5, 2021, https://www.inc.com/jessica-stillman/brene-brown-leadership-vulnerability-authenticity.html.
6. Paul Simon, "The Boxer," track 5 on *Bridge Over Troubled Water*, Columbia Records, 1970.

FOURTEEN: The Power of Your Story

1. Anton Wildgans, *Helldunkle Stunde*, 1916
2. Howard Gardner, *Leading Minds: An Anatomy of Leadership* (Basic Books, 1995).
3. John F. Kennedy, address at the University of California at Berkeley, March 23, 1962.
4. Sue Monk Kidd, *The Secret Life of Bees* (Viking Penguin, 2002), 107.
5. Warren E. Buffett, "Chairman's Letter – 1986," Berkshire Hathaway Inc., February 28, 1987.
6. 2 Corinthians 3:2, ESV.

Epilogue

1. Luke 12:24–25, ESV.
2. Luke 12:25, ESV.
3. Erma Bombeck, "At Wit's End," *Pampa Daily News*, January 7, 1975.
4. The subject of Les Csorba, *Trust: The One Thing That Makes or Breaks a Leader* (Thomas Nelson, 2004).
5. Cheri Ostroff, et al., "Understanding Self-Other Agreement: A Look at Rater and Ratee Characteristics, Context, and Outcomes," *Personnel Psychology, The Study of People at Work 57*, no. 4 (2007): 333–75, https://psycnet.apa.org/doi/10.1111/j.1744-6570.2004.tb02494.x.
6. Mukunda, interview with the author, October 21, 2024.
7. "Leading Across Boundaries and Divides," November 5, 2024, https://www.heidrick.com/en/insights/leading-across-boundaries-and-divides
8. Isaiah 51:1, ESV.
9. G. K. Chesterton, *Orthodoxy* (John Lane, 1908), 222–223.

APPENDIX A: The Raven Rules

1. Edgar Allan Poe, The Raven, in T*he Complete Poetry of Edgar Allan Poe* (Penguin Classics, 2008), 45–52.

Author's Note: A Last Word on Awareness

1. Anthony de Mello, *Awareness: The Perils and Opportunities of Reality* (Image Books, 1990), 56.
2. Ibid.
3. Ibid.
4. Ibid.

Notes

5. Ibid.
6. Ibid.
7. Ibid.
8. Carl Jung, *Aion: Researches into the Phenomenology of the Self*, trans. R.F.C. Hull, vol. 9, part II of *The Collected Works of C.G. Jung* (Princeton University Press, 1959), 126.
9. de Mello, *Awareness*, 16.
10. Ibid.
11. Ibid.
12. Ibid

Index

Accountability Ladder, 225. *See also* Senn, Larry
Adam I and Adam II, 57–61, 75, 110, 155, 190–91, 221–24, 261–62. *See also* Brooks, David; Soloveitchik, Joseph B.
adaptability, 99, 133–34, 137–39, 143, 146–47, 228, 259
agilist, 146–47
American Energy Partners. *See* McClendon, Aubrey
Apple (company). *See* Jobs, Steve
Armstrong, Alan (Williams Companies CEO), 175
artificial intelligence (AI), 20, 112, 132, 235–36, 255, 261, 263
Baker, James A., III (former US Treasury Secretary), 16, 239
Bear Stearns, 29–30, 79
Beasley, Stephen (El Paso Corporation CEO), 197–98
Becker, Greg. *See* Silicon Valley Bank
Berkshire Hathaway. *See* Buffett, Warren
Bernanke, Ben (former Federal Reserve chairman), 69
bias, 47, 94–98, 137–39, 236
"black swan" events, 131–32, 139, 150
Boyd, John (US Airforce Colonel). *See* OODA Loop
Brooks, David, 58–59, 193, 204–6, 209, 212. *See also* Adam I and Adam II; Soloveitchik, Joseph B.
Brown, Brené, 48, 105–6, 242
Brown, Jay (former Crown Castle CEO), 206–9
Bruegel, Pieter. See *The Parable of the Blind* (painting by Pieter Bruegel)

Index

Buffett, Warren: Annual Letter to Shareholders, 23; character, 60–61, 191, 230–31; discernment, 116–17; flaws, 20, 126–27; hiring, 256; humor, 116–17; investment strategy, 146, 176
Burke, James (Johnson & Johnson CEO), 88, 106
Burry, Michael (Scion Capital CEO), 31–33, 106–7, 131
Bush, George H. W. (forty-first US president), 15–16, 124, 174, 198
Bush, George W. (forty-third US president), 124
Calvert, Susanna Wu-Pong (Virginia Commonwealth University researcher), 125–26
capability spikes, 118
Chao, Elaine (former US Transportation Secretary), 124–25, 179, 251
Chesapeake Energy, 75–78, 140–42. *See also* Dell'Osso, Nick; Lawler, Doug; McClendon, Aubrey
CIA (Central Intelligence Agency), 15–16, 84, 234
Clayton, Dubilier & Rice. *See* Krenicki, John
Clifton Strength Online Talent Assessment, 120
coaching: author's role in, 52, 58, 60, 92–93, 97–98, 102, 170; blind spots and, 74, 99–101, 112–20; collaboration and, 160; need for, 33, 83–84, 127, 152–153; receiving, 91; strengths and, 118; studying, 179, 211–12.
See also mentorship
collaboration: culture of, 163–66; decision-making and, 160; leadership and, 162, 216; narcissism and, 171; self-control and, 91–92, 147; teams and, 151–52, 155, 157
Collins, Jim (*Good to Great* author), 88, 105, 136–37, 176, 217–18
conformist, 146–47, 256
ConocoPhillips, 77, 198
Cook, Tim, 20, 155
"Dare to Lead" program. *See* Brown, Brené
de Mello, Anthony, 22, 61–62, 275–79
decision-making, 31, 34–35, 87–88, 116–17, 160–61, 226
Dell'Osso, Nick (Chesapeake Energy CEO), 142
derailers, 80; avoiding, 126–27, 191; faults as, 19, 24, 100; ourselves as, 127; reflecting on, 127; teamwork and, 150; traits associated with, 54

INDEX

discernment, 110, 116–17, 130, 242
Digital Equipment Corporation (DEC). *See* Olsen, Ken
Dimon, Jamie, 34, 122–23, 133, 138–39, 143, 146–47, 203, 265
distributed leadership, 158, 161–63
Donahoe, John (former Nike CEO), 61
Dostoevsky (Fyodor), 28, 42, 181, 190
Dunham, Archie (former Chesapeake Energy chairman), 77–78.
    See also McClendon, Aubrey
Edelman Trust Barometer, 90
ego: bruised, 56, 64; driven, 168; managing, 34, 168–72, 176–85;
    unchecked, 31, 260
Eisenhower, Dwight, 20, 157
emotional intelligence (EQ), 137–38, 203, 228, 262
Enron, 32, 69–70, 91, 146, 175, 217, 249–51.
    See also Skilling, Jeff
Eurich, Tasha (*Insight* author), 35, 82, 84
executive recruiting: author's career in, 15–16, 22–23, 37, 44, 77,
    97n1, 123–124, 140, 167, 179; blind spots and, 90, 102,
    164; cautions in the field of, 31, 168; changes in, 164; character and, 195; integrity and, 62–63; interviews, 235, 242,
    254; leadership and, 105; self-forgetfulness and, 171–72,
    195; "superpowers" in the field of, 112–13, 120, 128; tension
    in, 52; vulnerability and, 115, 180
ExxonMobil, 87, 116, 143–45, 158–59, 178, 251.
    See also Darren Woods
feedback: 45, 48–49, 65–66, 83–84, 153, 207, 263. *See also*
    360-reference report
FLARE agility framework, 134–45
Fox, Ann (Nine Energy Services CEO), 101
Friedman, Milton, 30
Fuld, Richard S., Jr. (Dick), 28–29, 31, 33, 67–69, 79–80, 146.
    See also Great Recession; Lehman Brothers; 2008 financial crisis
Gardner, John T. (Heidrick & Struggles vice chairman), 49
Gates, Bill, 60–61, 74
George, Bill (former Medtronic CEO), 28
George, Robert, 97–98

INDEX

Getty, J. Paul (oil and gas pioneer), 139
Goldman Sachs. *See* Wolstencroft, Tracy
Good to Great. See Collins, Jim
gratitude, 42, 65, 181–82, 194, 228–30, 266–67
Gray, Rod (former Azurix CFO), 250–51
Great Recession, the, 25–28, 30, 35–36, 69, 76, 83, 115. *See also*
    Fuld, Richard S., Jr.; Lehman Brothers; 2008 financial crisis
Gregory, Joe (former Lehman president), 68–69
groupthink, 106, 139, 147, 243
Halliburton, 157, 176, 199n1, 245–46
Hamm, Harold (Continental Resources CEO), 142
headhunting: *See* executive recruiting
Heffernan, Margaret (*Willful Blindness* author), 33, 73, 156, 219–20
Hilcorp Energy. *See* Hildebrand, Jeff
Hildebrand, Jeff, 159–61, 187–90, 251
Hoffman, Gert. See *The Parable of the Blind* (novel by Gert Hoffman)
Hogan, Robert and Joyce, 54; Hogan Personality Inventory, 120–21
Hollub, Vicki (Occidental Petroleum CEO), 176
honesty, 19, 117, 157, 225, 249, 258, 262
Humble Inquiry. See Schein, Edgar
humor, 117–18, 182–83, 228
Hungary, 37–40, 95, 210, 230, 237
Icahn, Carl (investor), 76, 140–41. *See also* McClendon, Aubrey
Jackson, Alex (Quantum Capital Group partner), 100–101. *See also* Van Loh, Wil
Jekyll and Hyde, 51–53, 58, 66
Jesus, 42, 69, 71, 188, 193, 205–6, 260–61
Jobs, Steve, 20, 87, 121, 127, 155, 163, 256
Johnson & Johnson (J&J). *See* Burke, James
Jones, A. V. (investor), 135
JPMorgan Chase. *See* Dimon, Jamie
Keller, Tim (Redeemer Church pastor), 171–72
Krenicki, John (Clayton, Dubilier & Rice vice chairman), 117–18
Lawler, Doug (former Chesapeake Energy CEO), 140–42, 231, 251

Index

Lay, Ken (former Enron CEO), 69–70, 250. *See also* Jeff Skilling
Leach, Tim (Permian Strategic Partnership advisor to the CEO), 198–99
Leadership Acceleration Questionnaire (LAQ 360), 80–81. *See also* 360-reference report
Lehman Brothers, 25–30, 33, 67–70, 79. *See also* Fuld, Richard S., Jr.; 2008 financial crisis.
Level 5 leadership, 105, 176, 217, 220. *See also* Collins, Jim
Lewis, C. S., 169, 172, 179, 222
Liberty Energy. *See* Wright, Chris
listening, 32, 49, 68, 191, 207–8, 210–11
Lonely Man of Faith, The. *See* Soloveitchik, Joseph B.
Lumpkins, David and Kristi (Yellowstone Schools founders), 201–2, 210, 212, 261
McClaren, Bob (44 Farms CEO), 174–75
McClendon, Aubrey (former Chesapeake Energy CEO), 75–78, 140
McDonald, Larry (former Lehman vice president), 68–69, 79
Medtronic. *See* George, Bill
mentorship, 33, 49, 117–18, 175, 188, 229. *See also* coaching
META leadership framework, 22–23, 80
micromanaging, 47, 49, 64, 118–120
Miller, Jeff (Halliburton CEO), 157, 176, 199n1. *See also* Halliburton
Monahan, Tom (Heidrick & Struggles CEO), 90, 166n1, 282
Mood Elevator, 181, 228. *See also* Senn, Larry
moral licensing, 55–56, 76, 270
Munger, Charlie, 32, 60, 116–17, 122
Musk, Elon, 19–20, 87, 112, 127, 132, 136, 256
narcissism, 47, 52, 82–83, 128, 167–71
Nine Energy Services. *See* Fox, Ann
Nobel, Alfred B., 129–30, 147, 189
Nobel Prize. *See* Nobel, Alfred B.
objectivity, 65–66, 94–98, 127, 145, 256
Olsen, Ken, 74–75
OODA Loop (US Airforce leadership framework), 34, 133
open-book management, 159, 161

313

INDEX

ownership mindset, 65–66, 90, 92, 98, 225–260
Parable of the Blind, The (novel by Gert Hoffman), 71
Parable of the Blind, The (painting by Pieter Bruegel), 71–73
Paulson, Hank (US Treasury Secretary), 29, 79
people-pleasing, 45–47, 64, 85, 95–96, 180, 265, 270
Petraeus, David (former CIA director), 84, 101, 179
Powell, Jerome (Federal Reserve chairman), 69, 132
Pulitzer, Joseph, 39, 230
quantitative easing (QE), 69
Quantum Capital Group. *See* Van Loh, Wil
Reinemund, Steve (former PepsiCo CEO), 178, 180
Road to Character, The. *See* Brooks, David
Roche, Gerry (Heidrick & Struggles chairman), 117n1, 251, 253–54
Rockefeller, John D., 123, 170
Roosevelt, Theodore (Teddy), 20–21, 99, 129
Schein, Edgar (MIT sociologist), 59, 74, 154–55
Schultz, Howard (Starbucks CEO), 115
Scion Capital, 107. *See also* Burry, Michael
self-belief, 18, 174, 178, 189, 269
self-forgetfulness, 22, 171–76, 185, 269. *See also* selflessness
self-giving spirit, 45–46, 105, 109, 188, 195–99, 271
selflessness, 111, 152–53, 175, 189–91, 245, 265–66, 267. *See also* self-forgetfulness
Senn, Larry (Heidrick & Struggles chairman), 181, 224–26, 228
Silicon Valley Bank (SVB), 32–33, 79–80
Skilling, Jeff (former Enron CEO), 32–33, 69–70, 250. *See also* Enron
Smith, Adam, 30, 199
Soloveitchik, Joseph B., 57–60
Stephens, Autry (Endeavor Energy Resources founder), 231–32
Stice, Travis (Diamondback Energy CEO), 199n1, 222–24, 231–32
Taleb, Nassim Nicholas. *See* "black swan" events
Thiel, Peter (PayPal founder), 112, 235, 243
Thomas, Bill (EOG Resources CEO)

INDEX

Thompson, Jerry (TEPPCO COO), 237–38
360-reference report, 45, 92, 120, 122, 127, 135, 244. *See also* Leadership Acceleration Questionnaire (LAQ 360)
Tillerson, Rex (retired chairman and CEO, ExxonMobil), 145
transactional leadership, 22, 59, 155–56, 221
Trump, Donald, 27, 114, 124, 163
Tsuru, Frank (Diamondback Energy board member), 195–98, 251
2008 financial crisis, 24–36; ego and, 168, 171; executive recruiting after, 164; natural gas, 76; Richard Fuld and, 67–68, 79, 146; warnings, 106–7, 131. *See also* Fuld, Richard S., Jr.; Great Recession; Lehman Brothers
Untermeyer, Chase, 122, 174
VanLoh, Wil, 100–101, 134–35, 160
"VUCA" model, 133
Wall Street, 27, 67–68, 106–7, 140, 158, 198, 250
Walton, Sam (Walmart founder), 136
Weiner, Jeff (LinkedIn CEO), 61
Welch, Jack (General Electric CEO), 30, 117–18, 170, 238
West, Cornel, 97–98
White House, 15, 44, 122–24, 179, 239
Williams, Clay (NOV Inc. CEO), 181–82
Winfrey, Oprah, 111, 115, 210
Wolstencroft, Tracy (former Heidrick & Struggles CEO), 164–66, 216, 225
Woods, Darren, 18, 87, 116, 143–46, 158, 251, 265. *See also* ExxonMobil
Wright, Chris, 23, 114–15, 162–63, 177–78, 180, 265–66
Zuckerberg, Mark, 33, 116